Florida's Best Herbs and Spices

Native and Exotic Plants Grown for Scent and Flavor

Charles R. Boning
Illustrated and Photographed by the Author

Pineapple Press, Inc.
Sarasota, Florida

Inquiries should be addressed to:

Pineapple Press, Inc.
P.O. Box 3889
Sarasota, Florida 34230

www.pineapplepress.com

Library of Congress Cataloging-in-Publication Data

Boning, Charles R.
Florida's best herbs and spices : native and exotic plants grown for scent and flavor / Charles R. Boning ; illustrated and photographed by the author. -- 1st ed.
     p. cm.
Includes bibliographical references and index.
ISBN 978-1-56164-453-7 (pb : alk. paper)
1. Herbs--Florida. 2. Spices--Florida. I. Title.
SB351.H5B634 2010
635'.709759--dc22
                              2009047809

First Edition
10 9 8 7 6 5 4 3 2 1

Design by Charles R. Boning and Jennifer Borresen
Printed in China

Contents

Preface

Herbs and spices excite the senses with vibrant flavors and exotic scents. They enhance food. They bring the cuisines of distant lands into the home. Many are steeped in history, lore, and tradition. Herbs and spices also make attractive additions to the home garden. They surpass many ornamentals in visual appeal, combining beauty, intrigue, and utility.

Florida's warm climate provides residents with the opportunity to raise herbs and spices from around the globe. Unique tropical plants such as vanilla, pandanus, and curry leaf grow in southern portions of the state. By making minor adjustments, the Florida gardener can raise nearly any popular northern herb. Valuable native plants round out the possibilities.

This book introduces gardeners to 92 herbs and spices suited to cultivation in Florida. Each plant is covered in a detailed profile, which includes illustrations, growing techniques, climate requirements, and distribution maps. *Florida's Best Herbs and Spices* presents the gardener with a myriad of planting choices. We at Pineapple Press are confident that this book, like its companion volume, *Florida's Best Fruiting Plants*, will be regarded as a gardening classic.

Introduction

Raising herbs and spices within the home landscape provides several key benefits. First, the gardener can select plants based on personal preferences. Plantings can be tailored to match a particular cuisine or to provide access to ingredients that are not widely available. Second, the gardener has the ability to control the use of pesticides or other chemicals within the landscape. Third, substantial savings can be achieved by using herbs and spices grown within the garden, rather than those purchased from the market. Plants harvested directly from the garden are always fresher and more flavorful than their commercial counterparts. Finally, there is the sense of accomplishment that comes from establishing a successful herb and spice garden.

This book covers herbs and spices suitable for planting in every region of Florida. It includes both native and exotic plants. It describes familiar plants along with those that are rare or obscure. The plants described within these pages embody a unique mix of scents, flavors, textures, and colors.

For purposes of this book, a spice is defined as a plant part, devoid of significant nutritive value, which is used to enhance or alter the flavor of food. Spices may consist of seeds, roots, fruits, or leaves. While they are often dried for preservation, spices may be used fresh or may be processed in a number of ways, such as through fermentation or extraction.

An herb is defined as a green, leafy plant part used to flavor food, to provide aroma, or for medicinal or therapeutic purposes. Herbs are most often used fresh, although they may also be dried. Unlike spices, herbs may provide significant nutritive value.

Kanapaha Botanical Gardens in Gainesville, Florida, is home to one of the most extensive and diverse herb collections in the country.

Many herbs are highly ornamental and can be used in place of other groundcovers and bedded plantings. The pebbled leaves of golden sage, *Salvia officinalis* 'Icterina', add texture and color to the garden.

HISTORY OF HERBS AND SPICES

Humans have used herbs and spices since primitive times. Early uses may have been directed toward masking the effects of spoilage. However, our early ancestors may also have used herbs and spices for medicinal or ceremonial purposes, or simply for eating out of hand.

Prior to the advent of written history, herbs and spices stimulated commerce and communication between cultures. Evidence of the use of herbs, in both China and the Middle East, stretches back 5,000 years. As early as 2,000 BC, pepper, cinnamon, cardamom, and other spices were important items of commerce in the Middle East. Egyptians used spices for embalming and mummification. According to the New Testament of the Bible, three kings from the Orient bestowed rare spices—frankincense and myrrh—on the infant Jesus Christ.

Arab merchants, then Phoenician traders, supplied southern Europe with spices. Spices were symbols of status in the Roman Empire. Throughout early European history spices were expensive, and were only available to persons of wealth. Indeed, at various times, certain spices were worth more than their weight in gold. European interest was piqued as a result of the military expeditions of Alexander the Great, the crusades, and the travels of Marco Polo. The cities of Venice and Genoa grew and prospered for many centuries as a result of the Mediterranean spice trade.

The Age of Exploration was driven in large part by the quest for spice. Spain and Portugal sought to break the monopoly held by Italian merchants and Arab traders. When Christopher Columbus sailed the Atlantic in 1492, he sought to discover a sea route to India, the country of origin for many valuable spices. In 1498, Vasco de Gama sailed around the Cape of Good Hope and became the first European to discover a sea route to India. During the period that followed, Portuguese, British, Dutch, and Spanish navies competed for control of sea routes to India and Southeast Asia. Spices were the subject of wars, treachery, and complex colonial ambitions.

While the events described above occurred in the Eastern Hemisphere, several key spices originated in the Americas. The most noteworthy of these are vanilla, cacao (chocolate), and chili pepper. The Aztecs were familiar with these plants and their culinary uses. Native Americans used cacao as early as 1,000 BC. Spanish conquistadors, upon their arrival in the New World, swiftly recognized these plants as a source of potential wealth. The Spanish exploited native labor to establish and work vast plantations, shipping their produce to eager European markets. When a hurricane drove the Spanish plate fleet ashore on Florida's east coast in 1715, not only did its ships carry gold and silver, but they also carried a cargo of precious New World spices. These included annatto, sassafras, cacao, and vanilla.

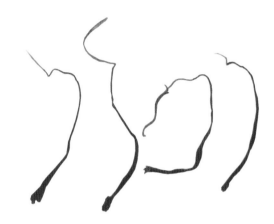

Pound for pound, saffron is the world's most expensive spice. The threads shown here are actually the dried stigmas of the saffron crocus, *Crocus sativus*. This plant is native to the Mediterranean region and may have originated on Crete.

Hot peppers come in many forms, sizes, and shapes. Peppers are native to the Americas and were not known in the eastern hemisphere prior to the voyages of Christopher Columbus. They have since been adopted as a key ingredient in many European, Asian, and African cuisines.

SCOPE, LIMITATIONS, AND CAUTIONS

This book does not cover every herb and spice that will grow in Florida. It focuses on 92 plants of merit. The species included are those with agreeable flavors and scents, those that are easy to grow in the home garden, and those with high landscape value. This book focuses on culinary herbs and provides reduced coverage of plants grown purely for scent.

This book includes more than a dozen descriptions of native herbs and spices. Some of these, such as Carolina allspice, Florida anise, wax myrtle, witch hazel, and yellow anise, are scent plants and are not suitable for human consumption. However, some native species such as bee balm, New Jersey tea, red bay, sassafras, spicebush, sumac, and vanilla, offer culinary uses.

While this book contains basic information regarding uses of the herbs and spices covered within its pages, it is not a recipe book or nutritional guide. The bibliography includes several excellent sources that provide expanded information about cooking. Further, while the culinary uses given for plants within this book comport with those recognized in current literature, they are not based on any specialized knowledge of the author or publisher. If information provided within this book conflicts with that of recent government advisories or scientific findings, the reader should exercise caution and should rely on the most recent information available.

The clove of commerce is the dried flower bud of a medium-sized evergreen tree, *Syzygium aromaticum,* thought to have originated in the Maluku Islands. The tree is extremely cold sensitive and suffers damage when temperatures fall below 50° F. Therefore, it is not suitable for growth as a dooryard tree in Florida

This book omits any references to the alleged medical or therapeutic qualities of herbs and spices. The author is not a physician and is unwilling to recommend any dubious forms of treatment. Many of the medical properties commonly ascribed to herbs have not been confirmed by science. In the author's opinion, any books or articles that "prescribe" herbal "treatments" for a broad range of ailments should be viewed with skepticism. That a single plant would reduce arthritic pain while preventing the common cold and eradicating various cancers is unlikely. That the writers of such literature have uncovered a "miracle" cure unknown to medical science is even less likely.

It should also be emphasized that not every plant in this book is edible. Some are only suitable for use as scent agents or as strewing herbs. Such limitations are pointed out within the plant profiles. A few species are poisonous. Unless the text specifically indicates that a plant is suitable for culinary use, it should never be ingested.

Many species of jasmine are grown as scent plants throughout the world's tropical and warm-temperate regions. Shown in the photographs above are downy jasmine, *Jasminum multiflorum* (left), and windmill jasmine, *Jasminum laurifolium* (right). In the Orient, especially in China, jasmine blossoms are used to flavor tea.

Contact with any new plant, even one that is regularly consumed by humans, carries some degree of risk. Individuals prone to allergic reactions should steer away from contact with unfamiliar plants. When using or ingesting any new herb or spice, the reader should start with small quantities until his or her personal tolerance is established. Use should be discontinued upon experiencing any adverse reaction, and a physician should be consulted immediately. Because it is impossible to completely eliminate the risks associated with allergies and other sensitivities, neither the author nor Pineapple Press may be held responsible for any ill effects that allegedly result from use of plants described within this book.

Finally, the reader should exercise special care when gathering any plant from the wild. Florida is home to some extremely toxic plants, including water hemlock, snakeroot, pokeweed, hairy vetch, atamasco lily, and mountain laurel. In addition, poisonous non-native species abound in Florida. Potentially deadly imports include oleander, castor bean, lantana, elephant ear, and angel's trumpet. Unless the reader is absolutely certain of the identity of the plant and has previous experience in collecting the same, the reader should not pick wild plants for culinary use.

This book is divided into two parts. Part I presents basic information related to cultivation. It contains a discussion of Florida's climate, growing conditions, garden pests, and other topics. Part II, which is the heart of this book, contains profiles of 92 plants. These are arranged alphabetically based upon the common name most often used in Florida.

Vicks plant, *Plectranthus tomentosa,* is a perennial species related to Cuban oregano. It will grow throughout peninsular Florida. The leaves smell like menthol or Vicks VapoRub when bruised or crushed. It is purely a scent plant and is not used for culinary purposes.

FEATURES OF THE PLANT PROFILES

The plant profiles furnish detailed information in a simple, consistent format. Each profile is two or four pages long. The first page relays basic data, including the plant's common name, scientific name, and classification. The most prominent feature is a full-color illustration depicting the leaves and, in some instances, the flower of a typical plant.

On the top right-hand side of the page, a state map shows the plant's range. Portions 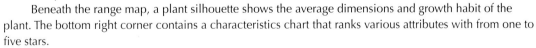 shaded in dark green denote areas to which the plant is best adapted. Portions shaded in light green show areas where the plant will grow, but where growing conditions are not optimal. Portions shaded in yellow show areas to which the plant is only marginally adapted. Where growing seasons differ in north and south Florida, the range maps are bisected by a dashed line.

Beneath the range map, a plant silhouette shows the average dimensions and growth habit of the plant. The bottom right corner contains a characteristics chart that ranks various attributes with from one to five stars.

The text follows a standard order and, in most cases, is organized under the following subheadings: Geographic Distribution, Plant Description, Flavor and Scent, Varieties, Cultivation, and Harvest and Use.

CLASSIFICATION OF HERBS AND SPICES Scientists classify plants through an array of features. Understanding the relationship between species can aid the gardener in several ways. Related species often share flavor characteristics, require similar regimens of care, succeed under similar conditions, and suffer from identical problems. Knowing that a species belongs to a particular family can assist the grower in making planting decisions and in tending to the needs of a plant.

A few of the plants described within these pages are isolated species within families that do not contain other members suitable for culinary use or as scent agents. However, most belong to one of a dozen spice- and herb-rich families: Alliaceae (onion), Apiaceae (carrot), Asteraceae (aster), Brassicaceae (cabbage), Fabaceae (bean), Lamiaceae (mint), Lauraceae (laurel), Myrtaceae (myrtle), Piperaceae (pepper), Rosaceae (rose), Rutaceae (citrus), and Zingiberaceae (ginger). Each plant profile identifies the family to which the plant belongs and lists related species.

The Jamaican caper, *Capparis cynophallophora,* is a native plant that is widely used as a hedge in south Florida. It is related to *Capparis spinosa,* a shrub native to the Mediterranean region that produces the edible capers sold in stores. Capers are the pickled flower buds of the plant. The fruits, known as caper berries, are also harvested, pickled, and used in cooking.

1
The Basics of Raising Herbs and Spices

Most herbs and spices are easy to grow. They are tenacious and will quickly rebound from minor setbacks. Herbs are inexpensive, fast growing, and have a short life span. Therefore, the death of a single plant need not be viewed as a monumental loss. Indeed, most gardeners expect to lose a few plants over the course of a season. Success is often, in part, the result of trial and error. While planting schedules may differ, care regimens for most herbs and spices are similar to those of many ornamentals.

GETTING STARTED

The first step in starting an herb and spice garden is to choose an appropriate location. While a few herbs will grow in shaded areas, most require at least 6 to 8 hours of direct sun per day. Some northern herbs, such as lemon balm and lavender, require shade during the summer. They may prefer locations where a canopy of a deciduous tree blocks the midday sun. To make intelligent planting decisions, the gardener should track the movement of sun and shadows across the yard through different seasons. In addition, the garden must have good drainage. Very few herbs and spices will succeed in low, damp locations. Where drainage is a problem, a raised planting bed may be the best solution.

The second step is to determine the size of the garden. A productive garden requires the input of some time and effort. The gardener should therefore make a realistic assessment of how much time he or she is willing devote to the project. A window box or container garden may be the best option for those with very limited time. There are advantages to starting small and gradually expanding the garden as time permits.

Pineapple mint is a variegated selection of apple mint. It performs well under Florida conditions and is frequently included in Florida herb gardens.

The third step is to determine the overall layout. A garden that is carefully designed will achieve better productivity with less effort. With medium and large gardens, it may be useful to draw a map to assist with the planning process. A garden that is laid out in a grid pattern has the advantages of accessibility and easy harvest. A less formal garden may be easier to maintain and may achieve a more natural look.

The fourth step in the planning process is to select appropriate plants. To reduce maintenance requirements, the gardener should select species that are reasonably well adapted to the location. This book provides detailed selection criteria that will assist the gardener with such decisions.

The leaves of aromatic aster, *Aster oblongifolius,* exude a pleasant scent when bruised or crushed. This plant is native to the eastern United States. It produces showy lavender-blue flowers in the fall.

The fifth and final step is to determine how the plants will be situated within the garden. As a rule of thumb, annuals should be segregated to facilitate removal at the end of the growing season. Plants should be sorted in terms of height. Taller specimens should be placed in a spot where they do not interfere with views, light, or access, generally toward the north or rear of the garden.

Many gingers are grown primarily for ornamental purposes. While some ornamental gingers are edible, few approach culinary gingers in flavor, quality, or utility. The gingers shown in the photographs above are red button ginger, *Costus woodsonii;* 'Moy Giant', *Hedychium* sp.; Hawaiian torch ginger, *Costus barbatus;* and torch ginger, *Etlingera elatior.* The flower buds and seedpods of torch ginger are used in Malaysian and Indonesian cooking. Gingers can be propagated by breaking up the rhizome and planting pieces near the soil surface.

PROPAGATING HERBS AND SPICES

Herbs and spices can be started from seed, vegetatively propagated, or purchased in containers from nurseries and retailers. The section that follows touches briefly on some common propagation techniques. In Florida, starting herbs and spices from seeds sown directly in the ground can be unreliable. Germination rates are often disappointing. A high percentage of newly spouted plants damp off or wither away under the intense sun. Other young plants succumb to insect pests. The odds of success increase with regular watering, a well-prepared planting bed, and seeds treated with fungicide. Some species may also benefit from a temporary shade cloth enclosure.

A less risky approach is to sprout seeds in small containers indoors or in a shaded location. Pressed-peat pots are ideal for this purpose. A mix of peat and sand, or sterile potting soil, should be used as the planting medium. When the plants reach a few inches in height, they can be incrementally exposed to direct sunlight. Once they are acclimated to full sun, they can be planted directly in outdoor beds.

A common mistake made by inexperienced growers is to plant seeds too deep. As a rule of thumb, seeds should be sown at a depth no greater than one and a half times the length of the seed. The seeds of some plants, such as oregano and lemon balm, can be sown directly on top of the soil. Other small seeds should receive only a light dusting of soil sufficient to cover the seeds.

Regular watering is critical in the periods leading up to and following germination. The planting medium must be kept damp. At the same time, it must not be permitted to become soggy. The best way to achieve even watering is to place the pots in a tray and to gradually fill the base until the pots soak up sufficient moisture. Any water remaining in the tray for more than a minute is an indication of over watering.

Another method of starting plants, especially woody perennials, is by rooting softwood cuttings. The branch should be severed with a sharp knife about 6 inches below the growth tip. A diagonal cut, made just below a node, will promote rooting. Leaves near the base of the cutting should be removed. The cutting should then be dipped in rooting hormone before being inserted about 2 inches deep into the growing medium. A combination of damp sand and peat works well as a medium. To maintain humidity and prevent evaporation, the top of the tray or container may be covered with cellophane. The cuttings should be stored in a shaded location until they resume robust growth.

Colony-forming herbs, such as bee balm, lemon grass, and thyme, can be propagated by subdividing clumps. A few species, such as rosemary, can be propagated through ground layering. This method involves bending over a flexible stem, scraping away some bark to expose the cambium, and burying the exposed portion in a mound of earth with the branch tip protruding. After a few weeks, roots will form along the buried section of the stem. At that point, the stem can be severed from the rest of the plant and replanted.

Woody species are typically reproduced through air layering or grafting. Air layering is accomplished by scraping away a segment of bark on a branch, wrapping the same in damp sphagnum moss, and sealing the wrap in cellophane covered with aluminum foil. After roots develop within the sphagnum moss, the branch is severed and replanted. Grafting involves joining a scion, which is a branch tip taken from one plant, with a rootstock, which is typically a young seedling plant from the same species. Both techniques are complex and should not be attempted without additional research and guidance.

FLORIDA GROWING CONDITIONS

Those who move to Florida from other regions of the country should not assume that the same gardening techniques they employed elsewhere are suitable for use here. The gardener must overcome special challenges posed by soil, pests, disease, and climate.

SOIL CONSIDERATIONS As a general rule, Florida's soil is mediocre to poor. It ranges from infertile sand to dense clay to oolitic limestone rubble. While most fruit trees and some ornamentals prosper when planted directly in native soil, most herbs benefit from some form of soil enrichment. The planting bed should be supplemented with some combination of topsoil, humus, peat, compost, and other organic matter. While manure is a valuable additive under certain circumstances, it should be used sparingly, as it can burn tender young roots.

Before planting, the gardener should ascertain the pH of the soil. Acidic soils have a pH value of less than 7.0. Alkaline soils have a pH value of greater than 7.0. Most herbs and spices prefer neutral or mildly

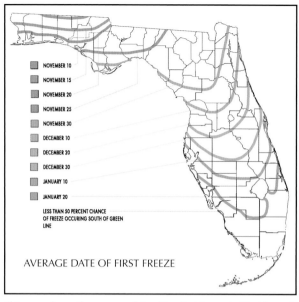

NOVEMBER 10
NOVEMBER 15
NOVEMBER 20
NOVEMBER 25
NOVEMBER 30
DECEMBER 10
DECEMBER 20
DECEMBER 30
JANUARY 10
JANUARY 20
LESS THAN 50 PERCENT CHANCE
OF FREEZE OCCURING SOUTH OF GREEN
LINE

AVERAGE DATE OF FIRST FREEZE

This map shows the average date of the first freeze in Florida each year. It is useful for determining when to harvest or take measures to protect cold-sensitive plants.

acidic soil. However, with proper care, many species will make acceptable growth in soils that are mildly alkaline. Strongly alkaline soils, such as those that are composed of limestone rubble, may cause nutritional deficiencies in many types of plants. Under such circumstances, it may be necessary to raise the acidity of the soil with sulfur or acidifying fertilizers. Applications of chelated iron, manganese, and other supplements may also be required.

CLIMATE CONSIDERATIONS Florida's climate is diverse. North Florida lies within the temperate zone. Winter freezes are frequent and can be severe. Much of peninsular Florida lies within the transitional zone between warm temperate and subtropical climates. The weather is characterized by long, humid summers, and mild winters punctuated with occasional freezes. South Florida has a subtropical climate. Winter freezes are rare. The climate of the Keys is classified as near tropical.

The growing season in Florida is longer than it is in most other locations within the continental United States. Even in north Florida, the gardener may be able to start and harvest more than one crop of short-lived annuals. However, in areas of the state from Orlando northward, it is important to know the average date for the first frost. When this date nears, the gardener should be prepared to harvest or protect any annuals that remain in the garden.

No part of mainland Florida is immune to the threat of winter cold, although several years may pass in which freezing temperatures do not occur south of Orlando. The main threat from freezing weather in

MARCH 10
MARCH 1
FEBRUARY 20
FEBRUARY 10
FEBRUARY 1
JANUARY 10
JANUARY 20

AVERAGE DATE OF LAST FREEZE

This map shows the average date of the last feeze in Florida. It is helpful for determining planting schedules.

peninsular Florida occurs in January and February. Northern perennials are hardy and are not affected by the cold. However, various annuals and several of the tropical species described within these pages may be damaged or killed.

When making planting decisions, gardeners should consider local microclimates. Fences, hedges, buildings, and stands of trees can inhibit the flow of cold air. Cold air drains away from elevated areas and collects in depressions. Cold-sensitive plants should be planted in high, protected locations that receive afternoon sun. On the other hand, hardy perennials may be placed in open or low locations.

When severe cold threatens, the gardener should act to preserve valuable and cold-tender specimens. Smaller plants, especially those in containers, can be moved indoors to avoid cold injury. Others can be covered with fabric. Plastic sheeting may provide

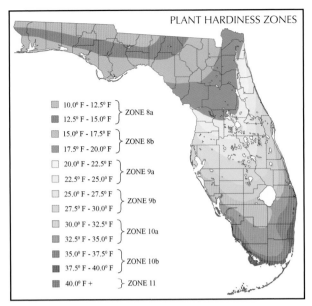

PLANT HARDINESS ZONES

10.0° F - 12.5° F	ZONE 8a
12.5° F - 15.0° F	
15.0° F - 17.5° F	ZONE 8b
17.5° F - 20.0° F	
20.0° F - 22.5° F	ZONE 9a
22.5° F - 25.0° F	
25.0° F - 27.5° F	ZONE 9b
27.5° F - 30.0° F	
30.0° F - 32.5° F	ZONE 10a
32.5° F - 35.0° F	
35.0° F - 37.5° F	ZONE 10b
37.5° F - 40.0° F	
40.0° F +	ZONE 11

This map is derived from NOAA data and the Plant Hardiness Zone Map published by the United States Department of Agriculture. It shows the average lowest temperatures that can be expected on an annual basis.

some protection, but tends to collect moisture and may burn those leaves that it contacts. Both micro-sprinklers and overhead sprinklers will provide several degrees of frost protection. The gardener might also consider taking cuttings from tender plants that cannot be adequately protected.

Florida's diverse climatic conditions also have an impact on when plants are started. In north Florida, planting schedules closely resemble those employed by gardeners in other parts of the southeastern United States. Annual herbs are planted in the spring, after the threat of frost has passed. They are harvested over the summer and fall, before the first frost.

Peninsular Florida is prone to hot summers with high humidity. This has a negative impact on a number of herbs that are common in northern gardens. Basil, caraway, dill, fennel, lavender, lemon balm, mint, parsley, sorrel, tarragon, thyme, and others tend to struggle or die out under such conditions.

To overcome this problem, gardeners living in the subtropics reverse typical planting schedules. Rather than planting the aforementioned herbs in the spring, south Florida gardeners plant these herbs in the fall and harvest them during winter and spring. South Florida gardeners discontinue most annuals over the summer. They treat other heat-sensitive biennial or perennial plants as annuals and permit these plants to die off as hot weather approaches. Some heat-sensitive plants can be protected with shade or can be taken indoors until the arrival of cooler weather.

AVERAGE ANNUAL RAINFALL

Niceville (55 inches)
Tallahassee (52 inches)
Jacksonville (52 inches)
Gainesville (50 inches)
Daytona Beach (49 inches)
Orlando (49 inches)
Tampa (47 inches)
West Palm Beach (51 inches)
Homestead (53 inches)
Ft. Myers (54 inches)

Less than 50 inches
50 to 60 inches
55 to 60 inches
Over 60 inches

This map shows the average annual rainfall in inches. It is derived from NOAA data and the Average Annual Precipitation map created by the Spatial Climate Analysis Service of Oregon State University. The actual amount of precipitation received by different areas of the state can vary dramatically from year to year, depending on the tracks of tropical weather systems and other factors.

Florida is one of the wettest states in the nation, averaging 54 inches of precipitation annually. However, this rainfall is not evenly distributed throughout the year. Peninsular Florida has a distinct dry season, which runs from November through May. Frequent irrigation may be necessary during these months. The wet season, characterized by afternoon showers and waves of tropical moisture, runs from June through October.

MAINTAINING THE GARDEN

Plants that receive proper care tend to be more vigorous and productive than those that are neglected. The discussion that follows outlines basic cultivation techniques.

IRRIGATION Herbs and spices require irrigation, particularly during periods of establishment, high growth, and low precipitation. A bi-weekly watering is sufficient for most of the plants covered within this book. However, requirements vary with the species, drainage characteristics of the soil, and the season.

Drip irrigation systems supply frequent applications of water at a low flow rate and at low pressure. Such systems are very efficient. Micro-sprinklers are slightly less efficient. However, they can be adjusted to cover a broader area. With both systems, the emitters have a tendency to clog. Soaker hoses work well for planting rows, but tend to deteriorate over time. Overhead sprinklers are inefficient, as they lose water to evaporation and runoff.

FERTILIZATION In many areas of the state, the soil lacks sufficient nutrients to promote the vigorous growth of many plants—other than weeds and native species. This means that the gardener seeking to grow non-native herbs and spices must fertilize. Most balanced, slow-release granular fertilizers will produce acceptable results. Many organic fertilizers are also effective. Composting is another eco-friendly method of adding nutrients to the soil.

Although supplemental nutrition is required in most areas of the state, it is better to under-fertilize than to over-fertilize. Over-fertilization can burn feeder roots and can send plants into shock. Further, excess nutrients are likely to wind up in ground water or runoff and add to the state's pollution woes. For similar reasons, fertilizer should not be applied immediately before a rainstorm. Nutrients will wash quickly through the root zone. Although it may seem counterintuitive, the best time to fertilize is immediately after a heavy rain. Capillary action works to draw nutrients into the root zone, where they are readily accessible.

MULCH AND WEED SUPPRESSON Plants grown in a bed of organic mulch are usually far more vigorous than those that emerge from bare earth. Organic mulch serves at least six important purposes. First, it conserves soil moisture by limiting evaporation and runoff. Second, it adds nutrients to the soil. Third, it draws earthworms into the root zone and encourages the development of beneficial microbes and mycorrhizal fungi. Fourth, it reduces the population of nematodes, microscopic worms that can harm the roots of the plant. Fifth, it moderates the temperature of the top layer of soil. Sixth, it suppresses weed growth.

Weed growth is a significant problem in most Florida gardens. Common weeds include pigweeds, nutsedges, pusleys, sandspurs, lamb's-quarters, beggar's ticks, goosegrasses, horse nettles, and purslanes. Weeds and grasses compete with herbs and other desirable plants for water and nutrients. Unless they are controlled or eliminated, they can rapidly take over the garden.

Use of chemical herbicides is rarely appropriate within an herb garden as spray drift is likely to kill or contaminate plants near those targeted. The only viable choices are to surround plants with a thick bed of mulch, to lay down weed-stop fabric, or to hand weed on a frequent basis. While grass clippings make valuable additions to the compost heap, they should not be used as mulch. They break down rapidly, generate heat as they decompose, and may harbor weed seeds.

Basil is one of the easiest herbs to grow in Florida and is well adapted to Florida conditions. It will tolerate considerable heat and humidity.

Gingers from the genus *Kaempferia* tend to be short and often have ornately patterned leaves. Several species are cultivated for culinary use. However, most are grown as ornamentals and are commonly referred to as peacock gingers.

Alabama wild ginger, *Asarum speciosum,* is not closely related to true ginger. It is a creeping evergreen that makes an attractive groundcover. The root gives off a pungent ginger scent. In the past, the root was used as a ginger "substitute." However, some authorities now regard all parts of this plant and its close allies as toxic.

The curry plant, *Helichrysum italicum,* is grown almost strictly as a scent plant. It is not an ingredient in Asian curries, which are actually spice mixes. While the scent may resemble that of an Indian curry, the flavor is not curry-like and is not particularly appealing.

Horehound is a member of the Lamiaceae or mint family. This European native is primarily used as a medicinal herb, although some species have been used to flavor teas, ales, and candies.

Caribbean oregano, *Lippia micromera,* is also sometimes referred to as Puerto Rican oregano and Spanish thyme. It is one of a large number of species that, while not closely related to true oregano, nevertheless carry the pungent flavor and scent of oregano.

Most members of the *Aloe* genus, including *Aloe* vera, are native to Africa. Aloes do not have a strong scent and are not regularly used for culinary applications. Aloe vera juice is marketed in the United States as a dietary supplement. The fluid from the interior of the leaves is used to sooth minor burns and skin irritations.

Catmint, *Nepeta faassenii,* is a member of the mint family that performs well throughout Florida. Like its close relative catnip, *Nepeta cataria,* catmint produces a euphoric effect in some domestic cats. The variety shown is 'Six Hills Giant'.

The photographs above depict two native trees that are planted, in part, for their fragrant white flowers. The magnolia, *Magnolia grandiflora* (left), is an ornamental evergreen tree that can attain a height of over 90 feet. The loblolly bay, *Gordonia lasianthus* (right), is medium-sized tree distantly related to tea.

Japanese honeysuckle flowers are attractive and strongly perfumed, and they draw many pollinators. Parts of the plant have also been used for culinary and medicinal purposes. However, this species has exhibited strong invasive tendencies and can be rangy and difficult to control within the garden. Its use within the landscape is therefore discouraged.

CONTROLLING PESTS Every gardener will suffer some damage as a result of garden pests. The following creatures rank as "frequent offenders" and deserve some additional comment:

Eastern Cottontail Rabbit The eastern cottontail rabbit, *Sylvilagus floridanus*, is found throughout Florida. It is a common, destructive pest of herb and vegetable gardens. The best way to prevent rabbit damage is to erect a chicken-wire fence or other exclusionary device.

Cutworms These thick-bodied caterpillars cause substantial leaf damage and can sever young plants at ground level. Cutworms can be controlled with approved pesticides.

Slugs and Snails Slugs and land snails emerge after dark to feed on herbs and other succulent plants. During the day they seek refuge in plant pot bases, foundation crevices, and other moist, dark places. Their presence is confirmed by the appearance of slime trails over walkways, soil, and plants. Metaldehyde baits can reduce populations, especially during dry weather. Slugs and snails will not cross a surface treated with copper sulfate. Various pesticides are also effective.

Grasshoppers Grasshoppers are common throughout Florida. These voracious herbivores can inflict significant damage over a short period. Some feed only on grasses. Others, such as the American bird grasshopper, *Schistocerca americana*, the eastern lubber, *Romalea microptera*, and the southern redlegged grasshopper, *Melanoplus propinquus*, can invade herb gardens. The only effective methods of control are through chemical insecticides or by using mesh screens to deny access.

Nematodes Nematodes are the most populous group of multi-celled animals on earth. Tens of

Butterflies and bees are frequent visitors to herb gardens. Pesticides are chemical poisons and can have a negative impact on a number of pollinators and other beneficial insects.

thousands of these microscopic worms can exist within a cubic foot of soil. Some are beneficial. Others, such as the root knot nematode, *Meloidogyne* spp., are parasitic and cause immense damage. Root knot nematodes are especially prevalent in loose, sandy soil. Plants beset by root knot nematodes experience poor growth or decline, and readily succumb to drought or other stresses. Mulch can reduce nematode populations. Nematodes appear to be less prevalent in raised planting beds. Nematodes can also be "cooked" out of the top layers of soil by using sheets of plastic film to trap heat. While nematodes affect many fruit trees and some spice plants, their attacks on herbs and other short-lived plants are less frequent or less noticeable.

Aphids The aphid is an extremely common pest of many herbs and spices. This pear-shaped insect is tiny, measuring less than 1/8 of an inch in length. It congregates on the underside of developing leaves. It can form dense colonies, sapping the energy of the plant and causing the distortion of new growth. Populations tend to peak in the spring. Insecticidal oils and soap solutions are effective in controlling aphids.

Other common pests within the herb and spice garden include thrips, scale insects, leaf miners, wireworms, armyworms, weevils, mites, and loopers.

The gardener should use restraint when applying pesticides within the herb and spice garden. Pesticides are chemical poisons and, to some extent, are bound to contaminate plant surfaces and tissues. Many are indiscriminate. They tend to kill beneficial insects and harmful insects at near-identical rates. Finally, when used in excess, pesticides can wash into local waterways and can have a devastating effect on zooplankton and other creatures that depend on such microorganisms.

The presence of some insect pests in the garden is natural, and minor damage should not be viewed as an invitation to drench the garden in toxins. The gardener should consider various low-impact approaches. Periodically rotating crops can suppress the tendency of pest problems to build over time. The gardener may be able to counteract minor pest problems by dissolving two tablespoons of dishwashing liquid in a gallon of water and applying the same as a spray. Pesticidal oils also have a relatively low impact on the environment. Serious pesticides should only be applied as a last resort, when insect problems become unmanageable. Even then, directions should be closely followed. The treatment should be targeted only toward those plants that are suffering infestations. Sprays should only be applied in periods of dry weather and low wind.

Coastal sweet pepperbush, *Clethra alnifolia,* is a deciduous shrub native to the eastern United States, ranging from central Florida to Maine. The flowers are sweetly fragrant and draw legions of bees, making this an attractive scent plant to include in natural gardens.

HARVEST AND STORAGE

Herbs and spices should be harvested during dry, warm weather, after any morning dew has evaporated. Plants harvested during wet weather tend to deteriorate rapidly and are susceptible to infection by mildew and mold. If herbs are clean and free of dust and pesticides, they can be used without additional preparation. If their cleanliness is in doubt, they should be briefly rinsed in cold water. The water should be gently shaken off before patting the leaves dry with paper towels. The idea is to minimize trauma to the leaves, as essential oils can be lost through the cleaning process.

Most herbs are at their best when they go directly from the garden to the pan or table. However, many species are annual or, for other reasons, produce a discontinuous supply. With the approach of summer in south Florida, and with the approach of winter in north Florida, the gardener may be forced to harvest and preserve any remaining cold- or heat-sensitive plants. Such herbs may be stored through refrigeration, freezing, or drying.

Herbs will usually remain fresh for between three days and a week if stored in the refrigerator. The best long-term storage method for leafy herbs is freezing. However, if left unprotected, they will suffer freezer burn and will deteriorate. The key to preservation lies in encasing the herbs in ice. This result is easily accomplished. Leaves should be placed in a small, sealable, plastic bag. The bag should be filled with water until all air has been eliminated. It should then be sealed and labeled with the name of the herb and the harvest date. Herbs stored in this manner will last for up to a year.

Both herbs and spices can be dried, though many herbs lose some flavor and much vitality when preserved in this manner. Nevertheless, rosemary, thyme, dill, mints, and bay leaves, among others, furnish a useful culinary additive when dried. Depending on the species, methods include sun drying, drying in an oven at low temperature, or drying in a dark location with good air circulation. Dried herbs and spices gradually lose their potency over time, especially when exposed to air or light.

Camphor basil, *Ocimum kilimandscharicum,* is native to Africa. The leaves are aromatic and exude a strong camphor scent. This plant is occasionally used as a flavoring agent in Indian cooking, although its safety has not been adequately assessed. Camphor is considered toxic to humans if consumed in heavy doses. Extracts of camphor basil have also been shown to repel or kill insects.

The Aztec sweet herb, *Lippia dulcis* or *Phyla scaberrime,* is native to the American tropics. While it has been promoted as a natural sweetener, its high camphor content makes it poorly suited for this role, and some authorities consider it unsafe for human consumption.

African okra is a member of the *Hibiscus* genus and is related to roselle, a flavoring agent profiled within these pages. Most okras are used as vegetables.

Madagascar jasmine, *Stephanotis floribunda* (left), which is not a true jasmine, nevertheless produces attractive blooms that give off a very pleasant fragrance. The curious seedpods (right) superficially resemble mangos in form.

Juniper berries are actually berry-like cones. The berries from a few species have been used as a spice, especially in the cuisines of northern Europe. However, the berries produced by most junipers are bitter and inedible. A few species are toxic. Overuse of even "edible" juniper berries is discouraged, and consumption should be entirely avoided by those who are pregnant and by those who suffer from kidney-related problems.

The blackberry jam fruit, *Randia formosa,* is a compact evergreen bush from the American tropics. Not only does it produce showy, fragrant flowers, but the pulp of the fruit is sweet and closely resembles blackberry jam in appearance and taste. This plant will succeed outdoors in coastal areas of south Florida.

The yaupon, *Ilex vomitoria,* is a native evergreen shrub. The Seminoles and other Native Americans used the leaves and twigs to brew a tea or "black drink" used in religious rituals. Consumption of large quantities of this caffeinated beverage on an empty stomach induced vomiting, giving rise to the scientific name of the species. Today, the yaupon is widely planted as an ornamental.

GEOGRAPHIC ORIGIN OF HERBS AND SPICES

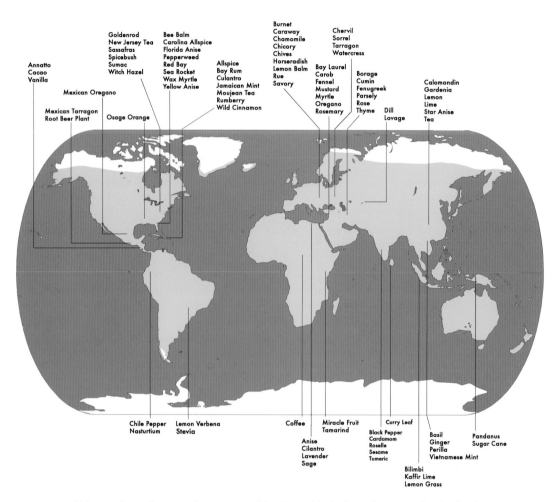

Annatto
Cacao
Vanilla

Mexican Oregano

Mexican Tarragon
Root Beer Plant

Osage Orange

Goldenrod
New Jersey Tea
Sassafras
Spicebush
Sumac
Witch Hazel

Bee Balm
Carolina Allspice
Florida Anise
Pepperweed
Red Bay
Sea Rocket
Wax Myrtle
Yellow Anise

Allspice
Bay Rum
Culantro
Jamaican Mint
Moujean Tea
Rumberry
Wild Cinnamon

Burnet
Caraway
Chamomile
Chicory
Chives
Horseradish
Lemon Balm
Rue
Savory

Chervil
Sorrel
Tarragon
Watercress

Bay Laurel
Carob
Fennel
Mustard
Myrtle
Oregano
Rosemary

Borage
Cumin
Fenugreek
Parsely
Rose
Thyme

Dill
Lovage

Calomondin
Gardenia
Lemon
Lime
Star Anise
Tea

Chile Pepper
Nasturtium

Lemon Verbena
Stevia

Coffee

Miracle Fruit
Tamarind

Anise
Cilantro
Lavender
Sage

Black Pepper
Cardamom
Roselle
Sesame
Tumeric

Curry Leaf

Bilimbi
Kaffir Lime
Lemon Grass

Basil
Ginger
Perilla
Vietnamese Mint

Pandanus
Sugar Cane

This map shows the approximate geographic origin of the herbs and spices within this book.

II
Plant Profiles

Allspice

SCIENTIFIC NAME: *Pimenta dioica*
FAMILY: Myrtaceae
OTHER COMMON NAME: Pimienta de Jamaica (Spanish)

Woody Perennial; Evergreen Tree

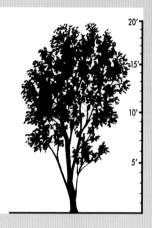

Characteristics

Overall Rating	★★★
Ease of Care	★★★★
Utility	★★★
Landscape Value	★★★★
Salt Tolerance	★
Drought Tolerance	★★★★
Heat/Humidity Tolerance	★★★★★
Cold Tolerance	★★
Shade Tolerance	★★
Longevity	★★★★

Known Hazards

The oils produced by this plant may cause dermatitis in hypersensitive individuals. Many closely allied species are poisonous. Allspice contains small amounts of estragole, which is considered a mild carcinogen. This plant should not be consumed by pregnant or nursing women. Allspice contains salicylates, and consumption may cause allergic reactions in those who are intolerant of these compounds.

Allspice is not a spice mix, as its name implies. Instead, the spice is composed of the dried fruit of a single species. Allspice is used in many cuisines and is especially popular in the Caribbean region, where it originated. The leaves can be used as a scent and flavoring agent.

GEOGRAPHIC DISTRIBUTION Allspice is native to Jamaica, Cuba, various other Caribbean islands, portions of southern Mexico, and Central America. The Aztecs and other indigenous people used it as a flavoring agent. Columbus is thought to have first brought allspice back to Europe. Today, major producers include Jamaica, Mexico, Guatemala, and Honduras. In Florida, allspice has been successfully cultivated as far north as Merritt Island on the east coast, and the Sarasota area on the west coast.

PLANT DESCRIPTION
Allspice is a small evergreen tree or large shrub. It can reach over 40 feet high under favorable conditions. In Florida, it typically reaches a height of between 15 to 20 feet. The bark is smooth and gray. Leaves are elliptic, dark green, and glossy. Small white flowers appear in

A mature allspice tree makes an attractive specimen within the home landscape.

clusters on short racemes near the branch tips. The species is dioecious, meaning some plants only bear male flowers while others only bear female flowers. However, male trees often produce some hermaphrodite flowers. These develop into fruits. The fruit is a small green berry, which can grow to about 1/3 of an inch in diameter. The berry turns purple or brown as it matures. Each fruit contains two kidney-shaped seeds.

The leaves of allspice are aromatic and give off a spicy fragrance when crushed or bruised.

FLAVOR AND SCENT The leaves and fruit are highly aromatic. The scent is complex and pleasant. The flavor resembles a mix of pepper, cloves, nutmeg, ginger, and cinnamon.

VARIETIES Several cultivars are propagated in Jamaica. These are not commonly available in Florida.

RELATIVES The Myrtaceae family contains more than 3,750 species. It is rich in food plants, including several fruiting plants and spices. Members described within this book include bay rum, *Pimenta racemosa*; rumberry, *Myrciaria floribunda*; and wax myrtle, *Myrica cerifera*. The clove, *Syzygium aromaticum*, is an important spice from this family that is not covered within these pages.

CULTIVATION Allspice is easy to grow in south Florida. It will withstand a brief frost. However, the plant suffers severe damage at about 28° F and is killed at about 27° F. In central and north Florida, allspice can be raised in containers, although it will eventually outgrow all but the largest containers. The plant can withstand some drought and should not be over-watered. Fruit production begins when the plant reaches 4 or 5 years of age. Male and female plants should be planted near each other to ensure adequate fruit production. Seeds will not germinate in cool conditions and, except in mid-summer temperatures, may require an artificial heat source to ensure germination. In addition, the seeds rapidly lose viability when removed from the fruit. Trees can be propagated through softwood cuttings.

HARVEST AND USE The fruit is harvested when it is still green, but after it has attained full size. In Florida, the fruit matures from August to October. The dried fruit is the primary source of the popular spice. However, the leaves also contain significant scent and flavor. The leaves can be used as a seasoning in the same manner as bay leaves, and are removed from the dish prior to serving. Unlike bay leaves, allspice leaves do not retain significant flavor after they have been dried. Allspice is used in Caribbean "jerk" seasoning, in various curry mixes, in marinades, in pumpkin pie, and in Mexican cooking. It is also used extensively in Germany and Scandinavia as a pickling agent and as meat flavoring.

Allspice flowers usually emerge from late spring to August.

23

Anise

SCIENTIFIC NAME: *Pimpinella anisum*
FAMILY: Apiaceae
OTHER COMMON NAME: Anís (Spanish)

Herbaceous Annual

Planted
in Spring

Planted
in Fall

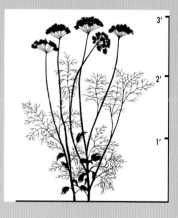

Characteristics

Overall Rating	★★★
Ease of Care	★★★
Utility	★★★
Landscape Value	★★
Salt Tolerance	★
Drought Tolerance	★★★★
Heat/Humidity Tolerance	★★
Cold Tolerance	★
Shade Tolerance	★
Longevity	★

Known Hazards

While anise is generally considered safe, it has estrogenic properties and should be avoided during pregnancy. Because this plant belongs to the same family as celery, those who are allergic to celery should exercise caution. Anise has been linked to photosensitivity in some individuals. Anise contains salicylates, and consumption may cause reactions in those who are intolerant of these compounds.

Anise is thought to have been cultivated at an early date and was used by the ancient Egyptians, Greeks, and Romans. The seeds are employed as a spice and the leaves are used as an herb. It is one of several spices that possess a licorice flavor. True licorice, *Glycyrrhiza* spp., is a root crop and is not related to anise. Anise is well suited to growth in Florida and succeeds as an annual throughout the state.

GEOGRAPHIC DISTRIBUTION Anise is native to the Middle East and eastern Mediterranean, and may have originated in Egypt. Commercial production occurs in Spain, Turkey, Italy, Greece, and Egypt. It will grow throughout Florida.

PLANT DESCRIPTION Anise is an herbaceous annual, attaining a maximum height of about 3 feet. Leaves on lower portions of the plant are deeply lobed, with uneven serrated edges. Leaves on the upper stem are divided into leaflets, and are lacy in appearance. Small white flowers are borne in dense umbels. Each flower has 5 petals, 5 sepals, and 5 stamens. The spice is made from the dried fruit of the plant, commonly referred to as the seed.

FLAVOR AND SCENT The scent and taste are similar to that of licorice. Anise is aromatic and slightly sweet.

RELATIVES Anise is a member of the large Apiaceae or carrot family. This family includes about 250 genera and 3,000 species. Several species are described within this book, including caraway, *Carum carvi*; chervil, *Anthriscus cerefolium*; cilantro, *Coriandrum sativum*; culantro, *Eryngium foetidum*; cumin, *Cuminum cyminum*; dill, *Anethum graveolens*; fennel, *Foeniculum vulgare*; lovage, *Levisticum officinale*; and parsley, *Petroselinum crispum*. Vegetables such as carrot, *Daucus carota*; celery, *Apium graveolens*; and parsnip, *Pastinaca sativa,* are placed within the Apiaceae family. Wild carrot, *Daucus carota*, also known as Queen Anne's lace, is also a member of the Apiaceae family. Special care should be employed when gathering this plant from the wild, as it closely resembles poison hemlock, *Conium maculatum*, which harbors a potentially deadly toxin. Anise is not related to Florida anise (*Illicium floridanum*), star anise (*Illicium verum*), or yellow anise (*Illicium parviflorum*), which are covered in subsequent sections of this book.

CULTIVATION Anise is moderately demanding in its cultural requirements. It prefers full sun and loose, well-drained soil, but will usually make acceptable growth on other soil types. In north Florida, seeds should be sown in the spring, once any danger of frost has passed. The plants flower in the summer and go to seed in late summer and early fall. In south Florida, anise is most often planted in the fall or early winter. Plants are spaced at about 12 inches. Seeds should be soaked in warm water for 24 hours prior to planting. Once established, the plant is moderately drought tolerant. Anise has a deep taproot and is therefore difficult to transplant.

HARVEST AND USE The ribbed seeds, when mature, are threshed or cut from the plants and dried in shallow trays. Several plants are required to obtain a significant quantity of seeds. Anise can be used whole or crushed in various recipes. It is employed as an ingredient in Middle Eastern cooking and in various European cuisines. It enhances the flavor of seafood. It is also used as a pickling agent. In India, anise is sometimes used as a breath freshener and palate cleanser. The anise-based drink absinthe was an immensely popular liquor in Belle Epoque France. Ingredients included anise, wormwood, and fennel. Absinthe was banned in the United States in 1912 and was banned in France in 1915. Recently, various nations have legalized absinthe, and this aperitif is making a comeback. Anise is also used to flavor ouzo, a liquor popular in Greece, and anisette, a liqueur popular in France, Spain, Italy, and Mexico. Anise has also been rubbed on fishing lures as an attractant. The leaves are edible, and can be used fresh as an addition to salads, dried for use in tea, or stewed as a potherb.

What is commonly referred to as anise seed is actually a fruit, specifically a dry schizocarp or seedpod. In form it resembles the fruit of other members of the Apiaceae family.

Annatto

SCIENTIFIC NAME: *Bixa orellana*
FAMILY: Bixaceae
OTHER COMMON NAMES: Lipstick Tree, Bixia, Achiote
  (Spanish)

Perennial; Evergreen Shrub

Characteristics

Overall Rating	★★★
Ease of Care	★★★
Utility	★★
Landscape Value	★★★
Salt Tolerance	★
Drought Tolerance	★★★★
Heat/Humidity Tolerance	★★★★★
Cold Tolerance	★★
Shade Tolerance	★
Longevity	★★★

Annatto (also spelled Annato) is primarily known as a coloring agent. It yields intense red and orange dyes that can be used in food, lipstick, soap, leather, candy, fabric, and other applications. The Mayans applied the dye as war paint. Annatto seeds are also used as a spice, lending a mild but distinctive flavor to various dishes. Annatto roughly parallels saffron in its applications and manner of use. It is a popular food additive in Latin America, the Caribbean, and the Philippines.

Known Hazards

Contact with the seeds can result in the staining of clothing and other items. On very rare occasions, this plant has been associated with allergic reactions.

26

GEOGRAPHIC DISTRIBUTION Annatto is native to the tropical rainforests of Central America and northern South America. Its precise origin is unknown, as it was widely disbursed by native people prior to the arrival of Europeans. The spice, often sold as a paste or in block form, is regularly available in Latin American markets. It is a common ingredient in the cuisines of Guatemala, southern Mexico, Jamaica, and the Philippines. The plant will succeed in most tropical and subtropical regions. However, it is frost sensitive. Growth in Florida is limited to the southern half of the peninsula.

PLANT DESCRIPTION This tropical evergreen shrub reaches a height of between 6 and 18 feet. The leaves, which measure up to 8 inches in length, are heart shaped with a pointed apex. The plant bears showy pink or white flowers with 5 petals. These form in loose clusters and measure about 2 inches in diameter. Clusters of spiny pods soon develop. These approximate an almond in overall shape. As the pods mature they turn from green to a bright, fiery red. The pods spit open, revealing between 25 and 75 triangular seeds set in a thick pulp. The triangular seeds are deep red, measuring about 1/8 of an inch in length.

FLAVOR AND SCENT The aroma of the spice is light, reminiscent of nutmeg. The taste is slightly peppery with a hint of sweetness. It is relatively weak and can be overpowered by other spices.

RELATIVES Although accounts of the Bixaceae family are inconsistent, it appears to contain 2 genera and between 5 and 20 species. Most are native to tropical America and the Caribbean. No members of the family other than annatto are covered in this book.

CULTIVATION The plant can be started from seed or from cuttings. Seeds should be planted at a very shallow depth. Annatto prefers full sun. It will grow on various soils. Once it has been established, annatto is a tough plant and will tolerate drought and other adverse conditions. While annatto can be container grown in north and central Florida, it is not the ideal container plant given its somewhat sprawling habit of growth.

HARVEST AND USE Production of seedpods is often profuse and may occur sporadically over much of the year. The dye is derived from the pulp within the seedpods. The spice is derived from the seeds. Following harvest, the seeds are separated from the pods and pulp and are then washed in cold water and dried. They can be ground into a paste or stored whole in an airtight container. The seeds can be steeped in hot water to produce a stock or to color and flavor rice. Frying the seeds in oil helps bring out the flavor. However, the cook should exercise caution, as the seeds tend to pop and jump when exposed to high temperatures. When used for stock or when fried in oil, the liquid may be kept and the seeds discarded. Annatto is used to color and flavor rice for paella. In Latin America, it is sometimes used as a spice for poultry and is often added to soups and stews.

The flowers and fruit of annatto are showy. The plant typically has multiple stems that branch close to the ground.

Basil

SCIENTIFIC NAME: *Ocimum* spp.
FAMILY: Lamiaceae
OTHER COMMON NAME: Albahaca (Spanish)

Herbaceous Annual

Planted in Spring

Planted in Fall

Characteristics

Overall Rating	★★★★★
Ease of Care	★★★★
Utility	★★★★
Landscape Value	★★★
Salt Tolerance	★★
Drought Tolerance	★★
Heat/Humidity Tolerance	★★★★
Cold Tolerance	★
Shade Tolerance	★★
Longevity	★

Known Hazards

Some sources discourage use of basil during pregnancy, while others consider this herb safe for consumption in amounts used for cooking and flavoring. Some forms contain minute quantities of safrole, which is considered a mild carcinogen. Basil contains salicylates, and consumption may cause reactions in those who are intolerant of these compounds.

This annual herb is one of the most popular culinary herbs on the planet. Basil is a significant ingredient in many of the world's finest cuisines, including those of Thailand, Italy, India, Vietnam, and France. Many varieties have been selected, and these give rise to a broad range of characteristics and flavors. Some have purple or ornamental leaves. Some are lemon-scented. Some are spicy, while others are sweet and mild. In 2003, the International Herb Association designated basil as the Herb of the Year.

28

GEOGRAPHIC DISTRIBUTION Members of the *Ocimum* genus are widely distributed throughout Africa, southern Asia, and tropical America. Commercial production takes place in Morocco, France, Italy, and Egypt. Some commercial production also occurs in California and Florida. Basil will grow throughout Florida.

Four forms of basil, from upper left to bottom right: 'Spicy Globe,' 'Cinnamon,' 'Thai,' and 'African Blue'

PLANT DESCRIPTION Basil is generally classified as an annual herb, although it may last for several seasons in south Florida. Depending on the variety, it can reach a height of between 1 and 3 feet. Leaves are opposite, oval, and measure between 1 to 3 inches in length. The leaves are diverse in shape and color. Flowers, which are borne on vertical spikes, are typically white, pink, or purple.

FLAVOR AND SCENT Basil tastes of mint and pepper, often with hints of lime, clove, and cinnamon. The aroma is complex, earthy, and pungent. Some types have a distinct citrus note.

VARIETIES Species within the genus, and even cultivars within a given species, show remarkable diversity. The dominant basil used as a spice within the United States is sweet or Mediterranean basil, *Ocimum basilicum*. Wild sweet basil, *Ocimum campechianum*, is a native plant, growing in widely scattered locations in Miami-Dade, Monroe, and Collier Counties. It is endangered and cannot be removed from the wild. However, when seeds or cuttings can be obtained from nurseries or other sources, it is well worth planting. It compares favorably with other basils from a culinary perspective. It is a resilient plant that prefers full sun and adequate drainage. Well-regarded basil cultivars include: 'African Blue,' 'Aussie Sweetie,' 'Basilico Green,' 'Cinnamon,' 'Green Bouquet' 'Indian Sacred Basil,' 'Lemon,' 'Licorice,' 'Magic Michael,' 'Minette,' 'Miniature Purple,' 'Purple Ruffles,' 'Red Rubin,' 'Thai Lemon,' 'Siam Queen,' 'Spicy Globe,' 'Sweet Dani,' and 'Wild Purple.'

RELATIVES The Lamiaceae or mint family contains several important herbs and spices. Species discussed within this book include: bee balm, *Monarda didyma*; Cuban oregano, *Plectranthus amboinicus*; Jamaican mint, *Micromeria viminea*; lavender, *Lavandula* spp.; lemon balm, *Melissa officinalis*; mint, *Mentha* spp.; oregano, *Origanum* spp.; perilla, *Perilla frutescens*; rosemary, *Rosmarinus officinalis*; sage, *Salvia officinalis*; savory, *Satureja* spp.; and thyme, *Thymus* spp.

CULTIVATION Basil prefers full sun and warm temperatures. It requires regular watering and will succeed in consistently damp parts of the garden. Plants should be spaced at 10 inches to a foot. Basil can be readily grown from cuttings or seed. Seeds are planted in the fall in frost-free areas of the state. In north Florida, seeds are sown in the spring after the danger of frost has passed. Cut stems should be suspended in water with a trace of rooting hormone until roots develop. During the growing season, basil should be regularly pinched or harvested to encourage branching and to prevent the plant from flowering and going to seed. Unlike many herbs covered in this book, most varieties of Basil thrive during the summer in south Florida. Plants are cold tender, though, and will ordinarily be killed by freezing temperatures.

HARVEST AND USE Basil is at its best when used fresh. Basil can be harvested as little as a month after planting. Where preservation is required, freezing is recommended, as the leaves retain most of their natural flavor that way. Immersing the fresh leaves in olive oil will also preserve the flavor. Basil is widely used in pestos, tomato sauces, and seafood dishes. The seeds are sometime harvested and used in drinks and desserts.

Dried basil, while less intense than fresh basil, still retains the essential flavor that makes this herb an important ingredient in many cuisines.

Bay Laurel

SCIENTIFIC NAME: *Laurus nobilis*
FAMILY: Lauraceae
OTHER COMMON NAMES: Bay, Sweet Laurel, Laurel
Común (Spanish)

Woody Perennial; Evergreen Tree

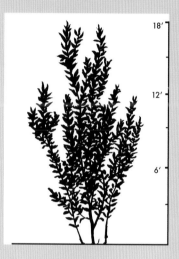

Characteristics

Overall Rating	★★★
Ease of Care	★★
Utility	★★★
Landscape Value	★★★
Salt Tolerance	★★★★
Drought Tolerance	★★★
Heat/Humidity Tolerance	★★★
Cold Tolerance	★★
Shade Tolerance	★★
Longevity	★★★★

This aromatic tree yields the bay leaves found in the spice section of supermarkets. The plant has a long and decorated history. Greek athletes and Roman emperors wore head wreaths composed of bay leaves. The International Herb Association designated bay laurel the Herb of the Year for 2009. The species requires a tropical or subtropical climate, and can only be grown outdoors in south Florida.

Known Hazards

The leaves present a choking hazard if they are not removed from food before it is served. Dried leaves, if consumed, can cause internal cuts to the gastro-intestinal tract. Must not be confused with cherry laurel, which is poisonous.

GEOGRAPHIC DISTRIBUTION The bay laurel originated in the western Mediterranean area or Asia Minor. Turkey is a major producer. The plant is cold sensitive. In Florida, bay laurel will grow as far north as Merritt Island on the east coast and Sarasota on the west coast.

A young 'Vanilla' bay laurel

PLANT DESCRIPTION The bay laurel is typically a small evergreen tree, and often assumes a shrublike form. However, under ideal conditions, it can attain a height of more than 50 feet. The rate of growth is slow. Leaves are borne alternately. They are deep green, leathery, 3 to 4 inches in length, with minute serrations in the margin. The yellow flowers are small and inconspicuous. The fruit is a tiny black berry.

FLAVOR AND SCENT The highly aromatic leaves of the bay laurel are somewhat bitter when first harvested. This trait is removed through the drying process. The flavor is reminiscent of pine, wintergreen, and cinnamon.

VARIETIES Several cultivars have been selected, including 'Angustifolia,' 'Aurea,' and 'Undulata.' However, these varieties are grown for their appearance and do not possess any special culinary properties.

RELATIVES The family Lauraceae contains about 50 genera and 2,000 species. It contains the notable fruiting plant avocado, *Persea americana*. Several other species from the family Lauraceae produce aromatic leaves used in cooking. The red bay, *Persea borbonia*, which is treated in a separate section of this book, is a native plant that can be used as a substitute for bay laurel. Other members of the Lauraceae family covered within this book include cinnamon, *Cinnamomum verum*; sassafras, *Sassafras albidumare*; and spicebush, *Lindera benzoin*. Other "bay" species such as Indian

bay, *Cinnamomum tamala*, and Indonesian bay, *Eugenia polyantha*, are used in a similar manner to laurel bay, but are not closely related. Another "bay" not closely related to bay laurel is bay rum. This species, which is not used for culinary purposes, is described in the next profile.

CULTIVATION Bay laurel has a reputation for being difficult to start. Seeds may require as long as 6 months to germinate. The plant is cold sensitive and will be greatly harmed at about 28° F and killed at 26° or 27° F. Bay laurel has moderate salt tolerance and can be grown on barrier islands.

Close-up detail of a dried bay leaf

HARVEST AND USE Bay leaves can be harvested at any time. Leaves are almost always dried before use, as flavors mature during the drying process. They are used in various Mediterranean cuisines, in French cooking, and in Cajun and Creole cooking. They are often used as an ingredient in fine Indian biryanis. Seafood boils, seafood dishes, and various soups and stews benefit from the distinctive flavor. In cooking, the leaves are generally used whole and strained from the dish prior to serving. They present a choking hazard if they are not removed from food prior to serving. The fresh leaves are tough and the dried leaves are hard and brittle.

Harvest is accomplished by clipping older leaves from the shoots. Insect pests rarely bother this species.

Bay Rum

SCIENTIFIC NAME: *Pimenta racemosa*
FAMILY: Myrtaceae
OTHER COMMON NAME: West Indian Bay

Woody Perennial; Evergreen Tree

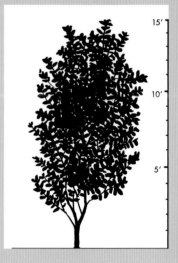

Characteristics

Overall Rating	★★★★
Ease of Care	★★★★
Utility	★★
Landscape Value	★★★★
Salt Tolerance	★★
Drought Tolerance	★★★
Heat/Humidity Tolerance	★★★★★
Cold Tolerance	★★
Shade Tolerance	★★★★
Longevity	★★★★

While leaves of this allspice relative have sometimes been employed as a cooking spice, they are not recommended for culinary use. Nevertheless, bay rum is undoubtedly one of finest scent plants available. It is best known for its incorporation into various aftershaves, lotions, soaps, and colognes. The aroma of the crushed leaves is lingering, pleasant, distinctive, and unforgettable.

Known Hazards

Not for culinary applications. The bay rum tree's fruit and essential oil are toxic. The leaves and other plant parts may be mildly toxic and should not be ingested.

GEOGRAPHIC DISTRIBUTION Bay rum is native to the Caribbean and is common in Trinidad, Cuba, Jamaica, the Virgin Islands, and Puerto Rico. It may also be native to the northern coast of South America. Commercial cultivation occurs on St. Johns, where trees are raised for the essential oils found in the leaves and twigs. The plant has been distributed to other tropical regions and is considered an invasive exotic on several Pacific islands, including Hawaii. In Florida, growth is limited to coastal areas of the southern peninsula. Leaf damage occurs at 30° F. Severe limb damage occurs at about 28° F.

PLANT DESCRIPTION Bay rum is a small to medium evergreen tree, with an upright, columnar habit of growth. It reaches a height of about 20 feet, but can be readily maintained in more compact form. The bark is smooth but is exfoliating and patchy. Leaves are deep green, shiny above, ovate to elliptic, measuring 2 to 5 inches in length. Emerging foliage is tinted red. The white flowers have a 5-lobed calyx. They are small but fragrant, appearing in loose panicles. The fruit is a small, black, oblong berry.

SCENT The leaves have a sweet, spicy fragrance, with notes of clove, balsam, and citronella. At least one strain is reported to have a lemon scent.

VARIETIES Several subspecies, *Pimenta racemosa grisea*, *Pimenta racemosa ozua*, *Pimenta racemosa racemosa*, and *Pimenta racemosa terebinthina* are mentioned in the literature. No named cultivars appear to be available in Florida.

RELATIVES The Myrtaceae family is made up of more than 3,750 species. The *Pimenta* genus also includes allspice, *Pimenta dioicia*, covered earlier within these pages. Other more distant relatives of bay rum discussed within this book include myrtle, *Myrtus communis*, and rumberry, *Myrciaria floribunda*.

CULTIVATION This species is undemanding in its cultural requirements. It is drought tolerant, although it benefits from regular watering during establishment. Soil should be well drained. Bay rum will grow in full sun, but appears to hold a slight preference for light, partial shade.

HARVEST AND USE The leaves can be harvested at any time. The essential oil, used for commercial purposes, is derived through steam distillation. It is the primary ingredient in bay rum aftershave and has been incorporated in various colognes, perfumes, lotions, rubs, and soaps. Curiously, an extract has also been marketed as an anti-fungal treatment for aquarium water. The fruit and oil are toxic, and all parts of the plant are suspect and should not be consumed.

A young bay rum planted as an accent. Eventually, the tree will fill in to occupy the entire space. Hardy, easily shaped, and well behaved, the bay rum can be adapted to many situations.

Bee Balm

SCIENTIFIC NAME: *Monarda didyma*
FAMILY: Lamiaceae
OTHER COMMON NAMES: Oswego Tea, Bergamot

Herbaceous Perennial

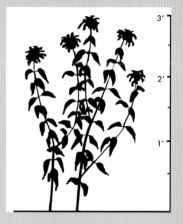

Characteristics

Overall Rating	★★★
Ease of Care	★★★
Utility	★★
Landscape Value	★★★★
Salt Tolerance	★★★
Drought Tolerance	★★★
Heat/Humidity Tolerance	★★★
Cold Tolerance	★★★
Shade Tolerance	★★★
Longevity	★★★

Bee balm is a native wildflower that has been adapted by nurseries and gardeners as a cottage herb. It is now cultivated in various warm-temperate and subtropical regions around the globe. Native Americans have long enjoyed this member of the mint family in teas and have used it for medicinal purposes. Bee balm is ornamental and relatively undemanding. In flavor and utility, it is equal to many better-known herbs.

Known Hazards

Bee balm should not be consumed during pregnancy.

34

GEOGRAPHIC DISTRIBUTION Bee balm is native to most of North America, including all 48 contiguous states. It can be grown throughout Florida. However, temperate selections tend to perform poorly in south Florida.

PLANT DESCRIPTION Bee balm is an herbaceous, clumping perennial. It dies back over the winter, but regenerates from underground rhizomes in the spring. The plant has an upright habit of growth and attains a height of 3 or 4 feet. The opposite leaves are lance shaped, slightly rough in texture, with toothed or lightly notched margins. Flowers, which appear during the summer, may be red, lavender, pink, white, or purple, depending on the variety.

A close-up of bee balm leaves showing the growth tip

FLAVOR AND SCENT The leaves are aromatic and give off a mintlike fragrance. They taste faintly of citrus.

VARIETIES Spotted bee balm, *Monarda punctata*, occurs naturally throughout the state. Like other bee balms, it is aromatic and fragrant. Lemon bee balm, *Monarda citriodora*, performs especially well in south Florida. Bee balm has been the subject of breeding to achieve flower variations. Cultivars, which may or may not be suited to growth in peninsular Florida, include: 'Adam,' a red-flowered selection; 'Blue Stocking,' a variety with good mildew resistance that bears violet flowers; 'Bowman,' a large, purple-flowered selection; 'Croftway Pink,' a variety with bright pink flowers; 'Gardenview Scarlet,' a medium-height variety that bears dark red flowers; 'Marshall's Delight,' a pink-flowered variety; 'Petite Delight,' a small, pink-flowered selection; 'Purple Crown,' a purple-flowered selection; 'Snow White,' a white-flowered selection; and 'Violet Queen,' a violet-flowered selection.

RELATIVES Lamiaceae or the mint family contains several important herbs and spices. Species discussed within this book include: basil, *Ocimum* spp.; Cuban oregano, *Plectranthus amboinicus*; Jamaican mint, *Micromeria viminea*; lavender, *Lavandula* spp.; lemon balm, *Melissa officinalis*; mint, *Mentha* spp.; oregano, *Origanum* spp.; perilla, *Perilla frutescens*; rosemary, *Rosmarinus officinalis*; sage, *Salvia officinalis*; savory, *Satureja* spp.; and thyme, *Thymus* spp. The *Monarda* genus consists of about 15 species. Wild bergamot, *Monarda fistulosa*, is native to the eastern United States and grows in open fields. It has lavender flowers and scent characteristics similar to those of bee balm.

CULTIVATION Bee balm is a relatively hardy plant. It can withstand minor drought, although the soil should never be permitted to dry out completely. It prefers partial shade. It is somewhat susceptible to attacks by powdery mildew. Bee balm spreads through rhizomes and can invade nearby sections of garden. Division is the preferred method of propagation. The root mass is unearthed in the spring and young plants are separated from the outer margin of the mat. Clumps will lose vigor unless they are divided every few years. Bee balm should be severely cut back prior to the advent of cool temperatures.

HARVEST AND USE The young leaves can be used as a salad herb. The blooms and leaves, if dried and steeped, yield a good-quality tea. They can also be used to flavor traditional tea. Teas brewed with bee balm are sometimes referred to as bergamot teas. However, they should not be confused with Earl Grey tea, which is flavored with

Bee balm makes a striking ornamental in addition to its use as a tea plant.

bergamot oil from the bergamot orange. Dried bee balm is sold commercially. The leaves make a flavorful salad ingredient. Flowers can be used as a garnish and can be added to salads for color. Bee balm attracts hummingbirds, bees, and butterflies to the garden.

Bilimbi

SCIENTIFIC NAME: *Averrhoa bilimbi*
FAMILY: Oxalidaceae
OTHER COMMON NAME: Cucumber Tree

Woody Perennial; Evergreen Tree

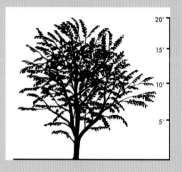

Characteristics

Overall Rating	★★
Ease of Care	★★★★
Utility	★★
Landscape Value	★★★
Salt Tolerance	★
Drought Tolerance	★★★★
Heat/Humidity Tolerance	★★★★★
Cold Tolerance	★★
Shade Tolerance	★★★
Longevity	★★★★

The bilimbi is closely related to the starfruit, or carambola. While the fruit of the carambola is used for fresh consumption, the fruit of the bilimbi is used as a flavoring agent. Its sour, acidic flavor lends tang to relishes, chutneys, and other dishes. The tree is attractive, very productive, and easy to maintain. However, it has never attained significant popularity in Florida. In most instances, it is grown in collections or as a novelty.

Known Hazards

Those with kidney stones, kidney disease, gout, or rheumatic ailments should avoid consumption due to oxalic acid content.

GEOGRAPHIC DISTRIBUTION The bilimbi probably originated in Indonesia, possibly in the Moluccas. It is widely grown in Malaysia, India, Sri Lanka, the Philippines, the Caribbean, and throughout Latin America. In Florida, cultivation is relegated to southern parts of the state.

PLANT DESCRIPTION The evergreen tree attains a maximum height of about 30 feet, but is usually much smaller. The alternate leaves are up to 24 inches long, and contain up to 20 pairs of leaflets. The leaflets are soft, with a rounded base and pointed apex. Small reddish-purple flowers appear on panicles dangling from the trunk and major branches. These panicles sometimes form dense clusters. The fruit is an elliptic berry. It has the approximate appearance and dimensions of a medium pickle. The flesh is crisp, although it grows less firm as the fruit ripens. Embedded within the flesh are from 3 to 6 flat brown seeds.

FLAVOR The fruit is generally too sour for consumption out of hand. However, the underlying flavor is pleasant, especially when the tartness is offset with sweetness.

VARIETIES No cultivars appear in the literature and none are available in Florida.

RELATIVES The bilimbi is a member of the Oxalidaceae, or wood-sorrel, family. This small family consists of 7 or 8 genera and about 900 species. Most species are tropical or subtropical, although a few grow in temperate climates. The fruiting plant, carambola, *Averrhoa carambola*, has already been mentioned as a relative. Several distant relatives are native to Florida. These include the yellow wood sorrel, *Oxalis stricta*, a common plant throughout the state, and tufted yellow wood sorrel, *Oxalis lyonii*, native to north Florida. The wood sorrels are delicate, low-growing plants with cloverlike leaves. The leaves are edible, pleasantly sour, and are sometimes used by hikers in salads or as a cooked vegetable.

CULTIVATION Bilimbi is generally grown from seed. It requires very little care. It should be watered during periods of establishment and during periods of drought. It is slightly more cold sensitive than its relative, the carambola. It is damaged by temperatures around 29° F, and is greatly harmed or killed by temperatures of about 27° F.

HARVEST AND USE In Florida, the bilimbi bears fruit sporadically over the warmer months, from May through November. In Southeast Asia, the fruit is often cooked with fish. The fruit can also be juiced to make a lemonade-like drink. The fruit can be pickled for later use, and can be fashioned into curries, chutneys, and relishes. The fruit contains oxalic acid. This compound is not harmful in small quantities or for those that are in good health. However, those with kidney stones, kidney disease, gout, or rheumatic ailments should avoid plants containing oxalic acid.

Fruit and flowers emerge directly from older wood. In cooking, bilimbi can be used for many of the same purposes as acid citrus.

Black Pepper

SCIENTIFIC NAME: *Piper nigrum*
FAMILY: Piperaceae
OTHER COMMON NAME: Pimienta Negra (Spanish)

Woody Perennial Vine

Characteristics

Overall Rating	★★★
Ease of Care	★★★
Utility	★★★
Landscape Value	★★★
Salt Tolerance	★
Drought Tolerance	★★
Heat/Humidity Tolerance	★★★★★
Cold Tolerance	★
Shade Tolerance	★★★
Longevity	★★

Black pepper is a spice with great historical significance. It is also important from a commercial perspective. It is the most popular condiment in the world after salt. Black pepper is an all-purpose seasoning, used in nearly every cuisine. The plant is not difficult to grow. However, it is tropical in habit and cannot endure winter cold.

Known Hazards

The essential oil from this plant contains minute quantities of safrole, which is considered a mild carcinogen. Some authorities suggest that use should be limited or avoided during pregnancy.

38

GEOGRAPHIC DISTRIBUTION Black pepper is native to southwestern India. It reached Egypt by 1200 BC and was used extensively by ancient Greeks and Romans. Traders and others used it as currency. Black pepper was the driving force behind the explorations of Vasco da Gama and others. The spice trade with India was controlled at various times by the Italians, the Portuguese, and the Dutch. Today, pepper accounts for about 20 percent of the world spice trade. Major producers include Vietnam, India, Indonesia, Brazil, Malaysia, Costa Rica, and Sri Lanka. In Florida, growth of black pepper is limited to coastal areas of the southern peninsula and the Keys.

PLANT DESCRIPTION Black pepper is an upright, woody vine, with trailing stems. It can climb to a height of about 20 feet, although it is usually maintained at 8 feet or less to facilitate harvest. Leaves are alternate, broadly ovate, tapering toward a pointed apex. The leaves measure from 3 to 5 inches in length. White flowers form on spikes during the summer. Between 50 and 100 tightly clustered pieces of fruit develop in a chain along each spike. The fruit is a small drupe, which contains a single seed. It is about 1/4 of an inch in diameter. The immature fruit is green, but turns dark-red or black upon maturity.

FLAVOR AND SCENT The flavor of black pepper is aromatic, slightly bitter, and hot, although the heat is less intense than that of a moderately hot chili pepper. The scent is sharp and irritates the nasal passages.

VARIETIES Types of black pepper that enjoy wide use in the United States include Lampong Pepper, from Indonesia, and Penang Pepper, from Malaysia. Tellicherry pepper is an expensive and highly aromatic form of black pepper from India.

RELATIVES The other member of the Piperaceae family covered within this book is the root beer plant, *Piper auritum*. Spiked pepper, *Piper aduncum*, is a non-native plant that has escaped cultivation in south Florida. Several plants not related to black pepper are nevertheless referred to as peppers. These include bell peppers and chili peppers. Brazilian pepper, *Schinus terebinthifolius*, is an invasive exotic that is not a member of the Piperaceae family. Its use as a spice is discouraged owing to safety concerns.

CULTIVATION The main limit to raising black pepper in Florida is temperature. Temperatures below 40° F result in growth setbacks. Even a light frost may be fatal. Pepper requires well-drained soil, but is not tolerant of drought. Regular irrigation is required during periods of low rainfall. Black pepper performs best in partial shade. A trellis or other support is necessary.

HARVEST AND USE Black pepper is usually harvested when the first berries in the chain ripen. The fruit, when dried, is referred to as a peppercorn. Black pepper is produced from the dried, green peppercorn. The fruit is cooked briefly in hot water following harvest. It is then allowed to ferment before it is dried. Used whole or ground, black pepper is one of the most common spices in many European cuisines. White pepper consists of the pepper seed with the surrounding flesh removed. To produce white pepper, ripe berries are soaked in water for 7 to 10 days, until the fruit swells, decomposes, and sloughs away from the seeds. Green pepper is produced from the dried unripe peppercorn. This is processed in a manner designed to retain the green color. The uses of pepper in the kitchen are extensive. It is frequently employed in spice blends, rubs, pickles, and marinades.

The fruit of black pepper, a small drupe, is referred to as a peppercorn. A single flower spike may produce between 50 and 100 peppercorns.

Borage

SCIENTIFIC NAME: *Borago officinalis*
FAMILY: Boraginaceae
OTHER COMMON NAMES: Starflower, Borraja (Spanish)

Herbaceous Annual

Planted in Spring

Planted in Fall

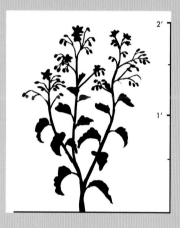

Characteristics

Overall Rating	★★★
Ease of Care	★★★★
Utility	★★★
Landscape Value	★★★★
Salt Tolerance	★★
Drought Tolerance	★★★
Heat/Humidity Tolerance	★
Cold Tolerance	★★★
Shade Tolerance	★
Longevity	★

Known Hazards

Borage should not be consumed during pregnancy, as it is thought to cause premature labor. Excessive consumption of borage oil or concentrates for prolonged periods may cause liver damage. Contact with the plant may cause skin irritation in hypersensitive individuals.

Borage is an attractive addition to the Florida herb garden. This annual can be used as a dried herb or as a fresh vegetable. It produces beautiful, edible flowers. Borage is easy to grow and requires little care.

GEOGRAPHIC DISTRIBUTION Borage is thought to have originated in Syria, but grows wild throughout the Mediterranean region. Spanish explorers brought this plant to the Americas prior to 1500. Borage is grown commercially for its seed, which contains gamalinolenic acid. Gamalinolenic acid is used as a supplement and for medicinal purposes. Large-scale producers of borage seed include the United States, Canada, England, Spain, the Netherlands, and New Zealand.

PLANT DESCRIPTION Borage is an annual herb reaching a height of 2 to 3 feet. It has a long central taproot and thick, branching stems. Stems, leaves, and flower buds are coated with bristly hairs. Leaves are gray-green, ovate to lanceolate, and typically measure between 3 and 5 inches in length. Flowers, which are usually a deep blue-violet, have five, pointed petals.

FLAVOR The leaves taste of cucumber and are slightly salty. The flowers also taste of cucumber and are slightly sweet. The plant is said to have a cooling quality.

VARIETIES Several cultivars exist. 'Alba' is a white-flowered selection. 'Flor Blanca,' which may be similar in form, is grown in Spain. There are also double-flowered varieties and pink-flowered varieties, selected for their ornamental qualities.

RELATIVES The Boraginaceae family consists of about 1,800 species in about 100 genera. With the exception of comfrey, *Symphytum officinale*, the family does not contain many notable culinary herbs. Comfrey, it should be noted, contains alkaloids with carcinogenic properties and is therefore not separately covered within this book. The Boraginaceae family also contains several familiar plants such as the forget-me-not, *Myosotis* spp.; the heliotrope, *Heliotropium* spp.; and the geiger tree, *Cordia sebestena*.

CULTIVATION Borage is typically grown from seed, which readily germinates. Borage is a hardy plant and is moderately drought tolerant. However, like many temperate herbs, it performs poorly over the summer in south Florida and often succumbs to the heat and humidity. Consequently, in areas from Orlando southward, it is planted in the fall and harvested over the winter and early spring. Borage prefers slightly alkaline soil, although it will readily tolerate a pH range of 6.6 to 8.0. It is considered difficult to transplant. Borage prefers full sun and good drainage.

HARVEST AND USE Young foliage can be harvested from the plant at any time. The fresh leaves add an interesting element to salads. They can also be battered, fried, and served with cheese. They are excellent in omelets and dumplings. The flowers are edible and are highly decorative. They make an exquisite garnish and can be floated on drinks or frozen in ice cubes. In Iran, the flowers are brewed into a purple tea. Dried leaves can also be used in teas and to flavor beverages. Borage is one of several herbs that make up Frankfurter Green (Grüne) sauce, popular in Germany.

Burnet

SCIENTIFIC NAME: *Sanguisorba minor*
FAMILY: Rosaceae
OTHER COMMON NAMES: Salad Burnet, Hierba del
    Cuchillo (Spanish)

Evergreen Perennial

Planted in Spring

Planted in Fall

Characteristics

Overall Rating	★★★
Ease of Care	★★★
Utility	★★★
Landscape Value	★★
Salt Tolerance	★
Drought Tolerance	★★★
Heat/Humidity Tolerance	★
Cold Tolerance	★★★★
Shade Tolerance	★★
Longevity	★★★

Burnet is an herb that is admired in Europe, but that has fallen into disuse in the United States. The plant is attractive and well behaved. The flavor is pleasant and unique. It is therefore unclear why burnet is not more widely cultivated in this country. Burnet is reasonably well adapted to growing conditions in north Florida. But, like so many temperate species, it deteriorates in the heat and humidity of the summer in peninsular Florida.

Known Hazards

The calyx is inedible. On very rare occasions, this plant has been linked to contact dermatitis in sensitive individuals.

GEOGRAPHIC DISTRIBUTION Burnet is native to portions of Europe and Asia. It has escaped cultivation in the northeast and western United States.

PLANT DESCRIPTION Burnet is a compact evergreen perennial. The plant reaches a maximum height of about 20 inches. It forms a low clump, with stems arching outward from the center. The leaves are composed of 6 to 11 pairs of leaflets. The leaflets have toothed margins. Small pink flowers are borne in rounded heads atop slim stalks.

FLAVOR The flavor of the leaves is mild, slightly bitter and slightly nutty. They taste of cucumber with hints of melon.

VARIETIES 'Dalar' is a cultivar of *Sanguisorba minor* that is available in the United States. Other *Sanguisorba* cultivars, many of which are derived from the species *Sanguisorba officinalis*, include 'Arnhem,' 'Lemon Splash,' 'Martin's Mulberry,' 'Red Thunder,' and 'Tanna.'

RELATIVES The Rosaceae or rose family is a large family containing about 100 genera and over 3,000 species. It contains several important herbs, many familiar ornamentals, and a number of well-known fruiting plants. Aside from the burnet, the only other member of the Rosaceae family covered within this book is the rose, *Rosa* spp. The genus *Sanguisorba* consists of about 20 species scattered throughout North America, Europe, and Asia. Several species within the *Sanguisorba* genus possess edible foliage. American great burnet, *Sanguisorba canadensis*, is native to eastern North America and the Midwest, ranging as far south as Georgia. Leaves are edible and the plant is sometimes used as a salad green. Great burnet, *Sanguisorba officinalis*, is found throughout Europe and in parts of Asia. Hybridization among various *Sanguisorba* species is common. No species within the genus is native to Florida.

CULTIVATION Burnet is relatively easy to grow in north Florida and can survive winter cold as far north as USDA zone 4. In south Florida it can be grown as an annual over the cooler months. It prefers loose, well-drained soil. It will tolerate sandy soil and poor soil, but does not fare well in areas prone to standing water or prolonged moist conditions. Burnet succeeds well in containers. While it generally prefers full sun, the plant may benefit from midday shade in the hot subtropics. Burnet has moderate watering needs and is capable of surviving short periods of drought. Burnet can be reproduced through division of roots and clumps. If the flowers are permitted to go to seed, seedlings will likely spring up around the original plant. Culling the flower heads promotes additional vegetative growth.

HARVEST AND USE When needed, leaves are stripped from the stems. Leaves tend to become increasingly tough and bitter as they age. Young leaves are preferred for culinary purposes. Burnet can be added for flavor to salads, yogurt, cream cheese, tomato-based dishes, iced tea, and cottage cheese. The flavor of burnet fades when the leaves are dried.

Burnet can form dense clumps. The leaves are almost always used fresh, as they quickly lose their characteristic flavor when dried.

Cacao

SCIENTIFIC NAME: *Theobroma cacao*
FAMILY: Sterculiaceae

Woody Perennial; Evergreen Tree

Characteristics

Overall Rating	★★
Ease of Care	★★
Utility	★
Landscape Value	★★★★
Salt Tolerance	★★
Drought Tolerance	★★
Heat/Humidity Tolerance	★★★★★
Cold Tolerance	★
Shade Tolerance	★★★★★
Longevity	★★★★

The cacao—source of chocolate—is tropical in habit, but can be grown in protected areas of south Florida and the Keys. The scientific name means "food of the gods." As a result of difficulties associated with processing cacao paste, the fruit of this tree is not regularly harvested in Florida. It is grown almost exclusively as a curiosity. Still, with its dark green foliage and colorful fruits, it rates as a very attractive curiosity.

Known Hazards

Cacao contains caffeine. Excessive consumption of caffeine can cause nervousness, anxiety, insomnia, headaches, heart palpitations, and other health disorders.

44

GEOGRAPHIC DISTRIBUTION Cacao is indigenous to Central America and northern South America, including portions of the Amazon basin. Indigenous peoples are thought to have spread the plant throughout tropical America at an early date. Significant commercial production occurs in Brazil, Ivory Coast, Indonesia, Ghana, Ecuador, Costa Rica, Nigeria, and Cameroon. In Florida, growth is relegated to coastal areas from Palm Beach County southward.

The cacao is cauliflorous; that is, the flowers and fruit form directly on the trunk and main branches. In weight, mature pods average about a pound. However, the pods come in many forms, sizes, and colors.

PLANT DESCRIPTION Cacao is a small evergreen tree, reaching a maximum height of about 30 feet. The leaves are alternate, ovoid, and entire. They are dark green and glossy, reaching a length of about 14 inches. The species is cauliflorous, producing white flowers directly on the trunk and older branches. These are about 3/4 of an inch in diameter. The fruit, a pod, is ovoid, and measures between 6 and 13 inches in length. The pod may be orange, red, yellow, or green in color. Each pod contains 20 to 55 flat brown seeds set within edible, whitish pulp.

FLAVOR The pulp is sweet and rich. The beans themselves are not sweet. Cacao is a bitter, complex spice. Only with the addition of sugar does it take on attributes commonly associated with chocolate. Most milk chocolate contains less than 20 percent cacao paste.

VARIETIES Several cultivar groups dominate commercial production. As a result of their hardiness and productivity, cultivars from the Forastero Group are most frequently planted. Cultivars from the less vigorous Criollo Group are used to produce gourmet-quality beans. Cultivars from the Trinitario Group, which is composed of hybrids of Forastero and Criollo, are also widely planted.

RELATIVES The Malvaceae or mallow family consists of about 200 genera and 2,000 species. It contains such important crops as cotton, *Gossypium* spp., and okra, *Abelmoschus esculentus*. Durian, *Durio zibethinus*, a popular fruit in Southeast Asia, is also a member of this family. The genus *Theobroma* is made up of about 20 species. The cupuaçu, *Theobroma grandiflorum*, of Brazil, produces a pod similar to that of cacao. The fragrant pulp inside the pod is used as a dessert and flavoring. Apart from cacao, the only member of the Malvaceae family covered within this book is roselle, *Hibiscus sabdariffa*.

CULTIVATION Cacao is an understory tree and requires some overhead shade. It prefers a humid climate with even, year-round precipitation. The tree will tolerate neither drought nor flooding. It prefers fertile, well-drained soil. Cacao is damaged by temperatures below 40° F and may be killed if temperatures drop below 31° F. The tree will typically begin to bear fruit at 3 to 5 years of age.

HARVEST AND USE The production of chocolate is a complex process. In commercial production, the pods are harvested from the tree when they have reached full size. Many superior varieties are harvested when the pods are still green. The pods are then split open and the contents extracted. The beans and pulp are left to ferment for several days. This process is known as "sweating." The beans are then dried either by the sun or with artificial heat. They are periodically stirred to promote even drying. The beans are then washed, roasted, and de-hulled. They are then ground into a fine cocoa paste. Cocoa butter and sugar are then added. Over 200 beans may be required to make a single pound of quality chocolate.

An immature cacao pod. The pulp of mature pods is edible, and has a sweet, pleasant flavor. However, the taste bears no resemblance to that of chocolate.

Calamondin

SCIENTIFIC NAME: *Citrus mitis*
FAMILY: Rutaceae
OTHER COMMON NAMES: Panama Orange,
    Philippine Lime

Woody Perennial; Evergreen Shrub

Characteristics

Overall Rating	★★★★
Ease of Care	★★★★
Utility	★★★
Landscape Value	★★★★
Salt Tolerance	★★★
Drought Tolerance	★★★
Heat/Humidity Tolerance	★★★★
Cold Tolerance	★★★★
Shade Tolerance	★
Longevity	★★★

Calamondin is a type of acid citrus, used as a flavoring agent
rather than as a fresh fruit. The tree is small, dense, and highly
ornamental. The beauty and cold hardiness of this species make it
a popular planting choice for homeowners throughout the state.

Known Hazards

Sharp spines present a
mechanical hazard. As with other
members of the citrus genus,
contact with the leaves and
fruit rind may cause dermatitis
and photosensitivity in some
individuals.

GEOGRAPHIC DISTRIBUTION Calamondin is native to China, but has spread throughout Southeast Asia. It is popular in the Philippines, India, Malaysia, and Thailand. Dr. David Fairchild first introduced this plant into Florida in 1899. Calamondin is one of the cold-hardiest varieties of citrus. It has been known to bear fruit as far north as the Alabama border.

The kumquat is another form of citrus that is often used as a flavoring agent. However, unlike the calamondin, several types are sweet enough that they can be enjoyed out of hand.

PLANT DESCRIPTION The tree is a small evergreen, rarely reaching over 15 feet in height. It has dark green, finely textured foliage. The alternate leaves are glossy and slightly toothed, reaching about 2 1/2 inches in length. The petioles have narrow wings. The white flowers reach about 1 inch in diameter. The fruit is a specialized berry, or hesperidium. It resembles a miniature tangerine, and reaches about 1 1/2 inches in diameter. The peel is glossy and smooth. The fruit contains 7 to 10 segments, with a scattering of seeds.

FLAVOR AND SCENT The flesh of the fruit is unpleasantly sour when eaten out of hand. The peel is aromatic, somewhat sweet, with a mild flavor. The flowers exude a sweet fragrance typical of other citrus.

VARIETIES A variegated clone has been produced that bears yellow and green fruit and white-fringed leaves. A dwarf variety is also available.

RELATIVES The family Rutaceae consists of about 150 genera and 900 species. It includes all varieties of citrus and such diverse species as the bael fruit, *Aegle marmelos*, and white sapote, *Casimiroa edulis*. Other citrus species discussed within this book include the kaffir lime, *Citrus hystrix*; the lemon, *Citrus limon*; and the lime,

Citrus spp. Non-citrus members of the Rutaceae family covered within this book include the curry leaf tree, *Muraya koenigii*, and rue, *Ruta graveolens*.

Another form of acid citrus that deserves mention is the sour orange, *Citrus aurantium*. Like calamondin, this species is used as a flavoring agent rather than as a fresh fruit. The tree is similar to that of the sweet orange, but is more compact. The peel of the fruit is thick and bitter. The pulp, as the name implies, is sour and acidic. The sour orange, like most citrus, originated in Southeast Asia. It spread to Europe at a very early date. It may have been the first variety of citrus planted by the Spanish at St. Augustine. It is a tough tree and can withstand adverse conditions, although it is not as cold tolerant as the calamondin. Like the calamondin, the sour orange is used in the production of marmalade and as a cooking spice where tartness is required.

CULTIVATION The calamondin is a low-maintenance tree. Its cultural requirements are similar to those of other citrus. It is somewhat drought tolerant, although irrigation enhances fruit set and development. Weeds and grasses should not be permitted to encroach into areas over the root crown. Several insect pests attack this species, including scale insects and various mites. It does not appear to be especially susceptible to citrus canker. Calamondin's vulnerability to citrus greening is unknown. Citrus greening is a very serious disease caused by the bacterium *Candidatus liberobacter* spp. An insect vector, the Asian citrus psyllid, is responsible for spreading the disease. Citrus greening was first detected in Florida in 2005. An infected tree displays various symptoms, including mottled foliage; stunted and misshapen fruit; small, narrow leaves; and reduced yield. Fruit do not ripen properly, remain green and bitter, and drop from the tree prematurely. Calamondin is highly resistant to citrus canker. The tree can be successfully raised from seed, and can also be reproduced from cuttings. Calamondin is cold tolerant. It suffers minor damage at about 22° F, but can survive temperatures as low as 18° F.

HARVEST AND USES The fruit ripen over much of the year. This species bears prolific quantities of fruit. The fruit is used to flavor drinks, marmalades, jellies, and various cooked dishes. It can be blended with honey to instantly produce an excellent sweet-and-sour sauce. It is especially popular as an ingredient in the cuisine of the Philippines.

Caraway

SCIENTIFIC NAME: *Carum carvi*
FAMILY: Apiaceae
OTHER COMMON NAMES: Persian Cumin, Alcaravea
  (Spanish)

Herbaceous Biennial

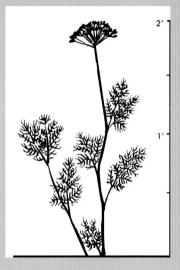

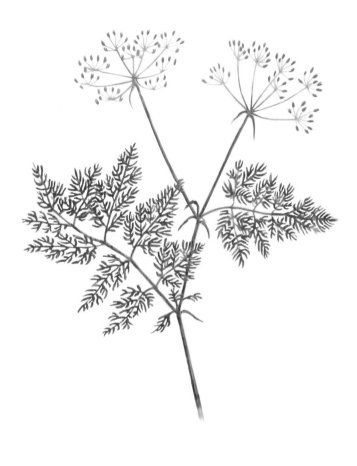

Characteristics

Overall Rating	★
Ease of Care	★★★
Utility	★★
Landscape Value	★★
Salt Tolerance	★
Drought Tolerance	★★★
Heat/Humidity Tolerance	★
Cold Tolerance	★★★
Shade Tolerance	★
Longevity	★★

Known Hazards

Those who are allergic to celery should exercise caution when handling or consuming this plant, which belongs to the same family. Moderate consumption is considered safe. However, there are reports that large doses of caraway oil over time can cause liver or kidney damage.

Caraway is a carrot relative, strongly associated with Germany and central Europe. This fragrant spice has many uses. Perhaps its most prominent role is as an ingredient in rye bread. It will grow in all regions of Florida. Like many members of the Apiaceae family, caraway is somewhat weedy in form. Yet, its white flowers, pliant stems, and feathery foliage bring a natural feel to the garden.

GEOGRAPHIC DISTRIBUTION Caraway originated in Europe and western Asia. It was used in cooking as early as the Stone Age. The name was taken from the Arabic *karawya*. Caraway has a long history of use in the cuisines of several European countries. Today, commercial production takes place in India, Iran, the Netherlands, Hungary, Morocco, and Russia.

PLANT DESCRIPTION This biennial herb is similar in appearance to the carrot. During its second year of growth, it attains a height of about 2 feet. The stem is slender and branched. Leaves are feathery, divided into thin fingers or filaments. The root is thick and tuberous. Small white flowers are borne on loose umbels at the top of the stalk. What is commonly called the "seed" is actually the fruit of the plant. It is curved, resembling a banana in overall shape. It has five light-colored ridges running along its length.

FLAVOR AND SCENT The aroma of caraway seed is earthy, pungent, and warm, with hints of anise, carrot, and citrus. The flavor of the seed echoes the scent, but is sharper and stronger. The flavor of the leaves approximates that of parsley.

VARIETIES 'Arterner' is an improved selection that produces large fruit. 'Karzo,' 'Kepron,' 'Mean,' and 'Record' are also highly regarded cultivars. A few selections bear fruit at the end of the first season of growth. However, annual varieties rarely match biennial varieties in terms of quality.

RELATIVES Caraway is a member of the Apiaceae or carrot family. Other species described within this book include: anise, *Pimpinella anisum*; chervil, *Anthriscus cerefolium*; cilantro, *Coriandrum sativum*; culantro, *Eryngium foetidum*; cumin, *Cuminum cyminum*; dill, *Anethum graveolens*; fennel, *Foeniculum vulgare*; lovage, *Levisticum officinale*; and parsley, *Petroselinum crispum*.

CULTIVATION Caraway is a hardy herb and grows wild in many areas of North America without any care whatsoever. Most first-year plants resemble carrots in their habit of growth. In the second season of growth, the plants generate vertical stalks. Plants started in the fall will usually bear fruit by the end of the following summer. Caraway prefers full sun and loose, well-drained soil. Seeds are somewhat slow to germinate. They should be soaked in warm water for a day before they are sown. They are then sown directly in the ground at a very shallow depth. As with several other members of the Apiaceae family, attempts to transplant this species often fail due to the long taproot. Weed control is important during all phases of development. The plant is negatively affected by high humidity, and may languish in wet, subtropical conditions. Caraway is reasonably drought tolerant once established.

HARVEST AND USE When the fruiting umbels have turned brown, they are severed from the plant and dried in the sun, in paper bags, or over light heat. The seed is then separated and stored in a dry location. Caraway is a popular flavoring agent for sauerkraut, sausage, coleslaw, rice, breads, cheeses, stews, and cabbage. The root can be prepared as a boiled vegetable. Some consider it to be equal to the parsnip in flavor. The leaves can be used in salads and are also sometimes incorporated into soups and teas.

Caraway seeds, which are actually the fruit of the caraway plant, are curved and resemble miniature bananas in form.

Cardamom

SCIENTIFIC NAME: *Elettaria cardomomum*
and *Amomum* spp.
FAMILY: Zingiberaceae
OTHER COMMON NAME: Cardamomo (Spanish)

Herbaceous Perennial

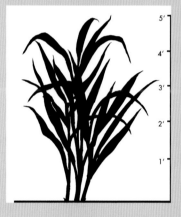

Characteristics

Overall Rating	★★★
Ease of Care	★★★
Utility	★★★
Landscape Value	★★★★
Salt Tolerance	★
Drought Tolerance	★★
Heat/Humidity Tolerance	★★★★★
Cold Tolerance	★★
Shade Tolerance	★★★★
Longevity	★★★

The common name cardamom actually applies to several species from two genera within the ginger family. While most spices from the ginger family are derived from underground rhizomes, the spice produced by cardamom is the dried seed of the plant. It is one of the world's most expensive spices. With its tropical appearance and curious flowering habit, cardamom makes an exotic addition to the Florida garden.

Known Hazards

Cardamom should not be consumed by those with gallstones. The plant contains elevated levels of salicylates, and consumption may cause reactions in those who are intolerant of these compounds.

GEOGRAPHIC DISTRIBUTION Cardamom is thought to be native to the Ghats region of southern India, although it also grows wild in Malaysia, Indonesia, and Sri Lanka. It is an understory plant, found in tropical rainforests. In India, cultivation takes place primarily in the states of Karnataka, Kerala, and Tamil Nadu. Large-scale production also occurs in Guatemala, which has become a major exporter. This spice is also grown to a lesser extent in Thailand, Vietnam, China, Sri Lanka, and Nepal.

The cardamom plant, like other members of the ginger family, can form dense clumps.

Cardamom pods are often used whole in Indian cooking. The flavor is dispersed by heat into the entire dish.

PLANT DESCRIPTION Cardamom is a large perennial herb, capable of growing to a height of 6 feet or more. Horizontal rhizomes send up between 5 and 20 shoots. Leaves are alternate, lanceolate, with the sheaths forming erect pseudostems. Leaves may be up to 2 feet in length. The flowers, which are borne on separate panicles that trail along the ground, are white with purple veins radiating from the center. The fruit is a dehiscent, thin-walled capsule, consisting of three segments. It contains about 20 brown, sticky seeds.

FLAVOR The seeds have a pungent, aromatic, pleasant flavor, with hints of eucalyptus. The scent is warm and pungent, with hints of camphor.

VARIETIES *Elettaria cardomomum*, the most common species, is also known as green cardamom. Three varieties of green cardamom are recognized: Malabar, Mysore, and Vazhukka. Cultivars grown in India include: 'CCS-1,' 'IRIC-1,' 'IRIC-2,' 'IRIC-3,' 'MCC-12,' 'Mudigere-1,' 'Najallani,' 'Palakkudi,' 'TDK-4,' and 'Veeraputhara.' Species from the genus *Amomum*, including *Amomum maximum, Amomum villosum*, and *Amomum tsao-ko*, are known as black or brown cardamom.

RELATIVES The Zingiberaceae or ginger family is composed of about 50 genera and 1,300 species. Most are stiff-leaved perennial herbs, widely distributed throughout the world's warm-temperate and tropical regions. Other members that are discussed within this book include the spices ginger, *Zingiber officinale*, and turmeric, *Curcuma longa*.

CULTIVATION Cardamom is not negatively affected by the heat and humidity of the summer in south Florida. However, the plant requires partial shade. It prefers rainfall to be evenly distributed throughout the year. Consequently, in Florida, irrigation is required during the dry season. The soil should not be permitted to dry out completely. Cardamom prefers acidic soil. The plant is propagated by seed and by removing and replanting suckers. The germination rate for seeds is often poor, perhaps as a result of the hard seed coat. Cardamom is tropical in habit and is seriously damaged by near-freezing temperatures. Therefore, it can only be grown outdoors in protected, southern-coastal areas of the state.

HARVEST AND USE The spice is the dried seed. Mature pods are removed from the plant and dried. The plant may come into production by the end of the second year, but more typically takes 3 or 4 years before it fruits. Cardamom is an important ingredient in the Indian spice garam masala, and is used in various biryanis and curries. Whole pods can be used to flavor rice. In the Middle East, cardamom is often added to coffee. It is also used extensively as a spice in Scandinavian cuisines.

Cardamom seeds can be used whole, but are often sold in ground form.

Carob

SCIENTIFIC NAME: *Ceratonia siliqua*
FAMILY: Fabaceae
OTHER COMMON NAMES: St. John's Bread,
   Algarrobo (Spanish)

Woody Perennial; Evergreen Tree

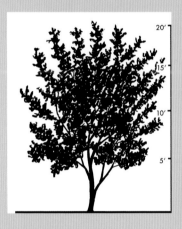

Characteristics

Overall Rating	★★
Ease of Care	★★★
Utility	★★
Landscape Value	★★
Salt Tolerance	★★★
Drought Tolerance	★★★★★
Heat/Humidity Tolerance	★★★★★
Cold Tolerance	★★★
Shade Tolerance	★★
Longevity	★★★★

The historic use of this legume as a sweetener and flavoring agent stretches back to ancient Egypt. Today carob is often promoted as a "health food" and as a chocolate substitute. Although the flavor does not measure up to that of real chocolate, the species has two distinct advantages for the home gardener. First, the tree will endure some cold and can be grown over a wider range. Second, the end product is much easier to process.

Known Hazards

May have some invasive potential

GEOGRAPHIC DISTRIBUTION The carob is native to the eastern Mediterranean. The name is derived from the Arabic *kharoub*. Carob has been cultivated extensively in various Mediterranean countries and is naturalized in some regions. Spanish missionaries first planted the tree in the Americas. The tree has been more widely planted in California than in Florida. It has escaped from cultivation in at least one location in California and, therefore, may have invasive potential in Florida. The carob has been grown in Florida since the mid-1800s. In Florida, the carob will grow as far north as Daytona Beach, on the east coast, and the Tampa area, on the west coast. Commercial production occurs in Spain, Italy, Portugal, Cyprus, Malta, and Turkey.

PLANT DESCRIPTION This slow-growing evergreen tree reaches a height of about 45 feet, although specimens rarely attain that size in Florida. The crown is rounded and roughly symmetrical. The alternate leaves are composed of 6 to 10 leaflets, about 2 inches in length. Small red flowers are borne on racemes that emerge from older wood and along the branches. The flowers may be male, female, or hermaphrodite. Most trees are monoecious, bearing all male or all female flowers. The fruit is a green indehiscent pod, ripening to reddish-brown. Each pod typically measures between 5 and 10 inches in length. The pod contains brown pulp surrounding a row of flat seeds.

FLAVOR The pods are naturally sweet with a slight bitter element. The flavor is similar, but certainly not identical, to that of cacao.

VARIETIES Two subspecies have been described, *Ceratonia siliqua oreothauma* and *Ceratonia siliqua somalensis*. Various cultivars have been selected, although few are available in Florida. Well-regarded varieties include: 'Amele,' 'Badan,' 'Bolser,' 'Clifford,' 'Cypriot,' 'Grantham' 'Matalafera,' 'Negra,' 'Santa Fe,' 'Sfax,' and 'Tantillo.' 'Clifford' and 'Santa Fe' are hermaphrodites and will bear without cross-pollination. These cultivars are common in California, and budded specimens may be available from mail-order nurseries. Grafted and budded selections tend to produce pods of superior quality to those borne by seedlings. Seedlings produce a high proportion of male plants that do not produce fruit.

RELATIVES The large Fabaceae family, commonly known as the legumes, contains over 600 genera and, perhaps, as many as 19,000 species. Many important food crops are members, including beans of various genera: lentils, *Lens culinaris*; peas, *Pisum sativum*; and peanuts, *Arachis hypogaea*. The family also includes ornamental plants such as the royal poinciana, *Delonix regia*. A member that is well known to residents of north Florida is the invasive exotic, kudzu, *Pueraria lobata*. This vexatious weed was first introduced to the United States from Japan in 1876. It drapes itself over the foliage of native plants and has taken over thousands of square miles of land throughout the southeastern United States. Members of the Fabaceae family described within this book include fenugreek, *Trigonella foenum-graecum*, and tamarind, *Tamarindus indica*.

CULTIVATION The carob tree requires well-drained soil. It is tolerant of drought and can survive in near-desert conditions. It generally does not require water in Florida, except for purposes of establishment. It benefits from some wind protection, especially during periods of establishment. The carob prefers slightly alkaline soil. Many trees have alternate bearing tendencies and produce a heavier crop every other year. Seedlings typically begin to fruit between 6 and 10 years after they are planted. The carob is most frequently propagated by budding. Lower branches are generally pruned away to encourage a more treelike habit of growth. The tree is not strictly tropical in habit and can withstand a light frost. It is said to be hardy to about 22° F.

HARVEST AND USES Pods turn dark brown as they ripen. Both the seeds and pods are edible. Whole pods can be chewed. They can also be processed in several ways. The pods can be ground into dry flour or powder. This powder can be substituted for cocoa powder in most recipes. It can be added to flavor milk or coffee. The carob pods can also be pulverized, mixed with sugar and water and boiled to produce thick syrup. Carob has gained favor as a chocolate substitute, because it has less calories, less fat, high protein, and no caffeine.

The ice cream bean is another member of the Fabaceae family. The pulp surrounding the seeds is occasionally used as an out-of-hand nibble or as a flavoring agent.

Carolina Allspice

SCIENTIFIC NAME: *Calycanthus floridus*
FAMILY: Calycanthaceae
OTHER COMMON NAME: Sweet Shrub

Woody Perennial; Deciduous Shrub

Characteristics

Overall Rating	★★
Ease of Care	★★★
Utility	★
Landscape Value	★★★
Salt Tolerance	★
Drought Tolerance	★★★
Heat/Humidity Tolerance	★★★
Cold Tolerance	★★★★★
Shade Tolerance	★★★★
Longevity	★★★★

Carolina allspice is one of several aromatic, native shrubs that can be used to bring scent into the garden. Attractive and easy to grow, this plant deserves to be planted on a wider scale. Although some sources promote Carolina Allspice for use in tea and home remedies, this plant is mildly toxic. It must not be used as a substitute for the familiar spice, allspice.

Known Hazards

All parts of the plant should be considered poisonous. It contains an alkaloid that affects the heart. Not for culinary use, literature that indicates otherwise notwithstanding.

GEOGRAPHIC DISTRIBUTION Carolina allspice is native to the southeastern United States, from Virginia to Florida. It inhabits woodland fringes, stream banks, and clearings. Carolina allspice grows naturally in scattered locations throughout the Panhandle, although it is considered endangered in Florida. It can be grown as far south as Orlando. It is available from various nurseries.

PLANT DESCRIPTION Carolina allspice is a deciduous shrub that reaches a height of about 9 feet. The rate of growth is medium. The habit of growth is dense, with a rounded crown. Suckers occasionally form around the base. Leaves are semi-glossy but rough textured, ovate, deep green, measuring 4 to 5 inches in length. They are opposite and entire. The leaves turn a bright golden-yellow in the fall. Two-inch dark, reddish-purple flowers form in the late spring and early summer. These are attractive and fragrant. They are followed by brown seed capsules, which persist through much of the year.

SCENT The scent of the bruised foliage is sweet and aromatic. The flowers exude a delightful fragrance of strawberry and pineapple. However, the intensity of this fragrance varies, and may be muted in some plants.

VARIETIES The cultivar 'Athens' has yellow flowers. Other cultivars include 'Michael Lindsey,' 'Mrs. Henry Type,' and 'Venus.' A cross of Carolina allspice with Chinese sweetshrub, *Sinocalycanthus chinensis*, has produced a selection dubbed 'Hartlage Wine.' This variety has large red blooms, but reduced scent.

RELATIVES The family Calycanthaceae, known as the strawberry shrub family, is small. It contains 3 genera and 6 species. Carolina allspice is the only member covered within these pages. The western sweetshrub, *Calycanthus occidentalis*, is native to California.

CULTIVATION Carolina allspice is easy to grow and is tolerant of various soil types. However, it prefers fertile, well-drained soil. This plant also prefers partial shade and does well when planted as a woodland border. Although it is an understory plant by habit, it may become somewhat leggy if planted in deep shade. Carolina allspice can be propagated through semi-hardwood cuttings rooted in a damp sand-peat mix. Suckers can also be dug up and transplanted. Seeds require cold stratification and should be planted in the spring.

HARVEST AND USE This plant is best enjoyed for its scent within the garden. However, the leaves and flowers can be gathered and brought indoors for their fragrance or used in potpourri. This plant was formerly used in teas and other herbal concoctions. However, it has been implicated in cattle poisonings and is now regarded as mildly toxic. The seeds contain higher concentrations of toxins, and have caused adverse symptoms in humans when consumed in quantity.

Leaves of Carolina allspice are aromatic, but are considered toxic.

Chamomile

SCIENTIFIC NAMES: *Chamaemilum nobile*
   and *Matricaria recutita*
FAMILY: Asteraceae

Herbaceous Annual or Perennial

Planted
in Spring

Planted
in Fall

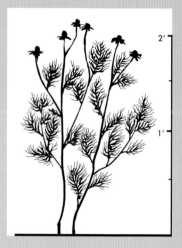

Characteristics

Overall Rating	★★
Ease of Care	★★★★
Utility	★★
Landscape Value	★★★★
Salt Tolerance	★★
Drought Tolerance	★★★
Heat/Humidity Tolerance	★
Cold Tolerance	★★
Shade Tolerance	★★
Longevity	★★

Known Hazards

Occasional allergen. In sensitive individuals, consumption has been known to cause swelling of the lips, tongue, and airways; hives; and gastrointestinal upset. Those who have suffered allergic reactions to ragweed should avoid this herb. Chamomile has been known to cause contact dermatitis in rare cases.

The common name "chamomile" refers to two species, Roman chamomile, *Chamaemilum nobile*, and German chamomile, *Matricaria recutita*. Both species are used in a similar manner. Chamomile is a garden herb with use dating from Egyptian and Roman times. In Europe, chamomile oil is used as an ingredient in various medicines. The primary use identified here is as an herbal tea or as a tea additive.

GEOGRAPHIC DISTRIBUTION This plant is native to Europe and western Asia. Chamomile has proven to be an invasive species in some areas, although this trait has not been a significant problem thus far in Florida. The name, derived from the Greek *chamaimelon*, means "earth apple."

Dried chamomile flowers exude a subdued but pleasant scent. The flavor is released when they are steeped in hot water and made into tea.

PLANT DESCRIPTION Chamomile is a low-growing herbaceous plant. Roman chamomile can attain a height of about 18 inches, while German chamomile can attain a height of up to 3 feet. Roman chamomile is a perennial. German chamomile is generally grown as an annual. Leaves are feathery in appearance, alternate, bipinnate, finely cut into multiple lobes. Flowers are daisylike, measuring about 1 1/2 inches in diameter, with white petals radiating outward from a yellow central disk.

FLAVOR AND SCENT The foliage and flower give off a light, sweet, applelike scent. The flavor is aromatic, with a trace of pleasant bitterness.

VARIETIES 'Bodegold' is an improved selection with large flowers. 'Double Roman' produces double blooms. Other cultivars include 'Dukat,' 'Mastar,' and 'Promyk.'

RELATIVES Chamomile is a member of the Asteraceae family. Other members of this large family covered within this book include: chicory, *Cichorium intybus*; goldenrod, *Solidago* spp.; Mexican tarragon, *Tagetes lucida*; stevia, *Stevia rebaudiana*; and tarragon, *Artemisia dracunculus*. A species with similar uses to chamomile is field chamomile, *Anthemis arvensis*. This plant is native to Europe, but is now naturalized in parts of the United States, including Florida. Pineapple weed, *Matricaria discoidea*, related to German chamomile, is an annual plant native to Canada and northern sections of the United States. It is sometimes used to make an herbal tea.

CULTIVATION Once established, chamomile is a hardy plant. It prefers loose, well-drained, slightly acidic soil. However, it will tolerate a wide pH range. While it usually grows best in full sun, some light shade may be beneficial under subtropical conditions. Chamomile cannot take the heat and humidity of the summer in south Florida. From Orlando southward, it is usually planted in the fall, harvested over the winter and spring, and allowed to expire upon the arrival of summer conditions. After it flowers, Roman chamomile should be cut back to stimulate new vegetative growth. If the old flower heads are not removed, chamomile will self-sow. Roman chamomile is usually propagated through division. German chamomile is started from seed. The seeds require light to germinate, so must be sown at a very shallow depth.

HARVEST AND USE A tea is made by steeping the flowers in hot water. The leaves can also be chopped and added to butter or sour cream to top baked potatoes. The dry flowers may be added to potpourri. Chamomile attracts butterflies and bees to the garden. While chamomile is generally regarded as safe for consumption, it has caused allergic reactions in some people.

German chamomile is a diminutive annual. The tea made from the flowers of this plant tends to be sweeter than the tea made from the flowers of Roman chamomile.

Chervil

SCIENTIFIC NAME: *Anthriscus cerefolium*
FAMILY: Apiaceae
OTHER COMMON NAME: Perifollo (Spanish)

Herbaceous Annual

Planted in Spring

Planted in Fall

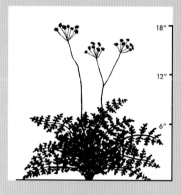

Characteristics

Overall Rating	★★★
Ease of Care	★★★
Utility	★★★
Landscape Value	★★
Salt Tolerance	★
Drought Tolerance	★★★
Heat/Humidity Tolerance	★
Cold Tolerance	★
Shade Tolerance	★★★
Longevity	★

Known Hazards

While consumption of chervil is considered safe by most authorities, at least one source states that its safety during pregnancy and nursing has not been adequately established. The roots are poisonous unless boiled prior to consumption.

The delicate young foliage of this plant enjoys considerable use in Europe as a salad ingredient, recipe ingredient, and garnish. It is one of the traditional *fines herbes* of French cooking. However, chervil is poorly known and rarely used in the United States.

GEOGRAPHIC DISTRIBUTION Chervil is thought to be native to the Middle East, southern Russia, and the Ukraine. It was probably introduced into Europe at an early date. The name may be derived from the Latin *chaeophyllum,* meaning "festival herb."

PLANT DESCRIPTION Chervil is a fast-growing annual that closely resembles carrot tops in appearance. It attains a maximum height of about 18 inches. Stems are grooved and much branched. The plant has a long, sturdy taproot. Leaves are finely cut, and are lacy in appearance. Leaves are light green at first, but turn reddish-brown or purple-brown as they mature. Flowering occurs in mid-summer. The plant bears umbels of small white flowers.

FLAVOR AND SCENT The flavor is mild, sweet, warm, and subtle, with a hint of anise and tarragon. Chervil's flavor is not dominant and can be overwhelmed by other herbs. The scent is aromatic and faintly resinous.

VARIETIES Chervil is sorted into flat-leaf types and curly-leaf types, which are roughly equal in flavor. 'Crispum' is a curly-leaf variety. 'Brussel Winter' is a vigorous selection that is slow to flower. Other cultivars include 'Altan' and 'Véga.'

RELATIVES As a member of the Apiaceae family, chervil is related to various plants discussed within this book. These include: anise, *Pimpinella anisum*; caraway, *Carum carvi*; cilantro, *Coriandrum sativum*; culantro, *Eryngium foetidum*; cumin, *Cuminum cyminum*; dill, *Anethum graveolens*; fennel, *Foeniculum vulgare*; lovage, *Levisticum officinale*; and parsley, *Petroselinum crispum.* The genus *Anthriscus* contains about 10 species, several of which go by the common name chervil. Cow parsley, *Anthriscus sylvestris,* is an invasive species that has escaped cultivation in the northeastern United States.

CULTIVATION Chervil prefers some shade and fairs poorly when placed in full sun in Florida. It is not especially tolerant of summer heat. If grown under hot conditions, it will rapidly bolt and go to seed. Removal of the flower buds will encourage continued vegetative growth. Successive plantings will ensure an extended harvest. Chervil is readily grown from seed. It is planted in the fall in south Florida, and is planted in the spring in north Florida.

HARVEST AND USE Sprigs of young foliage are clipped from the plant, most often in the spring or during periods of active growth. In France, Chervil is often used in combination with tarragon, chives, and parsley. It contributes its distinct flavor to Béarnaise sauce. It is excellent in mashed potatoes, salads, soups, herb butters, and poultry dishes. The flavor is diminished by exposure to heat, so chervil is usually added near the end of the cooking process. It also loses much of its flavor when dried. Although chervil is best used fresh, it may be preserved by immersion in white-wine vinegar and is sometimes used in vinaigrette salad dressings. Fresh leaves can be stored for up to a week in the refrigerator.

The chervil leaf is delicate in form and is sometimes used as a garnish. The flavor is mild.

Chicory

SCIENTIFIC NAME: *Cichorium intybus*
FAMILY: Asteraceae
OTHER COMMON NAMES: Chickory, Coffeeweed,
  Achicoria (Spanish)

Herbaceous Perennial

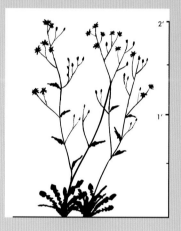

Characteristics

Overall Rating	★★
Ease of Care	★★★★
Utility	★★
Landscape Value	★★
Salt Tolerance	★★★
Drought Tolerance	★★★★★
Heat/Humidity Tolerance	★★★★
Cold Tolerance	★★★★
Shade Tolerance	★
Longevity	★★

Chicory is a common weed of roadsides, disturbed areas, and overgrown fields. The ancient Egyptians cultivated this plant for food and medicine. Introduced into North America from Europe during colonial times, chicory is now one of the most widespread non-native plants growing within the United States. It is included here for its culinary applications. The leaves can be used as greens. The roots are used as a coffee substitute.

Known Hazards

This herb should not be consumed during pregnancy. It has been identified as a contact allergen in very rare cases.

60

GEOGRAPHIC DISTRIBUTION Chicory is widely distributed throughout Europe, western Asia, and the Middle East. Because it has been cultivated for thousands of years, its place of origin is uncertain. Considered an invasive weed in many locations, it is present in all 48 contiguous states and in southern Canada. Chicory is not especially common as a wild plant in Florida. It appears along some north Florida roads and is also present in the Tampa area.

Chicory flowers tend to open in the morning and close later in the day.

PLANT DESCRIPTION Chicory is an herbaceous perennial, typically growing to about 2 feet, rarely attaining a height of 3 or 4 feet. The stalk is sparsely foliated, with alternate leaves. These are lanceolate, dentate or coarsely lobed. Leaves surrounding the base of the plant resemble those of a dandelion. The taproot is long and sturdy. It exudes bitter white latex when cut. Bright blue flowers grow directly on the main stalk. These measure up to 1 1/2 inches in diameter, but are usually smaller. Petals are fringed. Flowers open in the morning and close later in the day.

SCENT AND FLAVOR The root, when roasted, ground, and used as coffee has a pleasant, slightly bitter taste, not readily distinguishable from that of coffee. The scent is sweeter and lighter than that of coffee.

VARIETIES Some strains produce flowers that are lilac or violet, rather than sky blue. Several selections have been made based on improved root size or foliage, including 'Asparagus,' 'Brunswick,' 'Magdeburg' 'Radichetta,' 'Radicchio,' and 'Witloof.'

RELATIVES Chicory is the only representative of the *Cichorium* genus found growing wild throughout North America. Its close cousin the endive, *Cichorium endivia*, is a species cultivated specifically for use as a salad green. Other less-closely related members of the Asteraceae family discussed within this book include chamomile, *Chamaemilum nobile* and *Matricaria recutita*; goldenrod, *Solidago* spp.; Mexican tarragon, *Tagetes lucida*; stevia, *Stevia rebaudiana*; and tarragon, *Artemisia dracunculus*.

CULTIVATION Chicory is one of the toughest plants covered in this book. It is drought tolerant and thrives under difficult conditions. While it will grow in poor, sandy soils, it performs better in beds enriched with organic matter. Chicory prefers full sun. It is not negatively affected by the heat and humidity prevalent during the summer in south Florida. Chicory can be grown from seed.

HARVEST AND USE The roots are generally harvested between February and May, but can be collected at any time. Chicory coffee is easy to make. The roots must be thoroughly washed, then roasted in an oven at 350° F for 5 hours. The roots are then ground into a fine powder. When placed in the coffee machine they yield a pleasant, flavorful beverage that resembles coffee. Young chicory leaves can be used as salad greens. Older leaves are tough and bitter.

Chicory is a very common roadside weed throughout much of North America.

Chili Pepper

SCIENTIFIC NAME: *Capsicum* spp.
FAMILY: Solanaceae
OTHER COMMON NAMES: Hot Pepper, Pimienta
    Picante (Spanish)

Herbaceous or Semi-Woody Annual

Characteristics

Overall Rating	★★★★★
Ease of Care	★★★
Utility	★★★★
Landscape Value	★★★★
Salt Tolerance	★★★
Drought Tolerance	★★★
Heat/Humidity Tolerance	★★★
Cold Tolerance	★
Shade Tolerance	★★
Longevity	★★

Known Hazards

Hot peppers can burn eyes, ears, and sensitive skin. Gloves and eye protection should be worn during preparation. Hot peppers may also enhance reactions to certain medications. Some contain elevated levels of salicylates, and consumption may cause reactions in those who are intolerant of these compounds.

The chili pepper is an essential ingredient in many of the world's greatest cuisines: Thai, Mexican, Cajun, Indian, Korean, Indonesian, Malaysian, Persian, Szechuan, Filipino, and others. The plant is decorative and hardy, and it is a valuable addition to the Florida garden.

GEOGRAPHIC DISTRIBUTION The chili pepper is indigenous to tropical and subtropical regions of the Americas, including southern Mexico. Cultivation is thought to date back as far as 6,000 years. The chili pepper has spread to many regions of the globe. It has played an especially important role in the cuisines of India and Southeast Asia. Large-scale commercial production occurs in China, Mexico, the United States, Ghana, and India. Production also occurs in Costa Rica, Jamaica, Trinidad, Malaysia, and Thailand. In the United States, Texas, Florida, California, and New Mexico have significant production.

Pictured are immature tabasco peppers. This variety of *Capsicum frutescens* has an upright habit of growth and forms a dense bush. It is cultivated heavily in Louisiana, where it is used in the manufacture of the famed Tabasco sauce.

PLANT DESCRIPTION Peppers are frost-intolerant annuals, although in tropical climates they may persist as short-lived perennials. The plant is typically a low, herbaceous bush that may develop woody stems near the base. Leaves are variable. Some are nearly round, while others are tapering, elongated, or lanceolate. Most are dark green above and lighter below. Flowers are typically white or violet and star-shaped. These occur in leaf axils around growth tips. The fruit of hot peppers is typically smaller and more elongate than that of bell peppers.

FLAVOR AND SCENT The flavor ranges from mild to viciously hot. When a hot chili pepper is ingested, the mouth's pain receptors signal the brain that they have been exposed to extreme heat. The chemical responsible for this reaction is the alkaloid, capsaicin, and several related substances. The body responds by perspiring and by releasing

endorphins. The intensity of the heat is measured in Scoville units (SHU). The scale ranges from 0 to 16,000,000 SHU, for pure capsaicin. The hottest varieties of peppers discovered to date have topped 1,000,000 SHU. Growing conditions, fertilization, rainfall, and other factors can affect the amount of heat produced by the fruit of a given variety. The fruit possesses many flavors apart from the "heat" that is often thought of as its defining characteristic.

VARIETIES Half a dozen species of *Capsicum* are viewed as food species. *Capsicum annuum* includes jalapeño peppers, cayenne peppers, and common bell peppers. *Capsicum frutescens* includes tabasco pepper. *Capsicum chinense* includes Scotch bonnets and habañeros. *Capsicum pubescens* includes the rocoto peppers of South America. *Capsicum baccatum* includes the chiltepin. At least 250 selections of chili pepper are grown for culinary use. A few cultivars and cultivar groups are listed below:

'African Devil' (40,000–80,000 SHU) – This cultivar of the species *Capsicum frutescens* grows on a bushlike plant. The fruit, which may be red or green, are very hot.

'Aji' (25,000–50,000 SHU) – Varieties commonly referred to as Aji (pronounced "A-hee") are usually selections of *Capsicum baccatum*, originating in South America. At least 40 distinct selections come under the Aji umbrella. The typical fruit is yellow or orange, attaining a length of about 3 inches and a width of about 1 inch. Seeds of some selections may be difficult to obtain.

'Anaheim' (1,000–9,000 SHU) – This cultivar, within the New Mexico group of *Capsicum annuum*, was developed for canning and processing. The elongated, tapering fruit reaches a length of about 6 inches. It is typically harvested when dark green, although it eventually turns red. 'Anaheim' is a mild pepper, although the level of heat is somewhat variable.

'Banana' (100–400 SHU) – 'Banana,' also referred to as 'Hungarian Yellow Wax,' is a cultivar of *Capsicum annuum*. It is often pickled and used as a condiment on submarine sandwiches and pizza. The heat is mild and the flavor is fruity. The tapering fruit attains a length of 4 to 6 inches.

'Cascabe' (4,000–12,000 SHU) – 'Cascabe' is a Mexican cultivar of *Capsicum annuum*. It is medium hot, with a smoky, slightly bitter taste. The fruit is squat, with a rounded bell shape and purple-brown skin.

'Cayanne' (8,000–34,000 SHU) – This group of cultivars within the species *Capsicum annuum* is composed of medium hot peppers. These are widely used in Indian and Southeast Asian cuisines. The plant is bushlike, attaining a height

Pepper cultivars 'Candy Fest' (left) and 'Riot' (right)

of 3 or 4 feet. The cultivars 'Carolina Cayenne' and 'Charleston Hot' exceed the heat of typical cayanne peppers, with a rating of 65,000-100,000 Scoville units.

'Cherry' (1,500–4,000 SHU) – This selection of *Capsicum annuum* produces a round, relatively mild fruit approximating the size and shape of a cherry.

'Chilaca' (1,600–4,200 SHU) – This cultivar is also known as 'Pasilla,' especially when dried. It falls with the species *Capsicum annuum*. The fruit is long, tapering, often recurving in a broad arc. It ripens to purple-brown or a dark, reddish brown.

'Datil' (40,000–100,000 SHU) – This flavorful pepper is thought to belong to the species *Capsicum sinense*. An heirloom variety, it has been grown in the St. Augustine area since the 1800s, or perhaps as early as the 1700s. It is rumored to have come from Minorca, although its true origins are uncertain.

'Habañero' (140,000–400,000 SHU) – 'Habañero' falls with the species *Capsicum chinense*. This cultivar group contains some of the world's hottest peppers. These include 'Caribbean Red Hot,' 'Congo,' and 'Black Habañero.' 'Red

Savina' a selection of Habañero, formerly topped the world's hottest chili's list.

'Jalapeño' (4,500–5,600 SHU) – The 'Jalapeño' pepper is cylindrical in shape, with thick green flesh. It is a cultivar of the species *Capsicum annuum*. This pepper is often smoked, dried, and marketed as chipotle. Chipotle actually refers to the preparation process.

'Naga Jolokia' (800,000–1,000,000 SHU) – This cultivar from northeastern India recently displaced 'Red Savina' as the world's hottest pepper. Also known as the ghost chili, it is thought to be a cross between *Capsicum chinense* and *Capsicum frutescens*. The fruit is red, somewhat resembling that of 'Habañero.'

'Poblano' – This variety belongs to the species *Capsicum annuum*. It is called 'Ancho' when dried. The fruit is blocky, resembling a tapered bell pepper. It is often roasted and pealed. It is the preferred chili for use in the dish chiles rellenos.

'Santa Fe Grande' (18,000–13,0000 SHU) – This variety is a selection of *Capsicum annuum*. It is relatively mild and is popular in the southwestern United States.

This 'Shu' variegated pepper is extremely ornamental. The peppers, while edible, are of only marginal quality.

'Lil' Pumpkin,' recently licensed for retail sale, is primarily an ornamental pepper.

'Scotch Bonnet' (190,000–225,000 SHU) – This cultivar group, consisting of selections of *Capsicum chinense*, originated in the Caribbean. The fruits ripen to yellow, orange, and red. This pepper is an ingredient in "jerk" seasoning, popular in Jamaica.

'Serrano' (20,000–30,000 SHU) – This selection of *Capsicum annuum* originated in Mexico. It is a medium-heat pepper, and is often canned or pickled.

'Tabasco' (50,000–90,000 SHU) – This selection of *Capsicum frutescens* is used to create the classic Tabasco-brand pepper sauce produced by the McIlhenny Company on Avery Island, Louisiana, since 1868. The plant itself is vigorous and tough, and it is a prolific producer.

'Thai' (50,000–80,000 SHU) - Various chili peppers, primarily selections of *Capsicum annuum*, are used in Thai cuisine. Thai peppers tend to be small and are moderately hot to fiery.

RELATIVES The chili pepper is a member of the Solanaceae family, which includes several edibles and many poisonous plants. Important edibles include the tomato, *Solanum lycopersicum*; potato, *Solanum tuberosum*; eggplant, *Solanum melongena*; and cape gooseberry, *Physalis peruviana*. Toxic members of the family include Jimson weed, *Datura stramonium*; devil's trumpet, *Datura metel*; deadly nightshade, *Atropa belladonna*; and mandrake, *Mandragora* spp. Two members of the *Capsicum* genus native to Florida are bird pepper, *Capsicum annuum* var. *glabriusculum*, and *Capsicum frutescens*. Several indigenous groundcherries also belong to the Solanaceae family, including carpenter's groundcherry, *Physalis carpenteri*; clammy groundcherry, *Physalis heterophylla*; coastal groundcherry, *Physalis angustifolia*; cutleaf groundcherry, *Physalis angulata*; heartleaf groundcherry, *Physalis cordata*; longleaf groundcherry, *Physalis longifolia*; and Virginia groundcherry, *Physalis virginiana*.

CULTIVATION Seeds are typically started indoors. Growth is slow at first. While most hot peppers can endure some drought, irrigation may be necessary during dry periods. Chili peppers prefer full sun and any significant shade will result in lower production. If the gardener applies too much nitrogen fertilizer, plants will put their energy into vegetative growth, and fruit production will suffer. Hot peppers make excellent container-grown plants. The most prevalent diseases affecting hot peppers include bacterial spot, *Xanthomonas campestris*, and anthracnose, *Colletotrichum* spp. Both can be controlled with copper-based fungicides. Mites and aphids sometimes damage the foliage. Chili peppers are not negatively affected by the heat and humidity of the summer in south Florida, and are generally well suited to growth throughout the state.

HARVEST AND USE Hot chili peppers are picked when they color. Those handling the fruit should wear gloves and should never allow seeds or juice to contact the eyes, ears, nose, or other sensitive areas. When cutting chili peppers it is best to wear eye protection. A single seed that ricochets into the eye can cause intense agony. The hottest parts of the fruit are the interior ribs. Chili peppers can be put to a plethora of culinary uses. The fruit itself can be dried, ground, smoked, roasted, fried, grilled, fermented, sauced, or pickled. Chili peppers are an important ingredient in Thai red curry, Mexican chile con carne, Korean kimchee, Indian vindaloo, Cajun jambalaya, Szechuan mapo doufu, and so many of the world's great dishes.

The forms and colors of the fruit borne by pepper plants are almost unlimited. These living jewels can lend just as much color and interest to the garden as flowers.

The cultivar 'Marbles' is decorative, but also bears a flavorful pepper. The heat of this selection is rated at about 300 Scoville units.

Chives

SCIENTIFIC NAME: *Allium schoenoprasum*
FAMILY: Alliaceae
OTHER COMMON NAME: Cebolletas (Spanish)

Herbaceous Perennial

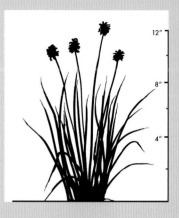

Characteristics

Overall Rating	★★★
Ease of Care	★★★★
Utility	★★★
Landscape Value	★★★★
Salt Tolerance	★★
Drought Tolerance	★★★★
Heat/Humidity Tolerance	★★★★★
Cold Tolerance	★★★★★
Shade Tolerance	★★
Longevity	★★★

Chives are attractive, hardy plants suitable for use as an edging or foundation planting. They are the first of two members of the onion family covered within this book. The culinary uses of chives differ from those of onions and garlic. Chives are grown for their leaves, rather than for their underground bulb. The common name of this species comes from the French word for onion, *cive*.

Known Hazards

Chives are a very rare allergen.

66

GEOGRAPHIC DISTRIBUTION Chives are native to Europe, Asia, and North America, and grow wild over much of the northern hemisphere. They were reportedly used in China as early as 3,000 BC. They did not find their way into most European cuisines until the 1500s.

The flower head of chives is composed of a number of closely packed flowers. Each has six petals and six stamens. The flowers are edible and have a strong onion flavor.

PLANT DESCRIPTION The plant is a clumping, herbaceous perennial, attaining a height of 12 to 20 inches. It is generally evergreen throughout Florida, but may go dormant over the colder months in north Florida. Each plant grows from an elongated underground bulb. Leaves are medium green, tubular, rounded, measuring about 1/8 of an inch in diameter. Small violet flowers appear in April or May. These are produced in a dense, rounded head that protrudes above the body of the plant. Seeds form in small capsules.

FLAVOR AND SCENT The flavor is similar to that of an onion, but delicate and without any "bite." Both the flavor and scent are considerably milder than those of garlic.

VARIETIES Slight variations occur within the species, depending on location. 'Album' is a selection that bears white flowers. The selection 'Glaucum' has curled leaves and violet flowers. The selection 'Jupiter' bears extra-large, purple flowers. A seed-free variety is also available.

RELATIVES The Alliaceae family contains about 1,500 species. This book covers garlic, *Allium sativum*, and various related members of the Alliaceae family, in a separate entry. Garlic chives, *Allium tuberosum*, have a sharper flavor than chives, midway between chives and garlic. The flowers are white, and the leaves are somewhat flattened and straplike.

CULTIVATION Chives are easy to establish and require little maintenance. They prefer well-drained soil with a high organic content and a near-neutral pH. However, they will tolerate a broad range of soils and pH values. They prosper in full sun and are not negatively affected by summer conditions in south Florida. They are somewhat drought tolerant. Chives will spread rapidly and, unless flower heads are removed, will self-seed and spread. They can be propagated from seed or by dividing established clusters.

HARVEST AND USE Chives are harvested when needed, usually by severing whole leaves from near the base of the plant. The leaves are typically minced before use. Chives have many culinary applications. They are an ingredient in various sauces, soups, dips, salad dressings, and breads. They improve omelets and scrambled eggs. They are a common topping of baked potatoes, usually in conjunction with sour cream. The *fines herbes* of French cuisine include chives, parsley, tarragon, and chervil. The entire plant is edible, from the bulb to the flower. Flower heads can be added to salads or used as a garnish. Chives spoil quickly once harvested and lose flavor when dried.

The rolled leaves are the part of the plant most often used in cooking. The bulb is too small to be taken seriously.

Cilantro/Coriander

SCIENTIFIC NAME: *Coriandrum sativum*
FAMILY: Apiaceae
OTHER COMMON NAME: Coriandro (Spanish)

Herbaceous Annual

Planted
in Spring

Planted
in Fall

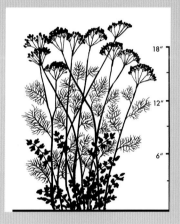

Characteristics

Overall Rating	★★
Ease of Care	★★
Utility	★★★
Landscape Value	★★
Salt Tolerance	★
Drought Tolerance	★★
Heat/Humidity Tolerance	★★
Cold Tolerance	★
Shade Tolerance	★★
Longevity	★

This versatile annual herb is used in many cuisines throughout temperate and warm regions of the globe. The leaves are commonly referred to as cilantro, while the seeds are known as coriander. This plant can be difficult to grow in Florida, since it achieves optimal growth under cool conditions.

Known Hazards

Those who are allergic to celery should exercise caution when handling or consuming this plant, which is a member of the same family.

68

GEOGRAPHIC DISTRIBUTION Cilantro is native to parts of north Africa, the Middle East, and western Asia. It was mentioned in the Bible and was cultivated by the ancient Greeks and Romans. The Spanish probably first introduced this species into the Western Hemisphere. Cilantro was planted in the 1600s in the colony of Massachusetts. Large-scale commercial production takes place in Canada, India, Morocco, Pakistan, Romania, and Poland. For reasons that are not clear, this spice is no longer widely used in European cuisines. Cilantro is grown on a small scale as a commercial crop in Florida.

PLANT DESCRIPTION Cilantro is a short-lived, herbaceous annual capable of attaining a height of about 20 inches. It closely resembles parsley in appearance. The lower leaves are compound or are deeply cut into multiple lobes. Leaves on the upper plant are finely divided and feathery. Small white or pink flowers are borne in umbels, measuring about 2 inches in diameter. Seed capsules are round, reddish brown in color when mature. They are divided into 2 single-seeded mericarps.

FLAVOR AND SCENT The leaves are pungent and, in flavor, resemble parsley with a touch of citrus. The seed capsules have an earthy, warm, slightly sweet flavor, with overtones of citrus and a hint of bitterness. However, full flavor does not develop until the ripe capsules have been dried.

VARIETIES Several selections have been made, although availability may be limited. 'Jantar' produces small white flowers and large seeds. Other cultivars include 'Bilbo,' 'Confetti,' and 'Santos.'

RELATIVES Cilantro is a member of the Apiaceae family. Members described within this book include: anise, *Pimpinella anisum*; caraway, *Carum carvi*; chervil, *Anthriscus cerefolium*; culantro, *Eryngium foetidum*; cumin, *Cuminum cyminum*; dill, *Anethum graveolens*; fennel, *Foeniculum vulgare*; lovage, *Levisticum officinale*; and parsley, *Petroselinum crispum*.

CULTIVATION Cilantro is almost always started from seed. The seed germinates readily, but young plants may fade quickly if exposed to hot temperatures. Weed control is important, as seedlings are slow to develop. In north Florida, a fall and spring crop can be grown. In south Florida, cilantro is planted in the fall and harvested over the winter.

HARVEST AND USE Leaves can be clipped from the plant at any time once the plant is established. The capsules are harvested shortly after the flower head turns brown. The top of the plant is severed and is hung upside down in a dark location in a paper bag. As the flower and foliage dry, the seeds can be shaken loose within the bag. The flavor of ground seeds diminishes in storage. Dried leaves lose most of their flavor and become tasteless with age. This plant is commonly used in the cuisines of India, Mexico, China, Vietnam, Portugal, and Thailand. Coriander is one of the most frequently used spices in both east- and west-African cuisine. Coriander is sometimes added to enhance the flavor of Belgian-style beers. It is also used in sausages and cured meats. Cilantro is often used in ceviche, salsa, chutney, and pesto.

Dried coriander seeds resemble miniature pumpkins in form. The seeds are sometimes briefly dry roasted before use to release aromas and to enhance the flavor.

Cinnamon

SCIENTIFIC NAME: *Cinnamomum verum* or *Cinnamomum zeylanicum*
FAMILY: Lauraceae
OTHER COMMON NAMES: Ceylon Cinnamon, Cinamomo (Spanish)

Woody Perennial; Evergreen Shrub

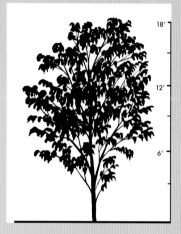

Characteristics

Overall Rating	★★
Ease of Care	★★★
Utility	★★
Landscape Value	★★★★
Salt Tolerance	★★
Drought Tolerance	★★★
Heat/Humidity Tolerance	★★★★★
Cold Tolerance	★
Shade Tolerance	★★★
Longevity	★★★★

Cinnamon is a handsome tree and, although frost sensitive, is reasonably well suited to growth in south Florida. Those who would consider growing this plant to produce spice should note that the spice consists of the inner bark. In other words, the tree must be severely pruned back to accommodate spice production. The leaves and fruits are aromatic and lend themselves to various uses.

Known Hazards

Essential oil of cinnamon should never be ingested. Plant material contains minute quantities of safrole, which is considered a mild carcinogen. Cinnamon contains salicylates, and consumption may cause reactions in those who are intolerant of these compounds.

GEOGRAPHIC DISTRIBUTION Members of the *Cinnamomum* genus are widely distributed throughout the world's warm regions. However, true cinnamon is probably native to Sri Lanka. Other closely related species are native to Southeast Asia, primarily China and Vietnam. Cinnamon was used in Chinese medicine prior to 2500 B.C. In Florida, it may be grown as far north as Palm Beach County. The tree suffers serious damage if the temperature drops to 29° F.

New flushes of growth are often tinted an attractive red.

PLANT DESCRIPTION This evergreen shrub or small tree reaches a height of about 20 feet in Florida. Flowers are white, with 6 petals and 6 stamens.

FLAVOR AND SCENT The spice is sweet and pleasant, with a delicate, slightly pungent flavor. The leaves are aromatic and smell of clove and anise. The flowers have a rank, disagreeable scent.

VARIETIES True cinnamon or Ceylon cinnamon is the most prized variety and is the type found on most spice shelves within the United States. Well-regarded Indian cultivars are 'Navashree' and 'Nithyashree.' Several relatives, identified below, though also used as spice, have a bitter note or lack the sweetness and delicacy of true cinnamon.

RELATIVES The family Lauraceae consists of about 2,000 species. Members covered within this book include: bay laurel, *Laurus nobiles*; red bay, *Persea borbonia*; sassafras, *Sassafras albidumare*; and spicebush, *Lindera benzoin*. The *Cinnamomum* genus contains over 250 species, several of which have properties similar to true cinnamon. Other notable species include camphor, *Cinnamomum camphora*; cassia, *Cinnamomum aromaticum*; malabathrum or tej patta, *Cinnamomum tamala*; Indonesian cinnamon, *Cinnamomum burmanii*; and Vietnamese cinnamon, *Cinnamomum loureiroi*. Camphor is a notorious invasive exotic in Florida. It is found over large portions of the state and has displaced native species. The leaf of tej patta is widely used as a flavoring and aroma agent in Indian cooking, but is not widely available in the United States.

CULTIVATION Cinnamon is usually grown from seed. However, superior cultivars can be vegetatively propagated through cuttings and air layers. Cinnamon is typically planted in the field after a year of container growth. In south Florida, it is best planted in the spring so that it can establish itself during wet-season precipitation. This species, especially when young, appears to benefit from partial shade. When cinnamon is raised in commercial plantings, it is kept at a height of less than 10 feet. Branches are periodically trimmed to stimulate the production of new branches from which bark can be harvested.

HARVEST AND USE Branches that reach a certain size are sheared from the tree. Both the outer and inner layers of bark are removed. The outer (corky) bark is scraped away, and the inner bark is allowed to dry. It curls upon drying, forming quills or cinnamon sticks. Cinnamon is an important ingredient in the Indian spice mix garam masala. The newly set fruit, termed cinnamon buds, are also used as a spice and do not require sacrificing parts of the plant. Cinnamon buds resemble cloves in physical appearance. They are sweet, with a complex flavor similar to cinnamon bark.

Quills can be used whole to flavor tea, warm apple cider, and hot cocoa.

Coffee

SCIENTIFIC NAME: *Coffea arabica*
FAMILY: Rubiaceae
OTHER COMMON NAME: Cafeto (Spanish)

Woody Perennial; Evergreen Shrub

Characteristics

Overall Rating	★★★
Ease of Care	★★★
Utility	★★
Landscape Value	★★★
Salt Tolerance	★★★
Drought Tolerance	★★★
Heat/Humidity Tolerance	★★★★
Cold Tolerance	★★
Shade Tolerance	★★★
Longevity	★★★★

Known Hazards

Coffee contains caffeine, which is a stimulant and mild diuretic. Excessive consumption can cause nervousness, anxiety, muscle twitches, insomnia, headaches, and heart palpitations. Some studies suggest that pregnant women should limit their intake of caffeine. Caffeine can raise intraocular pressure and may aggravate some types of glaucoma. Withdrawal from heavy and continuous use may cause unpleasant symptoms.

Coffee closely follows tea as one of the most widely consumed beverages on earth. It can be grown outdoors in protected areas of south Florida and will succeed as a container plant in other areas of the state. Lowland coffee rarely reaches the level of quality achieved by mountain-crown coffee. Coffee is nevertheless a worthwhile and interesting backyard crop for south Florida.

GEOGRAPHIC DISTRIBUTION Coffee is native to west-central Africa and first appeared as a cultivated crop in Ethiopia in the 800s. The word "coffee" may have been derived from the name of the Ethiopian province Kaffa. Coffee spread from Africa to the Middle East and north Africa by the 1400s and found its way to Europe by the end of the 1500s. Coffee was widely consumed by both sides during the American Civil War. Today, Brazil is the largest exporter of coffee. More than 50 countries produce coffee. Vietnam, Ethiopia, Nicaragua, Panama, Guatemala, and Columbia are considered major producers. High-quality "gourmet" coffee is grown in Kenya, Costa Rica, Hawaii, Jamaica, Indonesia, and a few other locations. It is typically grown at high altitude under partial shade, and undergoes careful hand selection.

Coffee flowers, immature fruit, and ripe fruit are sometimes present on the plant at the same time.

PLANT DESCRIPTION Coffee is an upright, evergreen, understory shrub. If left unpruned, it can reach a height of 20 or even 30 feet. Leaves are deep green, ovate, measuring 3 to 7 inches in length. Fragrant white flowers are borne in axillary clusters. These are followed by the fruit, which gradually change from green, to yellow, and then to red as they mature. The ripe deep-red drupe, which is referred to as a "cherry," encloses a thin pulp of sweet flesh. Each cherry contains two semi-hemispheric seeds or "beans," linked at their flat surface. When stripped of surrounding pulp and parchment, the beans are green to bronze. The coffee plant can live and bear fruit for up to 100 years, although commercial production usually ceases after about 30 years.

FLAVOR AND SCENT The flavor of coffee is a complex mix of acidic and bitter components, The scent is aromatic, and may contain earthy notes, floral notes, buttery notes, or notes of caramel, along with hints of other diverse aromas. Beginning in the 1970s, there has been a trend toward flavored coffees. However, most coffee aficionados believe that flavoring is added to mask flaws in the underlying product, that good coffee stands on its own.

VARIETIES About a half-dozen species of coffee are cultivated throughout the world. The species *Coffee arabica* is used for quality production. It is made up of at least two races or subspecies, Bourbon and Typica. Varieties include: 'Blue Mountain,' 'Bourbon Santos,' 'Catimor,' 'Caturra,' 'Columnaris,' 'Harrar,' 'Kent,' 'Kona,' 'Maragogipe,' 'Moka,' 'Mundo Novo,' 'Pache colis,' 'Pache comum,' and 'San Ramon.'

RELATIVES Coffee is a member of the large Rubiaceae family, which contains over 500 genera and as many as 10,000 species. The only other member of the family covered in these pages is the gardenia, *Gardenia angusta*. Other members of the *Coffea* genus have been used in much the same manner as *Coffea arabica*. Coffee robusta, *Coffea canephora*, may have originated in Uganda and is often used in blends and espressos. *Coffea liberica*, of Liberia, and *Coffea esliaca*, of Sudan, are also sometimes used as coffee, as coffee adulterants, or as coffee substitutes. Wild coffee, *Psychotria nervosa*, is a native Florida plant that has a similar habit of growth to *Coffea arabica*. Unfortunately, the beans produced by wild coffee are exceedingly bitter, do not yield an acceptable product, and should not be considered a coffee "substitute."

CULTIVATION Coffee requires a tropical or subtropical climate. It prefers rainfall of between 40 and 60 inches, evenly spaced during the year. In areas subject to winter cold, the coffee plant can be container grown or can be raised in a greenhouse. Substantial fruit production begins at about 4 or 5 years. To aid in harvest, most plants are maintained at between 5 and 8 feet in height. Coffee prefers partial shade and will tolerate significant shade. Coffee is severely injured at 32° F, and may be killed by lower temperatures.

HARVEST AND USE The annual production of a mature coffee plant ranges from 2 to 7 pounds of dried beans. The ripe cherries are harvested by hand. Because the fruit ripens unevenly, several pickings are required. After harvest, the beans must not be permitted to sit within the moist pulp for any extended period. Either the cherries are dried, or the beans are removed from the cherry by scrubbing or mechanical washing. When sun dried, the berries are placed in shallow trays and are frequently raked and turned. They are then de-hulled. Following this process, the beans are roasted. The color of the bean darkens with exposure to prolonged heat. This results in roasting gradations such as light, medium light, medium, medium dark, dark, and very dark. Physicians may advise those with hypertension and cardiovascular disorders to avoid coffee.

Cuban Oregano

SCIENTIFIC NAME: *Plectranthus amboinicus*
FAMILY: Lamiaceae
OTHER COMMON NAMES: Spanish Thyme, Orégano
   de la Hoja Ancha (Spanish)

Herbaceous Perennial

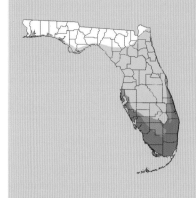

Characteristics

Overall Rating	★★★
Ease of Care	★★★★
Utility	★★★
Landscape Value	★★★★
Salt Tolerance	★
Drought Tolerance	★★
Heat/Humidity Tolerance	★★★★★
Cold Tolerance	★
Shade Tolerance	★★★
Longevity	★★★

This decorative, tropical plant is not a type of oregano. In fact, it is not even a close relative of oregano's. It is more closely associated with coleus. Nevertheless, its flavor is very similar to that of oregano. It can be used in the same manner. Cuban oregano is easy to grow and is well suited to growth in south Florida.

Known Hazards
None

GEOGRAPHIC DISTRIBUTION This plant is probably native to India, but grows wild in Malaysia. It has been widely distributed to many of the world's tropical regions.

PLANT DESCRIPTION Cuban oregano is an herbaceous perennial. It is evergreen. Stems are succulent, somewhat brittle, and angular. Opposite leaves are broad and fleshy. The plant may reach an overall height of nearly 2 feet. It produces small white or violet flowers.

FLAVOR AND SCENT The flavor closely resembles oregano, but has a mintlike, peppery sharpness. The scent is pungent and is very similar to that of oregano.

VARIETIES A few selections are available. These include 'Compact Grey,' 'Golden Ruffles,' 'Marble,' 'Silver Shield,' and 'Variegated.'

RELATIVES The Lamiaceae or mint family contains numerous herbs and spices. Species discussed within this book include basil, *Ocimum* spp.; bee balm, *Monarda didyma*; Jamaican mint, *Micromeria viminea*; lavender, *Lavandula* spp.; lemon balm, *Melissa officinalis*; mint, *Mentha* spp.; oregano, *Origanum* spp.; perilla, *Perilla frutescens*; rosemary, *Rosmarinus officinalis*; sage, *Salvia officinalis*; savory, *Satureja* spp.; and thyme, *Thymus* spp. The *Plectranthus* genus contains about 250 species. Most of these are succulent evergreens. One member of the genus that is grown as an herb in Florida is Vicks salve plant, *Plectranthus tomentosa*. When rubbed or crushed, this species exudes the fragrance of vapor rub. The little spurflower, *Plectranthus parviflorus*, is occasionally raised as an ornamental. It has escaped cultivation in at least two areas of central Florida.

CULTIVATION Cuban oregano is an easy plant to grow and will survive considerable neglect. It prefers full sun but will endure some shade, although it becomes leggy if planted in dense shade. It is not negatively affected by heat or humidity. Cuttings root easily. This species is cold sensitive and may be killed by freezing or near freezing temperatures. It makes a suitable container specimen in areas subject to frequent winter cold.

HARVEST AND USE The leaves can be harvested at any time. In fact, pinching the plant back occasionally encourages bushy growth. It is typically used fresh, although it is also dried and used in some jerk seasonings. Cuban oregano can be substituted for oregano in various dishes, including pizza. Diced Cuban oregano is used to flavor black beans to good effect. It is used in Cuban and Philippine cuisines. It is employed as an ingredient in medicinal teas in some cultures. That use is not recommended here, however, since—as noted within the introductory materials—this book makes no claims regarding the medicinal benefits of the herbs covered within these pages.

Variegated Cuban oregano makes a decorative addition to the herb garden. Although Cuban oregano is not closely related to true oregano, the flavor is similar.

Culantro

SCIENTIFIC NAME: *Eryngium foetidum*
FAMILY: Apiaceae
OTHER COMMON NAMES: Long Coriander, Recao
  (Spanish)

Herbaceous Biennial

Characteristics

Overall Rating	★★★★
Ease of Care	★★★
Utility	★★★
Landscape Value	★★
Salt Tolerance	★★
Drought Tolerance	★★
Heat/Humidity Tolerance	★★★★
Cold Tolerance	★
Shade Tolerance	★★★★
Longevity	★★

Culantro is a seasoning herb that enjoys considerable popularity in the Caribbean, Latin America, India, Singapore, Malaysia, Vietnam, and Korea. However, it is not widely known in the United States, except in certain ethnic communities. Although it has a different habit of growth, culantro is a distant relative of cilantro's. The flavor is comparable to that of cilantro, and both species are used in a similar fashion.

Known Hazards

May have some invasive potential

76

GEOGRAPHIC DISTRIBUTION Culantro is indigenous to Central America, southern Mexico, and the Caribbean. It is grown commercially in Trinidad and Puerto Rico. This non-native plant has escaped cultivation in Miami-Dade County.

PLANT DESCRIPTION Culantro is a biennial herb that attains a maximum height of just over a foot. Leaves form in a rosette around a shortened stem. They typically measure between 6 and 14 inches in length. Margins are serrated and are armed with tiny spines. Cream-colored flowers are borne on a short stalk that emerges from the center of the plant.

FLAVOR AND SCENT The scent is similar to that of cilantro, but stronger and more pungent. The flavor shares similar characteristics.

VARIETIES It does not appear that any named varieties exist. Packaged seed is sold under the species name.

RELATIVES The Apiaceae or carrot family contains several species covered within this book. These include: anise, *Pimpinella anisum*; caraway, *Carum carvi*; chervil, *Anthriscus cerefolium*; cilantro, *Coriandrum sativum*; cumin, *Cuminum cyminum*; dill, *Anethum graveolens*; fennel, *Foeniculum vulgare*; lovage, *Levisticum officinale*; and parsley, *Petroselinum crispum*. The genus *Eryngium* is composed of approximately 200 tropical and temperate species. Several are native to Florida, including Baldwin's eryngo, *Eryngium baldwinii*; blueflower eryngo, *Eryngium integrifolium*; creeping eryngo, *Eryngium prostratum*; fragrant eryngo, *Eryngium aromaticum*; rattlesnake master, *Eryngium aquaticum*; and the endangered scrub eryngo, *Eryngium cuneifolium*.

CULTIVATION Culantro prefers partial to relatively deep shade. With such protection, it will generally survive summer conditions in south Florida. In shaded locations the leaves tend to be larger and take on a darker shade of green. Shaded growth may also delay flowering, leading to an extended harvest. During the Florida summer, the plant exhibits a tendency to bolt and go rapidly to seed. Culantro prefers relatively heavy soils, high in organic matter. However, it also requires adequate drainage. Most plants are grown from seed. Seeds germinate after about 3 weeks. The plant is impervious to most pests and diseases, although it is occasionally affected by root-knot nematodes. Culantro has moderate salt tolerance.

HARVEST AND USE The leaves may be harvested at any stage. Fresh culantro has poor storage characteristics. Even when refrigerated, the leaves begin to deteriorate within 2 or 3 days after they are picked. The leaves are tough if left whole and are therefore finely chopped before use. Culantro is used as a seasoning and marinade for various meats. It is also used in chutneys, soups, and noodle-based dishes. It is a key ingredient in Puerto Rican sofrito and enhances various salsas and tomato-based dishes.

A bed of culantro gone to seed in the Florida sun

Cumin

SCIENTIFIC NAME: *Cuminum cyminum*
FAMILY: Apiaceae
OTHER COMMON NAME: Comino (Spanish)

Herbaceous Annual

Planted
in Spring

Planted
in Fall
or Winter

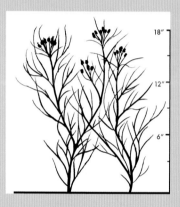

Characteristics

Overall Rating	★★★★
Ease of Care	★★★
Utility	★★★★
Landscape Value	★★★
Salt Tolerance	★
Drought Tolerance	★★★★
Heat/Humidity Tolerance	★★
Cold Tolerance	★
Shade Tolerance	★
Longevity	★

The flavor of cumin is instantly recognizable, distinct from that of other seed-based spices, such as anise, caraway, and fennel. Cumin is versatile, easy to grow, and can be stored for considerable periods without deterioration. Although it is a short-lived annual, cumin is one of the easiest and most worthwhile spices that will grow in the Florida garden.

Known Hazards

Consumption of cumin is discouraged during pregnancy. Cumin contains salicylates, and consumption may cause reactions in those who are intolerant of these compounds. Those who are allergic to celery or other members of the Apiaceae family should exercise caution when using this spice.

GEOGRAPHIC DISTRIBUTION Cumin is indigenous to southwestern Asia and the Middle East. Its native range is thought to have included Egypt, the eastern Mediterranean, and territory stretching east to India. It has been employed as a spice since biblical times. The Spanish introduced cumin to the Western Hemisphere. Commercial production takes place in Iran, India, Pakistan, Sri Lanka, Indonesia, Mexico, and Turkey. Cumin will grow throughout Florida.

PLANT DESCRIPTION Cumin is a small, herbaceous annual that reaches a maximum height of about 18 inches. The stem is heavily branched. The wispy, pinnate leaves measure 2 to 4 inches in length and somewhat resemble those of dill. Tiny flowers are borne in flattened umbels. The flowers are typically white, off-white, or pink. The fruit is an achene, measuring about 1/4 of an inch in length. Each fruit contains a single seed. The fruit has longitudinal ridges and tapers toward each end.

FLAVOR AND SCENT The flavor is warm, earthy, and rich, with mild heat and a slight bitter note. The scent is aromatic and spicy.

VARIETIES No cultivars are regularly available in Florida.

RELATIVES The Apiaceae or carrot family contains approximately 3,000 species. As a member of this family, cumin is related to numerous herbs and spices covered within this book. These include: anise, *Pimpinella anisum*; caraway, *Carum carvi*; chervil, *Anthriscus cerefolium*; cilantro, *Coriandrum sativum*; culantro, *Eryngium foetidum*; dill, *Anethum graveolens*; fennel, *Foeniculum vulgare*; lovage, *Levisticum officinale*; and parsley, *Petroselinum crispum*. So-called black cumin, *Nigella sativa*, is not related to cumin, although its seed is also used as a spice.

CULTIVATION Cumin is adaptable and relatively easy to grow. It performs best in full sun and prefers a dry, Mediterranean-like climate. It is fairly drought tolerant. Warm temperatures do not adversely affect this species. It will grow on a wide range of soils, but requires adequate drainage. Cumin is grown from seed. In north Florida, seeds are planted after the danger of frost has passed. In south Florida, seeds are usually sown over the winter. Temperatures below 32° F are generally fatal.

HARVEST AND USE The plant typically goes to seed about 5 months after it is set out. Following harvest, the seed heads should be hung upside down, suspended in paper bags in a dry, dark, well-ventilated location. Ground cumin will lose its potency unless stored in an airtight container. Toasting the seeds in a skillet enhances the flavor. Cumin is a key ingredient in Indian cuisine. It is found in garam masala, sambaar powder, and various curry mixes. In Mexican and Tex-Mex cuisines, it is an important ingredient in chili powder. It is used to flavor tacos, tamales, enchiladas, and salsas. It is also of special importance in Moroccan cuisine, where it is used for grilling kebabs, in stews, and to flavor couscous. It is used throughout the Middle East and north Africa.

A close-up view of cumin seeds (left) and ground cumin (right)

Curry Leaf Tree

SCIENTIFIC NAME: *Murraya koenigii*
FAMILY: Rutaceae
OTHER COMMON NAME: Kari-Pattha,
  Hojas de Curry (Spanish)

Woody Perennial; Deciduous Shrub

Characteristics

Overall Rating	★★★★★
Ease of Care	★★★★
Utility	★★★★
Landscape Value	★★★
Salt Tolerance	★★
Drought Tolerance	★★★★
Heat/Humidity Tolerance	★★★★★
Cold Tolerance	★★
Shade Tolerance	★★★
Longevity	★★★

The leaves of this small tree are considered an essential ingredient in southern Indian and Sri Lankan cuisines. In southern India, curry leaf is often grown in kitchen gardens to ensure a steady supply of this flavorful spice. The tree is well suited to growth in south Florida, and is much sought after by those who value authentic Indian cooking.

Known Hazards

The plant has some tendency to spread and colonize. Whole leaves, if left in food following cooking, may present a choking hazard. Seeds may be toxic.

GEOGRAPHIC DISTRIBUTION The curry leaf tree is native to India and Sri Lanka. It grows wild throughout much of the Indian subcontinent, forming stands in clearings or occurring as an understory plant in coastal forests. It is also grown on extensive tree farms. Curry leaf has been used as a spice in India for over 1,500 years. This plant is not the source of commercial curries marketed in the West, which are actually spice mixes meant to approximate the flavors of Indian cooking. While the curry leaf tree is regarded as semitropical, it has survived light frosts to about 28° F in Florida and southern California. It can be grown as far north as Orlando. However, it is likely to suffer cold-weather setbacks anywhere north of coastal areas of south Florida. Curry leaf is grown to a limited extent as a commercial crop in south Florida, but export to other states is restricted by citrus-related quarantines.

PLANT DESCRIPTION The curry leaf tree is a small semi-deciduous tree, reaching a height of about 25 feet under favorable conditions. In Florida, it is usually less than 15 feet tall. Although not closely related to sumac, it outwardly resembles sumac both in appearance and in habit of growth. Leaves are pinnate, containing 13 to 23 leaflets, which measure 2 or 3 inches in length. The flowers, borne in flat clusters at the branch tips, are small, white, with 5 or 7 petals. The flowers are followed by black, oblong berries, which are edible. The seed, though, is reportedly toxic. The plant reproduces, in part, by sending out underground runners. Unless some measures are taken to restrain new growth, curry leaf can rapidly form a thicket.

FLAVOR AND SCENT The leaf is highly aromatic, with a pungent, earthy component. The flavor is tangy, slightly hot, with a hint of citrus.

RELATIVES The Rutaceae or citrus family contains numerous fruiting plants. Those discussed within these pages include the calamondin, *Citrus mitis*; Kaffir lime, *Citrus hystrix*; lemon, *Citrus limon*; and lime, *Citrus hystrix* and *Citrus aurantifolia*. Leaves of the Kaffir lime are also used as a spice. Besides curry leaf, the only other noncitrus member of the Rutaceae family described within this book is rue, *Ruta graveolens*. The genus *Murraya* contains between 6 and 20 species. Orange jessamine or Chinese box, *Murraya exotica*, is grown as an ornamental. It has escaped cultivation in Florida and is considered an invasive exotic. The curry leaf tree should not be confused with the unrelated curry plant, *Helichrysum italicum*, which is native to Europe. While this herb exudes a currylike scent, especially when bruised or cut, it is rarely used as a flavoring agent.

CULTIVATION Curry leaf tree is not demanding in its cultural requirements. It is tough and resilient. It will grow on various soils, including sand, clay, and oolitic limestone. It prefers full sun but can endure a few hours of light shade. The tree can be grown from seed, although seeds are reportedly slow to germinate. Softwood cuttings, if treated with rooting hormone, can be started in a mix of gravel and potting soil. Because at least one other member of the *Murraya* genus has displayed invasive tendencies, some caution should be exercised when planting the curry leaf tree. An in-ground barrier may be needed to prevent this plant from colonizing large sections of the garden.

HARVEST AND USE The leaves are best when used fresh. Dried leaves rapidly lose much of the hot, aromatic quality that makes this spice so enticing. The leaves are used in vegetable curries, in coconut milk–based curries, in flat breads, and in connection with seafood and lentil dishes. The leaves are sometimes, but not always, removed from the dish prior to serving.

Curry leaf flower clusters are fragrant, and draw a wide assortment of flying pollinators.

Dill

SCIENTIFIC NAME: *Anethum graveolens*
FAMILY: Apiaceae
OTHER COMMON NAMES: Abesón, Eneldo (Spanish)

Herbaceous Annual

Planted in Spring

Planted in Fall or Early Winter

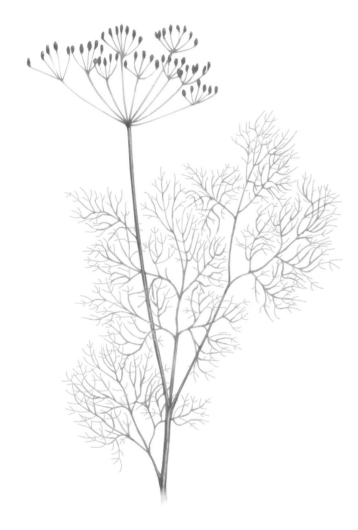

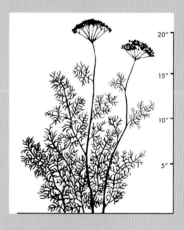

Characteristics

Overall Rating	★★★★
Ease of Care	★★★
Utility	★★★★
Landscape Value	★★★
Salt Tolerance	★
Drought Tolerance	★
Heat/Humidity Tolerance	★
Cold Tolerance	★
Shade Tolerance	★
Longevity	★

Known Hazards

Contact with the plant may cause skin irritation or photosensitivity in hypersensitive individuals. Dill contains salicylates. Consumption may cause reactions in those who are intolerant of these compounds.

Dill is a fast-growing, aromatic herb and is a popular dooryard crop in all regions of the country. It is easy to grow and adds interesting texture to the garden. The seeds are used as a spice and pickling agent. The leaves are used as an herb and flavor ingredient. The International Herb Association designated dill as the Herb of the Year for 2010.

82

GEOGRAPHIC DISTRIBUTION Dill is native to central Asia. Some commercial production occurs in Florida and California.

PLANT DESCRIPTION Dill is an annual herb, attaining a height of 10 to 30 inches. Leaves are alternate, finely cut, featherlike and delicate. The divisions appear as lacy filaments. Small white to yellow flowers appear in umbels of atop long stems. Seeds are about 1/4 of an inch in length with longitudinal ridges.

FLAVOR AND SCENT The leaves are highly aromatic, with a sweet, fresh, mown-hay smell. The taste is pleasantly sour and earthy. The seeds somewhat resemble caraway in flavor.

VARIETIES Several selections have been made and are available through seed catalogues. 'Bouquet' is a cultivar that produces heavy seed crops. 'Dukat' is well regarded for use as a green herb. Other cultivars include 'Fernleaf,' 'Hera,' 'Long Island Mammoth,' and 'Vierling.' Dill has been known to hybridize with fennel.

RELATIVES The Apiaceae family contains many plants of culinary import. Various species are described within this book, including anise, *Pimpinella anisum*; caraway, *Carum carvi*; chervil, *Anthriscus cerefolium*; cilantro, *Coriandrum sativum*; culantro, *Eryngium foetidum*; cumin, *Cuminum cyminum*; fennel, *Foeniculum vulgare*; lovage, *Levisticum officinale*; and parsley, *Petroselinum crispum*. Dill is one of two species within the genus *Anethum*. The other species, *Anethum sowa*, is native to Asia and has similar uses.

CULTIVATION Dill is generally planted from seed, with the seeds sown directly in the garden. In peninsular Florida, it should be planted in the fall. The plant tends to struggle and die out in the heat and humidity of the Florida summer. Dill is difficult to transplant and, if moved, may rapidly go to seed. Dill prefers direct sun, and significant shade will dramatically reduce yields. Dill also thrives in rich, well-drained soil. The planting bed should be enriched with organic matter. Although dill has moderate drought resistance, the gardener should provide regular irrigation during dry periods. While dill has escaped cultivation in the northeast and elsewhere, it does not appear to pose an invasive threat in Florida. However, if allowed to go to seed, it will readily self-sow and repopulate the garden over the next growing season.

Dill leaves are finely divided and threadlike. It is difficult to tell where the stems end and where the leaves begin.

HARVEST AND USE Sprigs can be clipped from the plant at any time. Dill should be used fresh whenever possible as the flavor diminishes when it is dried. Dill is frequently used to flavor baked and smoked salmon, and is employed in various fish recipes. The seed is harvested by clipping the umbels from the plant before the seeds disburse. The umbels are then hung upside down in a paper bag to dry. Seeds drop from the dried flower heads with gentle shaking. Dill seed is used in pickling solutions, as a curing spice for meat, and in marinades.

Fennel

SCIENTIFIC NAME: *Foeniculum vulgare*
FAMILY: Apiaceae
OTHER COMMON NAME: Hinojo (Spanish)

Herbaceous Perennial

Planted in Spring

Planted in Fall

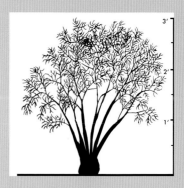

Characteristics

Overall Rating	★★★
Ease of Care	★★★
Utility	★★★★
Landscape Value	★★★
Salt Tolerance	★
Drought Tolerance	★★★★
Heat/Humidity Tolerance	★★
Cold Tolerance	★★★
Shade Tolerance	★★
Longevity	★★

Known Hazards

Fennel should not be used by individuals who have a history of abnormal blood clotting or estrogen-dependent breast tumors. It should be avoided by those taking birth control pills and should not be consumed during pregnancy. Those who are allergic to celery should exercise caution when handling or consuming this plant, which is part of the same family.

Fennel is an aromatic herb with multiple uses. All parts are edible. The seed (actually the dry fruit) is used as a spice. The leaf petioles, which weave together to form a "bulb," are consumed as a vegetable. The leaf is used as a garnish and as a flavoring agent. This handsome carrot relative is well suited to the Florida home garden.

GEOGRAPHIC DISTRIBUTION Fennel is indigenous to the Mediterranean, and its native range is thought to encompass portions of southern Europe, North Africa, and the Middle East. The Romans distributed this species to all regions of their vast empire. Today, China, India, Egypt, Argentina, and Indonesia are major producers. Fennel has become an exotic invasive in some regions.

The thickened base of Florence fennel can be used as a vegetable. The flavor falls somewhere between that of anise seed and that of celery.

PLANT DESCRIPTION Fennel is a short-lived perennial herb. It is capable of attaining a height of about 6 feet, although most cultivated types only grow to 3 or 4 feet. The stems (actually leaf petioles) are hollow and are somewhat celerylike in form. Leaves are deeply cut, with fine, wispy, threadlike filaments. Small yellow flowers are produced in erect umbels.

FLAVOR AND SCENT Fennel smells strongly of licorice or anise. This flavor is pronounced in the seed, but is subtle and is integrated with other flavors in the stems and foliage.

VARIETIES The species is divided into several distinct cultivar groups. Florence fennel is a widely grown cultivar group that is consumed primarily as a vegetable. It is an annual with swollen leaf petioles. Cultivars within this group include 'Romy,' 'Rubrum,' and 'Zefa Fino.' Sweet fennel is a perennial that attains a larger size than Florence fennel. The seeds are gathered and the leaves are used as a flavoring and garnish. Cultivars include 'Bronze' and 'Purpureum.'

RELATIVES Fennel is the sole species within the genus *Foeniculum*. Other relatives described within this book that fall within the family Apiaceae include: anise, *Pimpinella anisum*; caraway, *Carum carvi*; chervil, *Anthriscus cerefolium*; cilantro, *Coriandrum sativum*; culantro, *Eryngium foetidum*; cumin, *Cuminum cyminum*; dill, *Anethum graveolens*; lovage, *Levisticum officinale*; and parsley, *Petroselinum crispum*.

CULTIVATION Fennel can be readily grown from seed. It should be mulched to prevent competition from weeds and grasses. This temperate herb is negatively affected by the heat and humidity of south Florida summers. Consequently, in peninsular Florida, growing schedules are reversed. Fennel is planted in the fall and harvested during the winter and spring. In south Florida, fennel dies back over the summer but, usually, will regenerate from the bulb as temperatures cool. In north Florida, fennel is planted in the spring, goes dormant during the winter, and regenerates from its roots the following season. Fennel may be grown as an annual or as a biennial. It is typically removed after the second season of growth and replaced with fresh seedling stock.

HARVEST AND USE The seed heads should be severed from the plant after they turn brown and seeds begin to dislodge with gentle shaking. The heads can be hung upside down in a paper bag and stored in a dry, dark location. Seeds retain a gray-green tint after they are dried. The seed is used to flavor sausages and may be added to various breads. It is an ingredient in Chinese five-spice powder. It is used as palate cleanser and breath freshener in India. It is employed as a spice in the cuisines of Italy, China, India, Sri Lanka, Iran, Saudi Arabia, southern France, and central Europe. The leaves are used in a manner similar to dill, although they are different in taste. They may be added to salads, potato salads, pestos, and dips. Fennel pollen is also used as a spice. As a result of its scarcity and the amount of labor required to gather this item, the pollen rivals saffron in expense. The lower stems are excellent in salads and stews. However, when used in stews, fennel stems should be added toward the end of the cooking process, as heat tends to degrade the flavor.

In India, raw fennel seeds are sometimes eaten as a palate cleanser following a meal.

The flowers of Florence fennel, which form an umbel, are similar in form to those of other members of the Apiaceae family.

Fenugreek

SCIENTIFIC NAME: *Trigonella foenum-graecum*
FAMILY: Fabaceae
OTHER COMMON NAME: Methi, Alholva (Spanish)

Herbaceous Annual

Planted in Spring

Planted in Fall

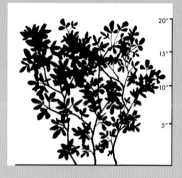

Characteristics

Overall Rating	★★★
Ease of Care	★★★
Utility	★★★
Landscape Value	★★
Salt Tolerance	★★
Drought Tolerance	★★★
Heat/Humidity Tolerance	★★
Cold Tolerance	★★★
Shade Tolerance	★★
Longevity	★

Known Hazards

Fenugreek is an occasional allergen. Contact with skin may cause rash in sensitive individuals. Heavy consumption may cause gastrointestinal distress and diarrhea. Those who are allergic to peanuts, chickpeas, or other members of the Fabaceae family should exercise caution. Fenugreek contains salicylates, and consumption may cause reactions in those who are intolerant of these compounds. This plant may have some invasive potential

This versatile spice is rarely found on spice racks in the United States and Europe, except as an occasional constituent in curry powder. However, fenugreek is widely used in other parts of the world. The seeds are the source of a potent spice. The leaves are used as a potherb in some regions and are also an important ingredient in Indian cooking.

GEOGRAPHIC DISTRIBUTION Fenugreek is believed to be native to the Mediterranean region and much of southern Asia. It is cultivated extensively in India, Turkey, and North Africa. It can be raised as a seasonal crop in locations that experience cold winters. It will grow throughout Florida.

PLANT DESCRIPTION Fenugreek is a short-lived, herbaceous annual, attaining a maximum height of about 2 feet. The rate of growth is rapid. The stem is smooth and hollow. The foliage is rough textured. Tripartite leaves are borne alternately along the stem. Leaflets are oval, toothed, and measure about 1 inch in length. White flowers appear during the summer, followed by sickle-shaped pods, which measure 4 or 5 inches in length. Each pod contains about 20 yellow-brown or light brown seeds. The seeds are hard and angular, with a crease down the center.

FLAVOR AND SCENT The flavor of the spice is musky, slightly bitter, and pungent, with a hint of maple, burnt sugar, and celery. The leaves are aromatic and exude the scent of freshly mown hay and curry. They impart a slight bitter element to the dishes they flavor.

VARIETIES Few cultivars are known or regularly available within the United States. Those appearing in the literature include 'Might,' 'Power,' and 'Tristar.'

RELATIVES Blue fenugreek, *Trigonella caerulea*, is closely related to fenugreek. It is native to mountainous regions of Europe. It has escaped cultivation in Miami-Dade County. Other members of the Fabaceae family described within this book include carob, *Ceratonia siliqua*, and tamarind, *Tamarindus indica*.

CULTIVATION Fenugreek prefers a dry, warm-temperate climate. It is generally grown from seed. Seeds should be planted in full sun. Soil should be well drained. The plant is tolerant of soils with a wide pH range. Planting typically takes place in the spring, after the danger of frost has passed. However, in south Florida, Fenugreek should be planted in the fall and harvested before the onset of the rainy season. Germination rates are high. Plants require 3 1/2 to 5 months to mature, flower, and produce ripened pods.

HARVEST AND USE The pods are harvested as they begin to turn brown. In the alternative, as the pods begin to brown, the entire plant is uprooted and permitted to dry. The pods or the foliage and pods are dried in a cool, dry location. As they dry, the pods split and dispel the seeds. The seeds undergo further drying and are sometimes lightly dry-roasted to dispel the bitterness and enhance underlying flavors. They take on an unpleasant flavor if over-roasted. Fenugreek is considered an important spice in Iran, where the leaves are a key ingredient in the vegetable sauce ghorme sabzi. It also frequently appears in Indian cuisine, where the leaves are an ingredient in curry mixes and some chutneys. Methi aloo is a potato-based Indian dish that makes heavy use of fenugreek leaves. Fenugreek is also found in recipes originating from the Republic of Georgia, Sri Lanka, Ethiopia, Morocco, Tunisia, Egypt, and from various Middle Eastern and African nations. Because of its bitter component, fenugreek should be used in moderation. The leaves can be used as a potherb or can be dried and used as a spice, although the flavor loses some of its intensity during the drying process. The sprouts can be added to salads.

Fenugreek seeds are hard, dense, and angular in shape. The plant's curious maple-syrup fragrance carries over into the flavor, which also has a nutty, slightly bitter quality.

Florida Anise

SCIENTIFIC NAME: *Illicium floridanum*
FAMILY: Illiciaceae
OTHER COMMON NAME: Florida Anisetree

Perennial; Evergreen Shrub

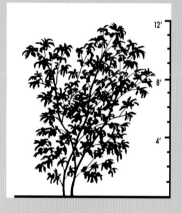

Characteristics

Overall Rating	★★
Ease of Care	★★★★
Utility	★
Landscape Value	★★★★
Salt Tolerance	★
Drought Tolerance	★★★
Heat/Humidity Tolerance	★★★★
Cold Tolerance	★★★
Shade Tolerance	★★★★
Longevity	★★★

Florida anise is closely related to the culinary spice star anise. However, Florida anise is toxic and must not be ingested. This native plant nevertheless makes an attractive addition to the home landscape and excels in natural settings. It somewhat resembles a rhododendron in its habit of growth and use within the landscape. The leaves, when bruised or crushed, exude a pleasant licorice-like fragrance. This feature makes Florida anise a worthwhile alternative to more commonly planted shrubs.

Known Hazards

The entire plant is considered toxic, and no part should be ingested. Florida anise is listed as threatened in Florida and must not be collected from the wild.

88

GEOGRAPHIC DISTRIBUTION The native range of Florida anise extends from the Florida Panhandle into southern Alabama, southern Mississippi, and southeastern Louisiana. It occurs as far east as the Tallahassee area, but does not occur naturally in peninsular Florida. Florida anise grows as an understory plant, occurring along ravine slopes, stream banks, and in other damp locations. The plant can be successfully raised throughout most of Florida, although its southern limits have not been adequately determined. Florida anise is classified as a threatened species in Florida and must not be taken from the wild.

The leaves of Florida anise give off an attractive scent. Unfortunately, all parts of this plant are considered toxic.

PLANT DESCRIPTION Florida Anise is an evergreen shrub. If left untrimmed, it can achieve the dimensions of a small tree, attaining a height of 12 to 16 feet. However, it can be easily maintained as a hedge or as a medium shrub. The growth rate is fast. The canopy is rounded and somewhat open. Dark, olive-green leaves measure from 4 to 6 inches in length. They are simple, elliptic to lanceolate, shiny, and leathery in texture. Flowers, which appear in the spring, provide visual interest. They measure about 2 inches in diameter and are typically maroon to reddish-pink, with considerable variation in color. Petals are elongated and somewhat strap-like in form. The flowers give off a rank, disagreeable odor. However, this characteristic does not detract from the overall beauty and utility of the plant. The fruit, which form at the branch tips, are star-shaped pods measuring about 3/4 of an inch in diameter. The young pods are green, but become brown and woody as they mature. Seeds, which number about a dozen, are disbursed though the explosive dehiscence of the pods.

SCENT The foliage is aromatic and exudes a scent similar to the odor of anise and star anise. The flowers produce an unusual odor that some have likened to the odor of rotting fish.

VARIETIES Several cultivars are available from nurseries that specialize in native plants. 'Album' and 'Florida Sunshine' are selections with white flowers. The foliage of 'Florida Sunshine' is said to take on an attractive yellow color during the winter. A variegated selection has also received some distribution. However, the availability of cloned plants is spotty.

RELATIVES The *Illicium* genus includes about 35 species. Two close relatives are covered within this book. The important culinary spice star anise, *Illicium verum*, is native to southern China. It is the only member of the genus that has been deemed safe for culinary use. Yellow anise, *Illicium parviflorum*, is a plant native to central Florida. Like Florida anise, it is toxic and cannot be used as a substitute for star anise. Yellow anise is covered in a separate section of this book.

CULTIVATION Florida anise is a very low-maintenance plant and will tolerate a broad range of conditions. Once established, it can withstand considerable neglect. It has low water needs and is moderately drought tolerant. The plant will adapt to various light exposures. However, when planted in full sun, the leaves tend to be less deep in color. When planted in deep shade, the plant tends to become somewhat leggy and sparse in appearance. Consequently, the preferred planting site is one that receives partial afternoon shade. Propagation is most often by seed, although selections can be reproduced by cuttings or through air layering. Florida anise does not suffer from any notable pest problems or diseases, and is not attractive to deer. It has low salt tolerance. Florida anise is cold hardy throughout the state of Florida.

HARVEST AND USE Florida anise is used strictly as a scent plant. It is toxic and has no culinary uses. The leaves can be used as a strewing herb or the plant can simply be enjoyed for its fragrance within the garden.

Gardenia

SCIENTIFIC NAME: *Gardenia augusta* (formerly *Gardenia jasminoides*)
FAMILY: Rubiaceae
OTHER COMMON NAME: Common Gardenia, Cape Jasmine

Perennial; Evergreen Shrub

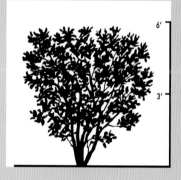

Characteristics

Overall Rating	★★★
Ease of Care	★★★★
Utility	★★
Landscape Value	★★★★★
Salt Tolerance	★
Drought Tolerance	★★★
Heat/Humidity Tolerance	★★★★★
Cold Tolerance	★★★★
Shade Tolerance	★★★★
Longevity	★★★

Gardenia is included within this book primarily as a scent plant, although the blossoms are considered edible. The aroma of the blossoms is magnificent. Along with jasmine, rose, and citrus, gardenia is universally considered among the elite of the scent world. Gardenia is a familiar landscape plant throughout Florida, and is frequently used for hedges, screens, and accents. Its handsome foliage and beautiful flowers certainly make this species worth planting for visual appeal alone, even if it lacked the other attributes described here.

Known Hazards

Sources describe the foliage of gardenia as inedible or as faintly toxic to humans. The entire plant may be dangerously toxic to pets. Cats are especially susceptible to gardenia poisoning.

90

GEOGRAPHIC DISTRIBUTION Gardenia is thought to have originated in southern China, although it was introduced into Japan and Taiwan at an early date. While the gardenia will grow throughout Florida, it may experience winter setbacks in northern parts of the state. Cold-hardy cultivars have been raised in protected locations as far north as Long Island, New York.

PLANT DESCRIPTION Gardenia is an evergreen shrub that can attain a height of between 3 and 12 feet. Cultivars differ in size and habit of growth. The rate of growth is moderately fast. Leaves are dark green, oval, glossy, and somewhat leathery in texture. They measure from 4 to 6 inches in length. Large, showy, creamy-white flowers are borne over an extended period. Flowers may be single or double, and may measure from 2 to 5 inches in diameter, depending on the cultivar. The flowers are followed by rounded seedpods that turn from green to yellow or orange as they mature.

SCENT AND FLAVOR The flowers are highly perfumed, with a fragrance that is sweet, alluring, heady, and pervasive. The flavor of the flower petals is light and sweet.

VARIETIES Many cultivars have been selected. Those grown in Florida include 'Aimee Yoshioka,' 'August Beauty,' 'Belmont,' 'Coral Gables,' 'Daisy,' 'Fortuneiana,' 'Miami Supreme,' 'Mystery,' 'Prostrata,' 'Radicans,' 'Shooting Star,' 'Summer Snow,' and 'Veitchii.' 'Shooting Star' and 'Summer Snow' have displayed slightly greater cold tolerance than other cultivars, making them good choices for planting in north Florida. Several other species within the *Gardenia* genus have been grown as ornamentals. These include brilliant gardenia, *Gardenia resinifera*, and Tahitian gardenia, *Gardenia taitensis*. However, these other species are not widely available in Florida.

RELATIVES The Rubiaceae family contains over 500 genera and as many as 10,000 species. The only other member of the family covered within this book is coffee, *Coffea arabica*. The Gardenia genus contains about 250 species.

CULTIVATION The gardenia prefers well-drained soil with a high organic content. It is partial to acidic soil, and may languish if planted in alkaline soils. When grown on even mildly alkaline soils, the plant tends to develop nutrient deficiencies. Iron deficiency is frequently encountered, and may cause the foliage to become chlorotic. The gardenia prefers full sun to light shade, but will usually survive even if planted in locations that only receive a few hours of direct sunlight. The plant can be started from seed or from cuttings. Cuttings taken during the summer months tend to be easier to establish. Grafted plants, which tend to be more vigorous, are sometimes difficult to find. In Florida, the gardenia is often grafted onto *Gardenia thunbergia*, a member of the genus that is native to Africa. This rootstock has exhibited some resistance to nematode damage. The gardenia is generally hardy and is not affected by any serious pests or diseases in Florida. Sucking insects, such as whiteflies, scales, and aphids, are rarely present in numbers sufficient to affect the health of the plant. Their secretions sometimes cause an accumulation of sooty mold, which can be eliminated by controlling insect populations. An application of 15-5-15 fertilizer, or fertilizer in some similar ratio, at the start of the warm season has been found to help stimulate flowering. The gardenia is not especially drought tolerant, and may require irrigation during periods of dry weather, especially when dry conditions correspond with the formation of flower buds. While plants have rebounded from temperature drops into the low teens, damage to peripheral branches begins to accumulate at about 20° F. Plants grafted onto *Gardenia thunbergia* rootstocks have significantly less cold tolerance. While the plant responds well to pruning, this task should only be performed after flowering is complete so as to avoid interrupting the bloom cycle.

HARVEST AND USE Flowering typically takes place from March through mid-summer, although off-season blooms are not uncommon. The flowers can be clipped and brought indoors, where their pleasant fragrance can permeate an entire residence. In China, the flowers are steeped in warm water and used to flavor tea, sometimes together with chrysanthemum. The petals can be added to salads or beverages, or can be used as a garnish. An edible yellow pigment has been extracted from the seeds and is marketed as a food additive. Flower extracts are used in the manufacture of perfume.

Garlic

SCIENTIFIC NAME: *Allium sativum*
FAMILY: Alliaceae
OTHER COMMON NAME: Ajo (Spanish)

Herbaceous Perennial

Characteristics

Overall Rating	★★★★★
Ease of Care	★★★
Utility	★★★★★
Landscape Value	★★★
Salt Tolerance	★★
Drought Tolerance	★★★
Heat/Humidity Tolerance	★★
Cold Tolerance	★★★★
Shade Tolerance	★★
Longevity	★★

This familiar and popular member of the onion family has been cultivated as a spice and flavoring agent since before the time of the ancient Egyptians. Following onion, garlic is the world's most important bulb crop. The International Herb Association selected garlic as the Herb of the Year for 2004. While garlic is usually thought of as a temperate species, garlic grows throughout Florida. It is a dooryard crop with untapped potential.

Known Hazards

Garlic is an occasional allergen. Sensitivity may manifest itself as eczema of the hands and other types of skin irritation. Those with blood clotting disorders should consult a physician prior to use.

92

GEOGRAPHIC DISTRIBUTION The species widely used for commercial production probably originated in southwest Asia. However, garlic has been widely introduced throughout Eurasia and the rest of the world. Close relatives grow wild in many locations throughout Europe and Asia. In the United States, the overwhelming bulk of the commercial garlic crop comes from California. While garlic will grow throughout Florida, several types are better suited to growth in north Florida.

PLANT DESCRIPTION Garlic is a perennial herb capable of reaching a height of about 2 1/2 feet. The stems are hollow and herbaceous. The leaves emerge from sheaths surrounding the bottom third of the plant. They are narrow, strap-like, and flat to slightly folded. A paper skin surrounds the bulb at the base, sometimes referred to as the "head." The head contains several bulbets or "cloves." Two modified leaves encase each of these cloves. Flowering occurs in the late spring or early summer. The flower head, an umbel, is composed primarily of bulbils, although it occasionally produces small white flowers. Most cultivars do not produce seed.

FLAVOR AND SCENT The flavor is pungent, earthy, and musky, with a sulfurlike component. Depending on the cultivar, the level of heat ranges from mild to sharp. The heat dissipates and the flavor mellows with cooking.

VARIETIES More than 150 cultivars have been identified. Most of these are grouped within two subspecies. Softnecked garlics belong to the subspecies *Allium sativum sativum*. These tend to be well suited to growth in warm climates. Hardnecked garlics belong to the subspecies *Allium sativum ophioscorodon*. Many hardnecks come from Russia and other nations that experience cold winters. Few are suitable for growth in south Florida. Cultivar groups are described below.

Creole – This cultivar group performs well in warm climates, and some members will succeed in all regions of Florida, including south Florida. Recommended cultivars include 'Ajo Rojo,' 'Burgundy,' and 'Creole Red.'

Artichoke – Members of this soft neck cultivar group produce large, mild-flavored bulbs. This type has good storage characteristics and is often stocked by supermarkets. It is among the most successful garlics for Southern gardens. Selections recommended for north Florida include 'Inchelium Red,' 'Lorz Italian,' 'Red Toch,' and 'Siciliano.'

Marbled Purple Stripe – Marbled Purple Stripes produce bulbs that contain 4 to 7 bulbets. As a general rule, the Marbled Purple Stripes outperform the Purple Stripes (described below) in warm climates. 'Chesnok Red' is a well-regarded cultivar and is reasonably well suited to growth in Florida.

Porcelain – Porcelain is one of the most successful hardneck cultivar groups. These garlics produce a very large bulb, measuring up to 3 inches across, with very few (3–12) cloves. A few selections are productive in warm climates. Cultivars that may be worth trying in north Florida include 'Georgian Crystal,' 'Georgian Fire,' 'Gypsy Red,' 'Music,' 'Romanian Red,' 'Wild Buff,' and 'Zemo.'

Purple Stripe – This hardneck cultivar group

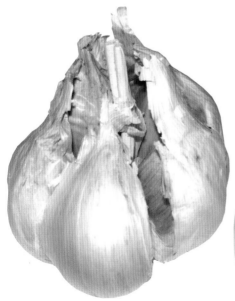

Compare a bulb of elephant garlic (left) with that of regular garlic (right). Elephant garlic is more closely related to the leek than to true garlic. The flavor is similar to that of true garlic, but milder. Elephant garlic can be grown throughout Florida, although performance has not been consistent.

contains a few selections suitable for growth in the South. Bulbs are richly flavored and deeply colored. They contain 8 to 12 cloves. Purple stripe varieties are well suited to roasting. The cultivars 'Metechi,' 'Persian Star,' and 'Siberian' have shown some promise for growth in the South. 'Metechi,' a hot garlic, is probably the most dependable of the three.

Silverskins – This is a softneck cultivar group that is marginally well suited to growth in the South. 'Locati' is an Italian selection that has shown some promise.

Turban – This cultivar group is sometimes classified as an early hardneck or as a subgroup of the artichoke group. Performance in the southern United States has been erratic.

Rocambole – This hardneck cultivar group produces a large bulb that is extremely flavorful. However, performance has been poor in Southern states. No selections are recommended for planting in Florida.

RELATIVES The Alliaceae or onion family is made up of herbaceous monocots. The largest and most important genus is *Allium*, which contains more then 900 species. Members of the genus include the onion, *Allium cepa*; leek, *Allium ampeloprasum*; and chives, *Allium schoenoprasum*. Chives are covered separately within this book. Scallions, *Allium fistulosum*, are clustering onions that are grown both for

their bulbs and foliage, although the bulbs are greatly diminished. Cultivars include 'Beltsville Bunching,' 'Feast,' 'Kyotot Market,' 'Red Beard,' 'Tokyo,' and 'White Lisbon.' The shallot, *Allium ascalonicum*, like garlic, is made up of multiple cloves. Elephant garlic, *Allium ampeloprasum*, is actually a bulb-forming leek. This plant forms enormous bulbs that are agreeable when roasted. However, overall, the flavor does not match that of true garlic. Performance in Florida has been fair to poor. Meadow garlic, *Allium canadense*, is an indigenous species and grows throughout north Florida. Striped garlic, *Allium cuthbertii*, is native to the state's northeast coastal region.

CULTIVATION Garlic is not grown from seed, but from cloves. Bulbs of specific cultivars can be obtained from mail-order and Internet suppliers. Bulbs obtained from the grocery may produce a satisfactory crop. The bulbs should be carefully divided into individual bulblets or cloves. These are typically planted in the fall and left in the ground over the winter. In north Florida, they should be planted about a month before the onset of freezing temperatures, to give the roots a chance to establish. In peninsular Florida, garlic can be planted at any time from November through January. However, bulbs of most cultivars that are intended for planting in areas of the state that receive less than 300 hours of winter chill must be cold stratified. Unless they are stored for

Flowers of society garlic have a sweet scent, unlike those of several other edible members of the Alliaceae or onion family. The plant is not as flavorful as true garlic, and some individuals have reportedly experienced gastric upset following consumption. Society garlic is a popular choice in Florida for median and foundation plantings.

Some members of the onion family produce decorative blooms. Garlic is sterile and does not reproduce sexually. Softnecked garlics have lost the ability to flower. The flowers on hardnecked varieties develop into bulbils rather than seeds.

several months in dry conditions at below 50° F, they may grow, but they will not form bulbs. The cloves should be set at a depth of about 2 inches, with the pointed end facing up and the fat end facing down. Garlic prefers loose soil enriched with organic matter. Irrigation should be supplied regularly once the bulbs have sprouted. Flower stalks should be removed to promote growth of the bulbs. Competing weeds must be controlled, preferably through the application of mulch.

HARVEST AND USE Garlic is harvested between 9 and 12 months after planting. In north Florida, this is usually between July and September. When the plant begins to experience foliage dieback, this is often taken as an indicator that the bulbs are mature. The bulbs may be dried in the sun for several days before they are hung in a cool, dry location. Garlic can be consumed raw or cooked. It can be sliced, diced, crushed, grated, and powdered. Garlic is an essential ingredient in southern European cooking, and is especially important in Italy and Greece. It is also widely used in Thai, Chinese, Vietnamese, Mexican, Cajun, and Indian cuisine. Young leaves are used to a limited extent in salads and cooking, primarily in Southeast Asia. The flowers are edible and have a mild onion-garlic flavor.

Ginger

SCIENTIFIC NAME: *Zingiber officinale*
FAMILY: Zingiberaceae
OTHER COMMON NAMES: Common Ginger, Jengibre
   (Spanish)

Herbaceous Perennial

Characteristics

Overall Rating	★★★
Ease of Care	★★★
Utility	★★
Landscape Value	★★★★
Salt Tolerance	★
Drought Tolerance	★★
Heat/Humidity Tolerance	★★★★★
Cold Tolerance	★★★
Shade Tolerance	★★★
Longevity	★★

This ancient spice of the Orient is also a showy, flowering plant, well suited to growth in Florida. The part of the plant used for culinary purposes is the rhizome or underground stem, which is sometimes misidentified as the root. In addition to its use as a spice, ginger reputedly has various medicinal properties, which are not covered here.

Known Hazards

Some sources indicate that consumption of large quantities should be avoided during pregnancy. Normal culinary quantities have not been linked with any adverse effects.

GEOGRAPHIC DISTRIBUTION Ginger may have originated in southern China. However, it has been widely grown throughout Southeast Asia and India since antiquity. In Roman times, India exported ginger to Europe. Today, commercial production occurs in India, Jamaica, Nepal, Taiwan, Haiti, Mexico, and Nigeria. Limited production has taken place in Hawaii.

In addition to its import as a spice, ginger is an attractive plant. The flowers vary in form and color between cultivars and species.

PLANT DESCRIPTION Ginger is a perennial plant that grows from a horizontal, subterranean rhizome. The vertical shoots that emerge from this tuberous rhizome attain a maximum height of about 4 feet. They are slender, stiff, and somewhat reedlike. Leaves are alternate, lanceolate, dark green, and strap-like. Flowering is rare. When it occurs, small yellow flowers emerge from a bulbous head borne on a separate stem.

FLAVOR AND SCENT The flavor of ginger is pungent, sweet, and slightly hot, with menthol and pepper undertones. The scent is aromatic and lemony. The flowers and stalks also emit a pleasant fragrance when crushed or bruised.

VARIETIES Several cultivars have been selected for commercial purposes in ginger-growing regions. The availability of these cultivars in Florida is limited.

RELATIVES The Zingiberaceae family contains about 1,300 species. Most of these are tropical in habit. Members covered in this book include cardamom, *Amomum subulatum*, and turmeric, *Curcuma longa*. Other spice plants within the family include galangal, *Alpinia galanga*, and grains of paradise, *Aframomum melegueta*. No members of the Zingiberaceae family are native to Florida. Bitter ginger, *Zingiber zerumbet*, and several other ornamental ginger relatives have escaped cultivation in various locations around the state. Wild ginger, *Asarum canadense*, is an herbaceous plant native to the eastern United States. It is not related to ginger. While the root was formerly used as a spice, the plant is a diuretic

and may not be safe for human consumption.

CULTIVATION When raised as a spice plant, ginger is treated as an annual. However, if the rhizome is left in the ground, the foliage will die back over the cooler months and repeat its growth cycle the following spring. Ginger is typically planted in the spring in north-central Florida, but can be planted at any time of the year in south Florida. It prefers a warm, humid climate. Ginger will grow in full sun, but prefers partial shade. Irrigation should be provided on a regular basis during periods of growth. Ginger prefers loose soil enriched with organic matter. The soil must be well drained, as rot will destroy plants grown in persistently wet soils. To propagate ginger the rhizomes should be divided into small sections. Each section should contain an eye or sprout. The rhizome sections should then be planted at a depth of about an inch.

A "hand" of ginger, sometimes referred to as the root, is actually a rhizome or underground stem.

HARVEST AND USE Ginger is usually harvested between 5 and 10 months after it is planted. Young roots are tender and mild. Roots tend to become fibrous and more intensely flavored with age. Indeed, the roots may form a dense mat if they are left in the ground over several seasons. The rhizomes are unearthed with a hoe or shovel. The hands, as they are called, are carefully cleaned and scrubbed. The gray epidermis is then scraped away. The hands can be used fresh or can be prepared and preserved in various manners. They can be boiled and sun dried. They can be candied. They can also be pickled in vinegar. Ginger in this form is often used as a condiment and palate cleanser accompanying sushi and other Japanese foods. It is an ingredient in lentil curries, confectionaries, ginger snaps, gingerbread, and ginger ale. Ginger finds widespread use in the cuisines of China, Thailand, India, Indonesia, Korea, and Japan. It is also used to a limited degree in European, Caribbean, African, and Middle Eastern cuisines.

Goldenrod

SCIENTIFIC NAME: *Solidago* spp.
FAMILY: Asteraceae

Herbaceous Perennial

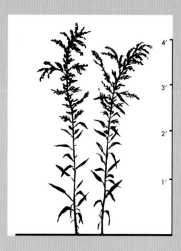

Characteristics

Overall Rating	★★
Ease of Care	★★★★
Utility	★★
Landscape Value	★★★★
Salt Tolerance	★★
Drought Tolerance	★★★
Heat/Humidity Tolerance	★★★★
Cold Tolerance	★
Shade Tolerance	★★
Longevity	★★

This common plant of pastures and roadsides was once considered an undesirable weed. It was blamed for pollen allergies because it bloomed at the same time as other virulent allergens. It has been absolved of this fault. Indeed, over the last few decades, goldenrod has become a staple in naturalized gardens. Although the habit of growth is somewhat unruly, the bright yellow plumes add a dramatic touch of color. Goldenrod is of interest here both for its natural beauty and as an herbal tea ingredient.

Known Hazards

Goldenrod is considered a mild allergen. Those who are allergic to other members of the Asteraceae family should exercise caution.

GEOGRAPHIC DISTRIBUTION Goldenrod is widely distributed throughout North America. A few species are also native to Europe, Asia, and South America. American goldenrod species are considered invasive in some areas of Europe.

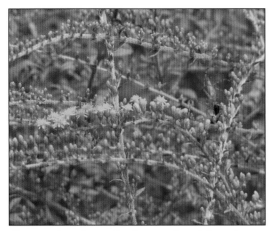

Close-up view of emerging flowers of rough-leaved goldenrod.

PLANT DESCRIPTION This perennial herb, depending on the species, may reach a height of between 2 and 7 feet. Leaves are lanceolate and alternate. Goldenrods have an unusual flowering habit, in that they flower from top to bottom. In most plants, flowering progresses from older inflorescences at the base of the plant to newer inflorescences at the top of the plant.

FLAVOR AND SCENT When crushed, the leaves emit a pleasant cedarlike aroma with hints of anise. When brewed into a tea, the flavor is a pleasant combination of floral notes and anise.

VARIETIES The Asteraceae family is the second-largest family of flowering plants, containing more than 20,000 species. The genus *Solidago* is composed of about 80 species. Due to similarity of appearance and the tendency of species to hybridize, it is difficult to distinguish between the species. However, several can be used to make tea. Fragrant goldenrod or anise-scented goldenrod, *Solidago odora*, is common throughout most of Florida, and is well suited to use as a tea ingredient. Other species indigenous to Florida include bluestem goldenrod, *Solidago caesia*; Canadian goldenrod, *Solidago canadensis*; Carolina goldenrod, *Solidago arguta* var. *caroliniana*; Dixie goldenrod, *Solidago brachyphylla*; downy goldenrod, *Solidago puberula*; giant goldenrod, *Solidago gigantea*; Leavenworth's goldenrod, *Solidago leavenworthii*; pinebarren goldenrod, *Solidago fistulosa*; seaside goldenrod, *Solidago sempervirens*; twisted-leaf goldenrod, *Solidago tortifolia*; and wand goldenrod, *Solidago stricta*.

RELATIVES The huge Asteraceae family contains many important herbs and spices. Members covered within this book include chamomile, *Chamaemilum nobile* and *Matricaria recutita*; chicory, *Cichorium intybus*; Mexican tarragon, *Tagetes lucida*; stevia, *Stevia rebaudiana*; and tarragon, *Artemisia dracunculus*.

CULTIVATION Goldenrod is a tough plant and demands little care. It is drought tolerant and, in fact, appears to prefer moderately dry conditions. It succeeds in a broad range of soil types, including infertile soils. As a result of these traits, it is a good choice for slopes, transitional areas, and other difficult locations. Goldenrod is not negatively affected by summer conditions in peninsular Florida. It can be grown throughout the state, although some species are better acclimated to north Florida. The plant can be grown in full sun or light shade, as long as it receives at least 5 or 6 hours of direct sun.

HARVEST AND USE Leaves are harvested in late summer and early fall, usually during periods of bloom. They are crushed and steeped for about 20 minutes in hot water. One tablespoon of crushed leaves should be used for 12 ounces of water. Goldenrod has also been used in wine making. In recent years, goldenrod hybrids have been grown for their use as cut flowers and commonly appear in floral arrangements.

Though it was once thought of as an undesirable weed, few plants are as attractive as goldenrod in bloom. The peak of flowering often coincides with the end of summer.

Horseradish

SCIENTIFIC NAME: *Armoracia rusticana*
FAMILY: Brassicaceae
OTHER COMMON NAMES: Red Cole, Rábano Picante
  (Spanish)

Herbaceous Perennial

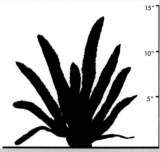

Characteristics

Overall Rating	★★★
Ease of Care	★★★★
Utility	★★
Landscape Value	★★
Salt Tolerance	★
Drought Tolerance	★★★
Heat/Humidity Tolerance	★★★★
Cold Tolerance	★★★
Shade Tolerance	★
Longevity	★★

Known Hazards

While adverse effects are uncommon, hypersensitive individuals may experience allergic reactions, which may include skin irritation, blistering, sneezing, mucus membrane inflammation, and other symptoms. Consumption should be limited by those who are pregnant or nursing or by those with high blood pressure, goiter, ulcers, or low thyroid activity. Those with kidney disorders should consult a physician before consumption, as horseradish has a diuretic effect. Horseradish contains salicylates. Consumption may cause reactions in those who are intolerant of these compounds.

Horseradish is an aggressive, weedlike plant grown as a root crop. This condiment is traditionally used with prime rib and various beef dishes. Horseradish grows well in north Florida, but appears to struggle somewhat over time in south Florida.

GEOGRAPHIC DISTRIBUTION Horseradish is native to southern Europe. It was used as a condiment in ancient Greece. It was introduced into North America during colonial times. Horseradish is grown as a commercial crop in the United States. It has escaped cultivation in various parts of the United States, primarily in the northern half of the country.

PLANT DESCRIPTION Horseradish is an herbaceous perennial that is typically grown as an annual. The taproot is light in color, thick, and tapering. The foliage, which forms in a rosette, attains a height of up to 2 feet. It consists of oval, toothed, dark-green leaves that can measure more than 18 inches in length. The plant bears white flowers on terminal panicles in late spring. Although the flowers are perfect and may be pollinated by various insects, the plant rarely produces viable seed.

FLAVOR AND SCENT The flavor is hot, biting, pungent, and somewhat bitter. When taken in excess quantity, it can irritate the eyes and sinuses. The scent is pleasant and aromatic, though fairly weak.

VARIETIES Several cultivars have been selected, including 'Big Top,' 'Bohemian,' 'Maliner Kren,' and 'Variegata.'

RELATIVES Horseradish is a member of the Brassicaceae or mustard family. This family consists of about 3,500 species. Other members covered within this book include: mustard, *Brassica* spp.; pepperweed, *Lepidium virginicum*; sea rocket, *Cakile edentula*; and watercress, *Nasturtium nasturtium-aquaticum*. Lake cress, *Armoracia aquatica*, is a close relative of horseradish that is native to a few locations in north Florida. Other, more distantly related members of the Brassicaceae family that are native to Florida include Jamaican capertree, *Capparis cynophallophora*; sand bittercress, *Cardamine parviflora*; shortpod whitlowgrass, *Draba brachycarpa*; sicklepod, *Boechera canadensis*; wedgeleaf whitlowgrass, *Draba cuneifolia*; and western tansymustard, *Descurainia pinnata*.

CULTIVATION Horseradish is reasonably easy to grow and requires little care. It prefers full sun and well-drained soil. The plant is propagated by planting pieces of the secondary roots. Once established, horseradish can be difficult to eliminate from the garden. Traces of root left in the ground at harvest will regenerate into new plants. The species will spread rapidly and form dense colonies unless the roots are periodically harvested. Horseradish does not appear to be negatively affected by summer conditions in peninsular Florida. It nevertheless seems to struggle in southern parts of the state, perhaps for lack of winter chill or as a result of nematodes in the soil.

HARVEST AND USE The root can be harvested at any time, but is typically dug up between six months and a year after planting. If the plant is put out in the spring, the root is usually harvested at the onset of winter or after the first frost. The root is often stored whole. It spoils more rapidly and loses flavor after it is cut or grated. However, grated horseradish mixed with vinegar tends to retain the essential flavor of the plant. To avoid irritating the eyes, the root should be grated in a food processor. The leaves are edible, but are rarely used as greens. Horseradish sauces are made from the finely grated root, cream, and other ingredients. Horseradish is an ingredient in shrimp cocktail sauces and Bloody Marys. It is also used in Western versions of wasabi. Horseradish is one of the 5 bitter herbs of Passover. When consumed in excess quantity, the root has been known to cause gastric upset. Horseradish is generally deemed safe for human consumption, but is an occasional allergen and irritant.

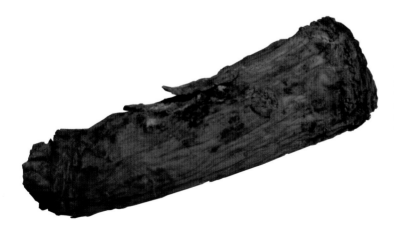

The surface of horseradish root can be shaved away with a vegetable peeler. The white core can be grated or sliced, or it can be diced and put in a blender with water and vinegar.

Jamaican Mint

SCIENTIFIC NAME: *Micromeria viminea*
FAMILY: Lamiaceae
OTHER COMMON NAMES: Costa Rican Mint Bush,
   Menta de Palo (Spanish)

Woody Perennial; Evergreen Shrub

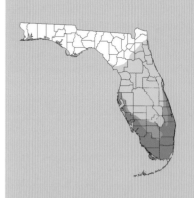

Characteristics

Overall Rating	★★★★
Ease of Care	★★★★
Utility	★★★★
Landscape Value	★★★★
Salt Tolerance	★
Drought Tolerance	★★★
Heat/Humidity Tolerance	★★★★
Cold Tolerance	★
Shade Tolerance	★★
Longevity	★★★

Although it does not belong to the mint genus, *Mentha*, Jamaican mint has the scent and flavor of peppermint. It is an extremely attractive addition to the home landscape and is easy to grow in south Florida. Yet, for reasons that are not clear, it is obscure, difficult to obtain, and rarely planted. It is one of the best herbs awaiting discovery.

Known Hazards

None

102

GEOGRAPHIC DISTRIBUTION Jamaican mint is native to Costa Rica. It also grows wild in Jamaica, Puerto Rico, and other Caribbean islands. Jamaican mint is damaged by temperatures below 32° F and is killed at about 30° F. It will grow as a perennial in south Florida, and can be grown in a container farther north.

PLANT DESCRIPTION Jamaican mint is a bushy, evergreen shrub that can attain a height of about 6 feet given ideal conditions, but that more typically attains a height of 2 or 3 feet in Florida. The rate of growth is moderate. Lower branches are woody. Suckers sometimes form at the base of the trunk. The foliage is fine in texture. Lime-green leaves are oval to spatulate, usually measuring less than 1/2 of an inch in length. White flowers appear sporadically over much of the year. These typically have 5 petals, with one slightly larger than the others.

FLAVOR AND SCENT All parts of the plant are aromatic and exude an intense peppermint scent. The leaves have a strong peppermint flavor.

RELATIVES The Lamiaceae or mint family is home to about 7,000 species of plants. It contains several important herbs and spices. Species discussed within this book include basil, *Ocimum* spp.; bee balm, *Monarda didyma*; Cuban oregano, *Plectranthus amboinicus*; lavender, *Lavandula* spp.; lemon balm, *Melissa officinalis*; mint, *Mentha* spp.; oregano, *Origanum* spp.; perilla, *Perilla frutescens*; rosemary, *Rosmarinus officinalis*; sage, *Salvia officinalis*; savory, *Satureja* spp.; and thyme, *Thymus* spp. Jamaican mint is closely associated with the savories, so much so that it is occasionally placed in the *Satureja* genus. The *Micromeria* genus contains about 130 species from regions including the Mediterranean, central Asia, the Canary Islands, Northwest Africa, Southeast Asia, the Arabian peninsula, and the Americas. Many members of this genus are aromatic. One species that is sometimes placed within the *Macromeria* genus, Browne's savory, *Micromeria brownie*, is native to Florida.

CULTIVATION Jamaican mint is easy to grow in south Florida. It is moderately drought tolerant, but benefits from weekly irrigation. It prefers neutral to slightly acidic soil. No serious pests or diseases appear to affect this plant. Unlike many true mints, Jamaican mint does not spread aggressively within the garden.

HARVEST AND USE The leaves can be substituted for those of mint leaves in any recipe calling for mint. The Jamaican mint is often used to season meats. It makes the perfect ingredient for preparing "real" tropical mojitos. In Jamaica it is made into a tea, sometimes in conjunction with ginger. The tea brewed from the leaves has a pleasant flavor and is said to have a mild sedative affect. Aside from its culinary uses, Jamaican mint is sometimes trained into bonsai and excels in this role.

Kaffir Lime

SCIENTIFIC NAME: *Citrus hystrix*
FAMILY: Rutaceae
OTHER COMMON NAMES: Wild Lime, Bai Makrut

Woody Perennial; Evergreen Tree

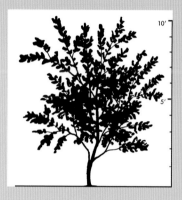

Characteristics

Overall Rating	★★★★
Ease of Care	★★★★
Utility	★★★★
Landscape Value	★★★
Salt Tolerance	★★
Drought Tolerance	★★★
Heat/Humidity Tolerance	★★★★
Cold Tolerance	★★
Shade Tolerance	★
Longevity	★★★

The fruit of the Kaffir lime is rarely consumed, although the zest from the rind is occasionally used in cooking. It is the leaves that are employed as an essential spice in Southeast Asian cooking. The flavor is relished by those who enjoy authentic Thai and Cambodian cuisine and cannot be duplicated by substituting the leaves of other types of citrus.

Known Hazards

Contact with the oils in this plant may cause photosensitivity, swelling, and rashes in some individuals.

GEOGRAPHIC DISTRIBUTION Kaffir lime is native to Indonesia. It is widely grown as a dooryard plant throughout Southeast Asia. Among citrus, Kaffir lime has medium sensitivity to cold and will grow in coastal areas and protected locations in central Florida. It can be grown in containers in north Florida.

PLANT DESCRIPTION Kaffir lime is a small evergreen tree which can attain a height of about 20 feet, but which is usually smaller. The habit of growth is somewhat shrublike. Sharp spines are present on the branches. Leaves are dark green and shiny, with winged petioles. The petioles give the leaves a distinctive double form. White flowers are borne in March and April, although the tree may bloom sporadically over much of the year. The fruit is about 2 or 3 inches in length. It is dark green, maturing to yellow-green, with lumpy skin and a knob at the apex. The flesh contains little juice.

FLAVOR AND SCENT The leaves are highly aromatic and exude a pleasant fragrance. When cooked with other ingredients, they impart a tangy lime flavor. The flavor is strong and distinctive. The fruit is intensely bitter.

RELATIVES Within the *Citrus* genus, relatives include the citron, *Citrus medica*; grapefruit, *Citrus paradisi*; mandarin, *Citrus reticulata*; orange, *Citrus sinensis*; pummelo, *Citrus maxima*; and tangelo, *Citrus tangelo*. Other citrus species covered within this book include calamondin, *Citrus mitis*; lemon, *Citrus limon*; and lime, *Citrus hystrix* and *Citrus aurantifolia*. The Kaffir lime is more distantly related to such fruiting plants as the bael, *Aegle marmelos*; wampee, *Clausena lansium*; and white sapote, *Casimiroa edulis*. Other distant relatives of the Kaffir lime covered within this book are the curry leaf tree, *Murraya koenigii*, which is also used as a leaf-based spice, and rue, *Ruta graveolens*.

CULTIVATION Cultivation techniques for most forms of citrus are applicable to Kaffir lime. The tree prefers full sun and well-drained soil. It is damaged when the temperature drops to 28° F and may be killed at 26° or 27° F. Kaffir lime's susceptibility to citrus greening is unknown, but is thought to be lower than that of the orange and other fruit-bearing citrus. This lethal bacterial disease was first detected in Florida in 2005, and has been spreading rapidly through the state's citrus regions.

HARVEST AND USE The leaves can be harvested at any time. They are best when fresh, but can be preserved by freezing or drying. The dried leaf, though, retains little of the essence of the fresh leaf. Before they are added to most dishes, the leaves are cut into fine slivers. They are used in this manner in curries and stir-fries. However, the whole leaves are sometimes used in the fashion of bay leaves, to impart flavor to stews and soups. Kaffir lime is especially popular in the cuisines of Cambodia, Indonesia, Laos, and Thailand. The leaves are occasionally employed as a flavoring agent in Myanmar, Malaysia, the Philippines, and Vietnam.

The aromatic leaves of Kaffir lime have frequently been employed in Asian cuisines. They may be used whole for simmering, in which case they are usually removed from the dish before it is served. They can also be shredded and made into pastes.

Lavender

SCIENTIFIC NAME: *Lavandula* spp.
FAMILY: Lamiaceae
OTHER COMMON NAMES: Lavanda, Alhucema (Spanish)

Semi-Woody Perennial

Planted
in Spring

Planted
in Fall

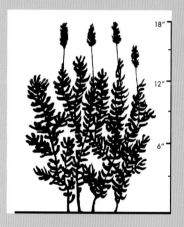

Characteristics

Overall Rating	★★★
Ease of Care	★★★
Utility	★★★
Landscape Value	★★★★★
Salt Tolerance	★★
Drought Tolerance	★★★
Heat/Humidity Tolerance	★
Cold Tolerance	★★★
Shade Tolerance	★
Longevity	★★

This mint relative is renowned for its fragrance, beautiful flowers, and attractive foliage. It is primarily a scent and strewing herb, and culinary applications are limited. The name is derived from the Latin *lavare*, meaning "to wash." This origin is perhaps demonstrative of the early use of this plant in soap and perfumery. The scent of lavender is said to have a soothing effect. Unfortunately, lavender is not especially well suited to growth in Florida, preferring a drier, Mediterranean-type climate.

Known Hazards

On very rare occasions, lavender has been associated with contact dermatitis. Some individuals are highly allergic to the essential oils and to the plant in general. Consumption should be avoided during pregnancy and while breast feeding.

106

GEOGRAPHIC DISTRIBUTION Lavender is native to Africa, the Mediterranean region, the Middle East, and southwestern Asia. It was widely used during Roman times. In the Middle Ages, it was used to prevent plague and to mask other odors. It is widely cultivated as an ornamental, especially in England, France, Bulgaria, and Australia. Lavender can be grown throughout Florida, but tends to fare poorly in south Florida.

'Provence' lavender, *Lavandula x intermedia,* is heavily cultivated in the Provence region of southeastern France. The plant is actually a hybrid between French lavender, *Lavandula angustifolia,* and spike lavender, *Lavandula latifolia.*

PLANT DESCRIPTION Lavender is a short perennial shrub that typically attains a height of about 2 feet. It tends to be evergreen in warm-winter areas and deciduous in colder climates. However, different species have differing habits of growth. Lower branches are woody and newer growth is composed of vertical, leafy shoots. The opposite leaves are fleshy, oblong, and coated with a silvery or blue-gray down. The bright purple flowers are borne on spikes.

FLAVOR AND SCENT The fragrance is perfumed, floral, sweet, and complex, with notes of camphor, citrus, and balsam. The flavor of lavender mimics the scent, but the sweetness is offset by a touch of bitterness.

VARIETIES The genus *Lavandula* contains over 30 species. Common lavender or English lavender, *Lavandula angustifolia,* is the species most frequently planted in the United States. Cultivars include 'Backhouse Purple,' 'Buena Vista,' 'Cedar Blue,' 'Compacta,' 'Gray Lady,' 'Hidcote,' 'Irene Doyle,' 'Lodden Blue,' 'Melissa,' 'Mitchem Gray,' 'Munstead,' 'Nana Alba,' 'Rosea,' 'Royal Velvet,' and 'Sachet.' Notable sterile hybrids include 'Abrialii,' 'Dutch Mill' 'Grosso' 'Hidcote Giant,' 'Provence,' 'Seal,' 'Silver Gray,' and 'White Spike.' Other species that are planted with some frequency include fern-leaf lavender, *Lavandula multifida*; fringed lavender, *Lavandula dentata*; Spanish lavender, *Lavandula stoechas*; spike lavender, *Lavandula latifolia*; and wooly lavender, *Lavandula lanata.* Many of the cultivars listed above will succeed in north Florida. Among varieties that may be able to withstand conditions on the peninsula are 'Goodwin Creek' (*Lavendula x intermedia*), 'Quasti' and 'Kew Red' (*Lavandula*

stoechas), and 'Spanish Eyes' (*Lavandula multifida*).

RELATIVES Lamiaceae or the mint family contains several important herbs and spices. Species discussed within this book include basil, *Ocimum* spp.; bee balm, *Monarda didyma*; Cuban oregano, *Plectranthus amboinicus*; Jamaican mint, *Micromeria viminea*; lemon balm, *Melissa officinalis*; mint, *Mentha* spp.; oregano, *Origanum* spp.; perilla, *Perilla frutescens*; rosemary, *Rosmarinus officinalis*; sage, *Salvia officinalis*; savory, *Satureja* spp.; and thyme, *Thymus* spp. Sea lavender, *Limonium carolinianum*, although it bears a slight resemblance to lavender, is not closely related and is a member of the Plumbaginaceae family.

CULTIVATION Lavender prefers full sun and loose, well-drained soil. It prefers slightly alkaline soils, and will grow on limestone-based soils and in gravelly locations. Plants should be adequately spaced to promote air circulation. Lavender is drought resistant. Wet and humid conditions have a detrimental impact on this plant. It also cannot endure extreme heat. As a result, lavender fares poorly in the summer in peninsular Florida. Therefore, it is often planted in the fall and treated as an annual. Lavender can be started from seed, from cuttings, or by root division. Seed germination rates tend to be low.

While lavender is not an easy herb to grow in south Florida, the result can be well worth the effort. The flowers are worked heavily by bees and other flying insects. The dried flower buds are sometimes used for culinary purposes.

HARVEST AND USE The flowers and flower buds are gathered, dried, and used in potpourri. The flowers are also used to scent lotions, soaps, shampoos, and bath water. Lavender is used to some extent as a cooking herb, especially in Provence, France. The fresh or dried flower buds may be added to various dishes. However, it should be used sparingly, as the flavor can overpower that of other herbs. Lavender is also sometimes added to tea as a flavoring agent. The flowers are attractive to bees and yield a high-quality honey.

Lemon

SCIENTIFIC NAME: *Citrus limon*
FAMILY: Rutaceae
OTHER COMMON NAME: Limón (Spanish)

Woody Perennial; Evergreen Tree

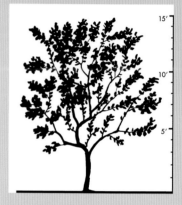

Characteristics

Overall Rating	★★★★
Ease of Care	★★★
Utility	★★★★★
Landscape Value	★★★
Salt Tolerance	★★
Drought Tolerance	★★★
Heat/Humidity Tolerance	★★★
Cold Tolerance	★★
Shade Tolerance	★
Longevity	★★★

The lemon is the world's most popular acid-citrus fruit. Several cultivars are reasonably well suited to Florida conditions. The tree is productive and bears fruit over much of the year. This quality, combined with the fact that the fruit has multiple uses, makes the lemon a good choice for dooryard planting in central and southern portions of the state.

Known Hazards

Contact with the leaves and fruit rind may cause photosensitivity or contact dermatitis in some individuals.

GEOGRAPHIC DISTRIBUTION The lemon is native to southern Asia. It reached the Mediterranean prior to the year 1000 and was carried to the Americas by Christopher Columbus. During the late 1800s and early 1900s, the lemon was an important commercial crop in Florida, but it is rarely grown commercially today.

Many varieties of lemon have been developed. A few, such as 'Berna,' 'Perrine, ' and 'Ponderosa' have distinctive necks or collars.

PLANT DESCRIPTION The lemon is a small evergreen tree, usually attaining a height of 12 or 15 feet. Branches are often armed with sharp spines. The dark green leaves are alternate, elliptic in shape, and measure between 3 and 4 inches in length. Margins are dentate. The petioles bear narrow wings. The flowers measure about an inch in diameter and have 4 or, more typically, 5 white petals, often with a pink blush on the underside. The fruit, which ranges from oval to elliptic in shape, measures between 2 1/2 and 5 inches in length. Mature fruit is generally yellow. The rind is of medium thickness. The flesh ranges from pale yellow to off-white and is composed of between 8 and 10 segments, which may contain a scattering of seeds.

FLAVOR AND SCENT The outer peel is aromatic and sweetly scented. The flesh is tart and acidic, but is pleasant and delicious when sweetened or when combined with other flavors.

VARIETIES Dozens of cultivars have been selected. Several are suitable for dooryard planting in Florida. 'Bearss' and 'Avon,' both selected in Florida, are excellent choices for the home garden. 'Meyer,' a cultivar discovered in China in 1908, is thought to be a cross between a lemon and mandarin. It performs well under Florida conditions. 'Eureka' and 'Lisbon,' are often planted in Florida, but have not proven entirely satisfactory.

RELATIVES The family Rutaceae includes all varieties of citrus. Members of the family discussed within this book include calamondin, *Citrus mitis*; curry leaf tree, *Muraya koenigii*; Kaffir lime, *Citrus hystrix*; lime, *Citrus latifolia* and *Citrus aurantifolia*; and rue, *Ruta graveolens*.

CULTIVATON General cultivation techniques for citrus apply to the lemon. Mites and scale insect may attack the tree, but can be readily controlled with pesticides. In Florida, the lemon is susceptible to several diseases, including anthracnose, branch knot, scab, greasy spot, gummosis, leaf spot, and various root rots. The lemon is highly susceptible to the bacterial disease citrus canker. It is also moderately susceptible to citrus greening, a very serious disease that is spreading rapidly in Florida. Citrus greening is transported from one tree to another by an insect vector, the Asian citrus psyllid. Once a tree is infected, foliage becomes mottled, fruit are often misshapen and fail to properly ripen, and the tree goes into a gradual decline. The cold tolerance of the lemon is greater than that of the lime, but not equal to that of the orange. Fruit suffer damage at about 28° F. Defoliation and limb damage may occur with a temperature drop to 26° F. The 'Meyer' lemon appears to have greater cold tolerance than other varieties. High summer temperatures have an adverse impact on the lemon. Like other forms of citrus, the lemon can be propagated through budding or grafting.

HARVEST AND USE In Florida, the 'Meyer' cultivar ripens from November through March. Other cultivars ripen over different periods. The lemon has good storage characteristics. If picked before maturity, the fruit will store for several weeks with or without refrigeration. The fruit can be juiced or used as a garnish. The juice can be frozen and will store for many months. The pulp and juice serve as ingredients in numerous recipes, ranging from seafood dishes to soups to confectionaries and pies. The grated peel or zest makes an aromatic spice. Many of the world's great cuisines make extensive use of the lemon.

The lemon flower exudes a very sweet scent. It provides no hint of the acidity of the fruit that will soon develop in its place.

Lemon Balm

SCIENTIFIC NAME: *Melissa officinalis*
FAMILY: Lamiaceae
OTHER COMMON NAME: Melisa (Spanish)

Semi-Woody, Deciduous Perennial

Planted in Spring

Planted in Fall

Characteristics

Overall Rating	★★★
Ease of Care	★★★★
Utility	★★★
Landscape Value	★★★
Salt Tolerance	★★★
Drought Tolerance	★★★
Heat/Humidity Tolerance	★
Cold Tolerance	★★★
Shade Tolerance	★★
Longevity	★★★

Known Hazards

Those with a thyroid condition should consult with a physician before using this herb, as it may interfere with production of the hormone thyrotropin, a thyroid-stimulant. There is insufficient data on the safety of lemon balm while pregnant or nursing, and use is therefore discouraged.

Lemon balm is one of several herbs grown for their "lemony" scent and flavor. The International Herb Association designated lemon balm as the Herb of the Year for 2007. This species does very well in north Florida and can be grown throughout the state.

GEOGRAPHIC DISTRIBUTION Lemon balm is indigenous to southern Europe. It has been planted in most warm temperate regions of the globe. In some areas it is viewed as an invasive pest. It is capable of spreading by seed and displacing native species. To date, these invasive tendencies have not been apparent in Florida.

In its habit of growth, lemon balm resembles many other members of the mint family.

PLANT DESCRIPTION Lemon balm is a perennial herb. It attains a height of about 3 feet. Leaves are opposite, glabrous, somewhat wrinkled, with dentate margins. Clusters of small off-white to pale-yellow flowers appear in the leaf axils in the late spring and summer. These turn pink with age.

FLAVOR AND SCENT Leaves are aromatic and exude a faint lemon scent, which is accentuated when the leaves are crushed or bruised. The lemon flavor is pleasant, but not as strong as that of lemon verbena.

VARIETIES A few cultivars appear to have been selected. A yellow-leaved variety dubbed 'All Gold' and a variegated type, 'Variegata,' are sometimes available.

RELATIVES Lemon balm is a member of the Lamiaceae or mint family. This family consists of about 625 genera and 7,000 species. Other Lamiaceae species discussed within this book include basil, *Ocimum* spp.; bee balm, *Monarda didyma*; Cuban oregano, *Plectranthus amboinicus*; Jamaican mint, *Micromeria viminea*; lavender, *Lavandula* spp.; mint, *Mentha* spp.; oregano, *Origanum* spp.; perilla, *Perilla frutescens*; rosemary, *Rosmarinus officinalis*; sage, *Salvia officinalis*; savory, *Satureja* spp.; and thyme, *Thymus* spp. The Melissa genus is small and contains only about five species. None are native to North America.

CULTIVATION Lemon balm can be grown throughout Florida. With some protection, it can succeed as far north as USDA hardiness zone 4. In north Florida, it is deciduous. It is killed to the ground by the first frost, but regenerates from its roots upon the return of warmer weather. In south Florida, lemon balm suffers decline in the heat and humidity of the summer. It is therefore grown as a winter crop and is treated as an annual. Although the plant performs well in full sun, it will tolerate light shade. Lemon balm has moderate salt tolerance. The plant can be cut back as it begins to flower to prevent it from self-sowing. Lemon balm can be started from seed, cuttings, or clump division. The seed is tiny and should be planted at a very shallow depth.

HARVEST AND USE The leaves can be harvested at any time after the plant is established. Lemon balm leaves are used fresh in salads, steeped as herbal tea, and used as a flavoring agent for beverages, sauces, salad dressings, soups, seafood dishes, and desserts. Dried leaves are used in potpourris, although the scent diminishes when the leaves are dried. Those taking thyroid medications should not consume lemon balm, as it is thought to interfere with the absorption of these drugs. Otherwise, this species is considered safe for human consumption.

Close-up photograph of lemon balm growth tip

Lemon Grass

SCIENTIFIC NAME: *Cymbopogon citratus*
FAMILY: Poaceae
OTHER COMMON NAMES: Takrai,
    Pasto de Limón (Spanish)

Herbaceous Perennial Monocot

Characteristics

Overall Rating	★★★★★
Ease of Care	★★★★
Utility	★★★★
Landscape Value	★★★★
Salt Tolerance	★★★
Drought Tolerance	★★★
Heat/Humidity Tolerance	★★★★★
Cold Tolerance	★★★
Shade Tolerance	★★★
Longevity	★★★

Known Hazards

Contact with lemon grass has been linked to minor skin irritation in hypersensitive individuals. The blades are fibrous and may present a choking hazard if consumed whole.

Lemon grass is one of the most rewarding herbs that can be raised in the Florida garden. It is tough and easy to grow. It is an important ingredient in Thai cuisine, which has become very popular in the United States. Lemon grass makes an attractive edging or foundation planting.

GEOGRAPHIC DISTRIBUTION This species is thought to be native to Malaysia. Some lemon grass is grown for commercial purposes in Florida and California. Lemon grass is frost tender. In north Florida, lemon grass goes dormant over the winter and may not regenerate in locations that have experienced severe cold.

There are many grasses that are planted as ornamentals in Florida. There is only one—lemon grass—that lends itself to a multitude of culinary uses.

PLANT DESCRIPTION This perennial grass reaches about 4 feet in height. It forms dense clusters that expand by adding stalks to the outer perimeter from the base. Leaf blades are slender, semi-erect, and sharp edged. Under ideal growing conditions, small, greenish-red flowers may appear during the summer.

FLAVOR AND SCENT Lemon grass has a pleasant lemony aroma and taste with a hint of ginger and mint. The flavor is mild and lacks any sour or bitter component.

VARIETIES While *Cymbopogan citratus* is the main species available in the United States, the related Malabar grass, *Cymbopogon flexuosus*, is also used in cooking. Malabar grass is native to Cambodia, Thailand, Myanmar, and India.

RELATIVES The family Poaceae contains the true grasses and is made up of about 600 genera and 10,000 species. The other grass covered in this book is sugar cane, *Saccharum officinarum*. The genus *Cymbopogon* contains about 55 species, most of which are native to Australia and Southeast Asia. Citronella grass, *Cymbopogon nardus*, is used in the production of citronella oil, which is used in insect repellents, candles, soaps, and lotions. Palmarosa or Rosha grass, *Cymbopogon martinii*, is grown for its essential oils, which are used in perfumes and lotions.

CULTIVATION Lemon grass is typically started through subdivision. Side shoots that contain some root material can be removed and transplanted. Entire clumps can be dug up, divided, and distributed to new locations. Lemon grass can be difficult to start from seed, as seeds have a low germination rate. Seeds should be sown at very shallow depth in damp, but never wet, medium. Temperature must be maintained near 70° F. The plant prefers full sun, but will take some shade. Lemon grass requires sufficient moisture, and the plant will go dormant and begin to turn brown under drought conditions. Once lemon grass is established, it is easy to grow and requires little care. Small plants should be kept free of weeds. As the plant matures and fills in, its dense habit of growth serves to exclude most weeds. Lemon grass thrives in summer conditions that affect peninsular Florida.

HARVEST AND USE The plant is harvested by cutting shoots from around the base at ground level. The bulb and thickened portions of the lower stalk are used in most recipes. The outer sheath is removed and the inner core is sliced, grated, or minced. The upper leaf blades are tough and are not suited for human consumption. However, newer, more tender sections of the blades can be finely sliced and added to soups or used as a garnish. Fresh lemon grass can be stored in the refrigerator for up to 3 weeks if kept in a plastic bag with the air removed. It can also be frozen for extended periods. Lemon grass is an ingredient in Thai, Malaysian, Sri Lankan, and Vietnamese cooking. It is added to curry pastes and seafood dishes. However, it is also enjoyed as a raw snack, as a salad ingredient, and as a flavoring for tea and beverages. Lemon grass, like its cousin, citronella, serves as an inspect repellent.

Lemon grass base before (left) and after (right) preparation

Lemon Verbena

SCIENTIFIC NAME: *Aloysia triphylla* (formerly *Lippia citriodora*)
FAMILY: Verbenaceae
OTHER COMMON NAME: Hierba Luisa (Spanish)

Perennial; Deciduous Shrub

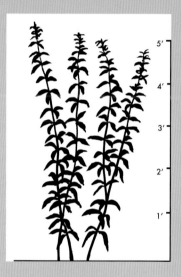

Characteristics

Overall Rating	★★★★
Ease of Care	★★★★
Utility	★★★★
Landscape Value	★★★
Salt Tolerance	★★★★
Drought Tolerance	★★★
Heat/Humidity Tolerance	★★★★★
Cold Tolerance	★★★
Shade Tolerance	★★
Longevity	★★

The sweet, lemony flavor of this herb makes it one of the best choices for the home garden. Many herb aficionados believe that lemon verbena has the finest and most subtle flavor of all the lemon-scented herbs, which include lemon balm, lemon basil, lemon grass, lemon savory, lemon thyme, and lemon mint. This plant is considered moderately difficult in Florida.

Known Hazards

Those with kidney disorders should consult a physician prior to consumption.

114

GEOGRAPHIC DISTRIBUTION Lemon verbena is indigenous to warm regions of the southern half of South America, including Peru, Chile, Argentina, Paraguay, Uruguay, and portions of Brazil. The Spanish introduced this plant to Europe. Some commercial production occurs in France. Essential oils from this plant are used in the production of perfume. The plant is frost tender and may experience winter dieback in north Florida. However, it will grow throughout the state.

Lemon verbena can be a robust plant and can rapidly take over its corner of the garden. Unlike many herbs that rapidly lose their scent, the dried leaves of lemon verbena retain their fragrance for years.

PLANT DESCRIPTION Lemon verbena is a perennial shrub capable of attaining a height of about 15 feet, but generally maintained at 5 or 6 feet. It is deciduous in north Florida and is evergreen in south Florida. The plant is somewhat sprawling in habit and can become leggy with age. The rate of growth is rapid. The leaves are lanceolate, serrated, and measure between 3 and 4 inches in length. They form whorls of three at nodes along the branches. Inconspicuous flowers are borne on branched terminal panicles during the summer. These are white with a trace of purple.

FLAVOR AND SCENT This plant has the fragrance and taste of lemon or lemon zest, but without the sourness and acidity of lemon.

VARIETIES No cultivars are known for this species.

RELATIVES The Verbenaceae family contains about 80 genera and 800 species, and is closely associated with the Lamiaceae or mint family. Teak, *Tectona* spp., is the primary member of the family with commercial import. Several common garden ornamentals, such as lantana and verbena, belong to this family. It should be noted that several lantanas are considered invasive exotics in Florida. Native members of the Verbenaceae family include: American beautyberry, *Callicarpa americana*; blue porterweed, *Stachytarpheta jamaicensis*; and Florida fiddlewood, *Citharexylum spinosum*. The *Lippia* genus, in which lemon verbena was formerly placed, consists of about 200 species and includes herbs such as the Aztec sweetherb, *Lippia dulcis*, and Mexican oregano, *Lippia graveolens*. Aztec sweetherb is a natural sweetener that is vigorous and easy to grow in Florida. However, its use for culinary purposes is not recommended here. It contains high levels of camphor, a carcinogen. The other members of the Verbenacea family covered within these pages are moujean tea, *Nashia inaguensis*, and Mexican oregano, *Lippia graveolens*.

CULTIVATION Lemon verbena prefers full sun, but will adapt to light shade. It should be planted in a location protected from strong winds. It is not negatively affected by the warm, humid conditions that occur during the summer in Florida. Soil should be loose and well drained with a near-neutral pH. Irrigation may be necessary during periods of low precipitation. The plant has a moderately high nitrogen requirement, and performance is enhanced with periodic fertilization. Lemon verbena can be propagated through leafy cuttings. The plant is somewhat susceptible to attack by mites and whiteflies.

HARVEST AND USE The leaves can be harvested at any time, but they tend to be especially flavorful at the time of flowering. They can be thinly sliced and used to add a lemony character to various dishes, and are especially useful in light sauces for seafood and poultry. They are also used effectively in marinades and stuffing. The leaves can be steeped to produce a tea or can be used to flavor tea. If the leaves are added to vodka with a bit of sugar, allowed to sit for a month, then strained, the liquor will be infused with the flavor of the herb. Lemon verbena is also a popular potpourri ingredient. The dried leaves retain their fragrance for several years.

Lime

SCIENTIFIC NAMES: *Citrus aurantifolia* and *Citrus latifolia*
FAMILY: Rutaceae
OTHER COMMON NAME: Lima (Spanish)

Woody Perennial; Evergreen Tree

Characteristics

Overall Rating	★★★★
Ease of Care	★★★★
Utility	★★★★
Landscape Value	★★★★
Salt Tolerance	★★★
Drought Tolerance	★★★
Heat/Humidity Tolerance	★★★★★
Cold Tolerance	★★
Shade Tolerance	★
Longevity	★★★

Known Hazards

Contact with the foliage and fruit rind has been known to cause a severe reaction in a few individuals, which may include phototoxicity, painful swelling, skin irritation, and other symptoms. Sharp spines are capable of causing mechanical injury.

The common name "lime" embraces several citrus species, usually characterized by skin that remains green through harvest. The two species covered here are the Key lime (or Mexican lime) and the Tahitian lime. The lime is highly recommended for planting as a dooryard tree in south Florida. It is a superb flavoring agent for drinks and marinades, and is the vital ingredient in Key lime pie.

116

GEOGRAPHIC DISTRIBUTION Like most forms of citrus, the lime originated in Southeast Asia, possibly on the Malaysian peninsula or in eastern portions of the Indian subcontinent. The Tahitian lime is grown commercially in Florida. The smaller and more aromatic Key lime has faded as a commercial crop, but excels as a dooryard crop. In Florida, growth is relegated to southern areas of the peninsula as a result of the tree's cold sensitivity.

Compare a typical Persian lime (top) with the diminutive Key lime (bottom). If left on the tree, limes eventually turn yellow.

PLANT DESCRIPTION The lime is a small evergreen tree, usually less than 15 feet in height. The branches of most varieties have prominent thorns. The leathery leaves are aromatic, dark green above and somewhat paler below. They are elliptic to oblong ovate in shape. Flowers, which measure between 1 and 2 inches in diameter, have 4 to 6 petals. They are white, sometimes tinged with pink or purple. The fruit is an elliptical hesperidium. It usually measures less than 3 inches in diameter. The skin typically turns from green to pale yellow at maturity. Most fruit are picked before they reach maturity. The pulp is contained in from 6 to 15 segments, which may contain a few to numerous seeds.

VARIETIES The Key or Mexican lime, *Citrus aurantifolia*, is the most aromatic species of lime. The tree is compact and somewhat shrublike in form. The Tahitian lime, *Citrus latifolia*, is thought to be a hybrid of the Mexican lime and the lemon or citron. Both the tree and the fruit are larger than those of the Key lime.

RELATIVES The family Rutaceae consists of about 150 genera and 900 species. The *Citrus* genus is made up of between 12 and 24 species. Other members of the Rutaceae family profiled within this book include the calamondin, *Citrus mitis*; curry leaf tree, *Muraya koenigii*; Kaffir lime, *Citrus hystrix*; lemon, *Citrus limon*; and rue, *Ruta graveolens*. The citron, *Citrus medica*, is another citrus species that is sometimes used as a spice or flavoring agent. The zest or outer peel is extremely fragrant. The thick inner rind or albedo is often candied in a sugar solution and dried.

CULTIVATION The lime is a low-maintenance tree. It grows well on sand and oolitic limestone, although it performs poorly on heavy clay. The Key lime is tolerant of drought and can withstand minor salt spray. The Tahitian lime is less drought tolerant. Red citrus mites, rust mites, broad mites, and scale insects occasionally bother the tree. Withertip, a fungal disease, affects the Key lime, but not the Tahitian lime. Scab sometimes develops during periods of wet weather. The lime is moderately vulnerable to citrus greening. Citrus greening is a bacterial disease that was first detected in Florida in 2005. It has been spreading rapidly. Signs of infection include blotched foliage, low yield, and stunted, misshapen fruit that fail to properly ripen. The lime is also extremely vulnerable to citrus canker. The lime is not tolerant of freezing temperatures and is more sensitive to cold than the sweet orange and the lemon. It suffers serious damage when the temperature falls to about 27° F. Like other forms of citrus, the lime is usually propagated by budding.

HARVEST AND USE In south Florida, production occurs over large portions of the year. The Key lime undergoes periods of high productivity in early summer and early winter. The Tahitian lime bears primarily during the summer and early fall. The fruit is often harvested at the first color shift from dark green to light green. It is used as a flavoring, marinade, ingredient or garnish in a wide range of dishes. Some people are allergic to oils produced by the leaves, the rind of the fruit, and other parts of the plant. The reaction may be touched off by exposure to sunlight and may result in swelling, severe dermatitis, and other symptoms.

Lovage

SCIENTIFIC NAME: *Levisticum officinale*
FAMILY: Apiaceae
OTHER COMMON NAMES: Maggi Herb, Apio de Monte
  (Spanish)

Herbaceous Deciduous Perennial

Planted
in Spring

Planted
in Fall

Characteristics

Overall Rating	★★
Ease of Care	★★★★
Utility	★★★
Landscape Value	★★★
Salt Tolerance	★
Drought Tolerance	★★★
Heat/Humidity Tolerance	★★
Cold Tolerance	★★★
Shade Tolerance	★★
Longevity	★★★

Known Hazards

There are some counter indications against the consumption of lovage during pregnancy. On rare occasions, contact with the plant has caused photosensitivity and consumption has resulted in food allergies. Those who are allergic to celery should exercise caution when handling or consuming this plant.

This member of the carrot family produces seeds that are used as a spice, leaves that are used as a garnish or green, and hollow stems that are used as a vegetable. Indeed, all parts of the plant are edible. For reasons that are unclear, this adaptable herb is little known and rarely used except in southern Europe. It is certainly a species worth growing in Florida.

GEOGRAPHIC DISTRIBUTION Lovage probably originated in central Asia. The curious name of this plant is not the result of any association with romanticism. Instead, it evolved from the old French, *luvesche*, which is traced through Latin to the Liguria region of Italy. Lovage was used in Roman times and was widely distributed throughout southern Europe at an early date. It has escaped cultivation and grows wild in England and over parts of Europe.

PLANT DESCRIPTION Lovage is a short-lived perennial herb capable of attaining a height of more than 7 feet under ideal conditions. In Florida, it is typically less than half this tall. It is a stout plant, bearing some resemblance to angelica (*Angelica archangelica*) in its habit of growth. It has a central taproot. Leaves are medium green, compound, with from 3 to 7 leaflets. Leaflets are deeply lobed and wedge-shaped, with roughly serrated edges toward the apex. As with many other members of the Apiaceae family, flowers are borne on flattened umbels atop long stalks. The flowers are light yellow. The seeds (actually fruits) are thick bodied, elliptical, and yellowish-brown, with three longitudinal ribs.

FLAVOR AND SCENT The flavor is similar to celery, but is stronger, yeasty, more resinous, and distinct. All parts of the plant are pleasantly aromatic.

 RELATIVES The family Apiaceae is large and is home to a wide array of vegetables, herbs, and spices. Herbs not covered within this book that belong to the Apiaceae family include angelica, *Angelica archangelica*; cicely, *Myrrhis odorata*; and licorice, *Glycyrrhiza glabra*. Members of the Apiaceae family covered within this book are anise, *Pimpinella anisum*; caraway, *Carum carvi*; chervil, *Anthriscus cerefolium*; cilantro, *Coriandrum sativum*; culantro, *Eryngium foetidum*; cumin, *Cuminum cyminum*; dill, *Anethum graveolens*; fennel, *Foeniculum vulgare*; and parsley, *Petroselinum crispum*.

CULTIVATION Lovage is a vigorous plant and is easy to grow in Florida and elsewhere. However, it is not especially drought tolerant. Irrigation should be supplied regularly during establishment and during periods of low rainfall. The plant will rapidly wilt if the soil is allowed to dry out completely. Lovage is tolerant of a wide range of soil types, including clay, heavy soil, and slightly alkaline soil. It is planted from seed. Fresh seed is preferred, as the rate of germination declines over time. In south Florida, seed may require cold stratification to germinate. Lovage is planted in the late summer or fall in south Florida. It fairs poorly during summer conditions and is treated as an annual.

HARVEST AND USE Leaves can be harvested at any time. They can be used fresh, or can be dried or frozen for storage. They are added as a seasoning to tomato-based sauces. They can also be used in soups, salads, potato salads, stuffing, and poultry dishes. The seeds are also employed as a flavoring agent and can be substituted for caraway or celery seeds. The stems can be blanched and used as a vegetable. The fresh stems can also be used as drinking straws. If divided lengthwise and placed in ice-cold water, they curl, creating a unique garnish. Young shoots are sometimes gathered in the spring. The root is strongly flavored and may be used as a flavoring agent. It is a weak diuretic.

Mexican Oregano

SCIENTIFIC NAME: *Lippia graveolens*
FAMILY: Verbenaceae
OTHER COMMON NAMES: Sonoran Oregano, Té de Pais
(Spanish)

Perennial Shrub; Semi-Evergreen

Characteristics

Overall Rating	★★★★
Ease of Care	★★★★
Utility	★★★★
Landscape Value	★★★
Salt Tolerance	★★
Drought Tolerance	★★★★
Heat/Humidity Tolerance	★★★
Cold Tolerance	★★★
Shade Tolerance	★
Longevity	★★★

Like Cuban oregano, addressed earlier, Mexican oregano is not closely related to oregano. However, it closely duplicates the scent and flavor of oregano. This is a tough plant that grows well in Florida and is not beset by any serious problems. This herb is very popular in Mexico and is becoming more widely available in the United States.

Known Hazards
None

GEOGRAPHIC DISTRIBUTION This species is native to southern Texas, New Mexico, Mexico, and Central America. It has long been used by the Seri Indians, of northwestern Mexico, as a culinary and medicinal herb. The plant is not frost tolerant. It can be grown outdoors in south Florida. It should be grown as a container plant in northern areas of the state.

Mexican oregano is not closely related to either oregano or Cuban oregano. It is a tough plant and is easy to cultivate.

PLANT DESCRIPTION Mexican oregano is a perennial shrub that attains a maximum height of 5 or 6 feet. The rate of growth is medium. The plant has an open, coarse, somewhat sprawling habit of growth. Branches are stiff and somewhat brittle. The opposite, dark green, oval leaves are entire. They are usually less than 1/2 of an inch in length. Flowers are borne sporadically throughout the year and tend to be most numerous after heavy precipitation. The flowers are small, white, and fragrant, borne in clusters at the leaf axils.

FLAVOR AND SCENT The leaves have an intense flavor similar to that of true oregano. The taste is considered to be slightly sweeter and more robust than that of true oregano. The scent is warm and pungent.

RELATIVES The Verbenaceae family contains about 80 genera and 800 species. Native members of the Verbenaceae family include American beautyberry, *Callicarpa americana*; blue porterweed, *Stachytarpheta jamaicensis*; and Florida fiddlewood, *Citharexylum spinosum*. A Mexican species closely related to Mexican oregano, *Lippia berlandieri*, is also used as an oregano substitute. The Aztec sweetherb, *Lippia dulcis*, has been used as a natural sweetener. However, this plant contains high levels of camphor and has a bitter aftertaste. Stevia, *Stevia rebaudiana*, an unrelated plant described later within this book, has far more potential as a sugar substitute. The other Verbanaceae species covered within this book are lemon verbena, *Lippia citriodora*, and moujean tea, *Nashia inaguensis*.

CULTIVATION Mexican oregano prefers full sun. Seeds require between 1 and 2 weeks to germinate. The plant is also easily propagated from leafy cuttings. This plant is drought tolerant. It is not bothered by wet and humid conditions, but requires proper drainage. It has few pest or disease problems. All told, Mexican oregano requires very little care.

HARVEST AND USE Mexican oregano can be harvested at any time. It is generally dried before use, which does not diminish the flavor. It should not be overused, as it can quickly overpower other flavors. Mexican oregano can be substituted for oregano in any dish. It is considered an essential ingredient in several regional styles of Mexican cooking. It is a key ingredient in Mexican cheesecake, pay de queso. It is also used in soups, salsas, tomato-based sauces, and various bean dishes.

Mexican Tarragon

SCIENTIFIC NAME: *Tagetes lucida*
FAMILY: Asteraceae
OTHER COMMON NAMES: Winter Tarragon,
   Hierba de Anis (Spanish)

Herbaceous Perennial

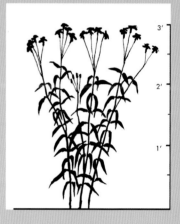

Characteristics

Overall Rating	★★★★
Ease of Care	★★★★
Utility	★★★★
Landscape Value	★★★★
Salt Tolerance	★
Drought Tolerance	★★★★
Heat/Humidity Tolerance	★★★★
Cold Tolerance	★★★
Shade Tolerance	★★
Longevity	★★

This tarragon substitute is hardier than tarragon, exceeds tarragon in visual appeal, and very nearly equals tarragon as a flavoring agent. It actually falls within the marigold genus, and is not closely related to true tarragon. Unlike true tarragon, Mexican tarragon is not bothered by the heat and humidity of the Florida summer.

Known Hazards

None. Those who are allergic to other members of the Asteraceae family should exercise caution when using this herb.

122

GEOGRAPHIC DISTRIBUTION Mexican tarragon is endemic to the Sierra Madre de Oaxaca mountains of southern Mexico and is also present in parts of Guatemala. It grows on hillsides, rocky terrain, disturbed areas, and woodland borders. The Aztecs used this plant as an ingredient in cacao-based drinks. Mexican tarragon will grow throughout Florida. However, in north Florida it may be killed to the ground by frost.

Mexican tarragon is easier to grow, more robust, and slightly stronger-tasting than true tarragon.

PLANT DESCRIPTION This is a perennial herb that forms a small, upright bush. It is grown as an annual in cooler climates. Mexican tarragon reaches a maximum height of 2 to 3 feet. Older stems are woody. Leaves ascend the shoots in four orderly columns, giving the plant an attractive appearance. The leaves are narrow, lanceolate, dark green above, lighter below. They measure from 2 1/2 to 4 inches in length. Half-inch yellow-orange flowers with from 3 to 5 petals are produced in loose clusters in the fall. As with other marigolds, the flowers are actually a composite of several smaller flowers. They are hermaphroditic and are pollinated by insects.

FLAVOR AND SCENT The leaves have a mild anise/tarragon flavor and fragrance. The taste also combines a touch of mint, cinnamon, and sweetness. The flowers have a sweet scent but are essentially tasteless and are not regularly used for culinary purposes.

RELATIVES Other members of the Asteraceae family discussed within these pages include: chamomile, *Chamaemilum nobile* and *Matricaria recutita*; chicory, *Cichorium intybus*; goldenrod, *Solidago* spp.; stevia, *Stevia rebaudiana*; and tarragon, *Artemisia dracunculus*. The *Tagetes* or marigold genus contains about 50 species. Several serve as ornamentals. Others have been used in teas, as condiments, and for medicinal purposes. The familiar garden marigold, *Tagetes erecta*, has been brewed into a tea in some regions of the southern United States. Chinchilla, *Tagetes minuta*, an herb native to northern South America, is valued as a tea plant and flavoring agent in Chile, Bolivia, Peru, and Paraguay. No member of the *Tagetes* genus is native to Florida.

CULTIVATION Mexican tarragon should be planted in full sun. Although it has shown some drought tolerance, Mexican tarragon benefits from regular irrigation. It will grow in a broad range of soil types. The plant is generally grown from seed. Seeds are sown at a very shallow depth after the danger of cold weather has passed. They germinate in about 2 weeks. Ground layering is also an effective method of propagating this species.

HARVEST AND USE This herb can be substituted for tarragon in any recipe calling for tarragon. It loses flavor if cooked for prolonged periods and is thus generally added toward the end of the cooking process. Mexican tarragon makes a superb Béarnaise sauce. In addition, the fresh leaf can be used to flavor beverages. Whole leaves may be added to cider, punch, or sangria. In Mexico it is used to make an herbal tea. One disadvantage of Mexican tarragon is that it loses its flavor if dried. It should be frozen for extended storage.

Mint

SCIENTIFIC NAME: *Mentha* spp.
FAMILY: Lamiaceae
OTHER COMMON NAME: Menta (Spanish)

Herbaceous Annual

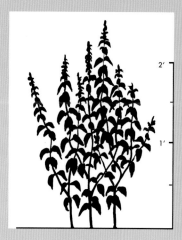

Characteristics

verall Rating	★★★★★
O se of Care	★★★★
Ea ility	★★★★★
Ut ndscape Value	★★★
La t Tolerance	★★★
Sa ught Tolerance	★★★★
D at/Humidity Tolerance	★★★★
H ld Tolerance	★★
Co ade Tolerance	★★★
Sh ngevity	★★★
Lo	

Known Hazards

Mints contain salicylates and have been associated with allergic reactions in those who are intolerant of these compounds. Pure mint oil or menthol is poisonous and must not be ingested. Some non-native mints have displayed invasive tendencies.

The mints are among the most important, numerous, and widely cultivated herbs. In fact, so many varieties of mint are available that one could dedicate an entire herb garden to the genus. These aromatic plants are easy to grow and have many uses.

124

GEOGRAPHIC DISTRIBUTION Members of the *Mentha* genus can be found on every continent except Antarctica. Some are considered invasive where they have been introduced into new locations. Some mints are grown as a commercial crop in Florida.

From top left to bottom right: Kentucky mint, spearmint, pineapple mint, and peppermint

PLANT DESCRIPTION Mint species differ somewhat in form and habit of growth, but share many common characteristics. The vast majority are perennial herbs, forming vertical stems atop horizontal rhizomes. The rate of growth tends to be rapid. Stems tend to be squared. Flowers are tubular. Leaves are opposite with toothed or serrated margins. The shape is variable, ranging from oblong to lanceolate. Leaf color is also variable. The leaves of some selections are tinted with silver-gray, red, or purple.

FLAVOR AND SCENT Mints are highly aromatic, with a pleasant, sweet, cooling flavor. Depending on the variety, the flavor may hint of cedar, citrus, or wintergreen.

VARIETIES There are about 30 species within the *Mentha* genus. Many members hybridize with one another. Over 200 cultivars have been selected. Some of the more common varieties include: apple mint, *Mentha suaveolens*; Asian mint, *Mentha asiatica*; Bergamot mint, *Mentha citrata*; Corsican mint, *Mentha requienii*; garden mint, *Mentha sachalinensis*; ginger mint, *Mentha gracilis*; Hart's pennyroyal, *Mentha cervina*; horse mint, *Mentha longifolia*; pennyroyal, *Mentha pulegium*; peppermint, *Mentha piperita*; slender mint, *Mentha diemenica*; spearmint, *Mentha spicata*;

and water mint, *Mentha aquatica*.

RELATIVES The Lamiaceae family, which consists of about 200 genera and 7,000 species, contains many important herbs and spices. Species discussed within this book include basil, *Ocimum* spp.; bee balm, *Monarda didyma*; Cuban oregano, *Plectranthus amboinicus*; Jamaican mint, *Micromeria viminea*; lavender, *Lavandula* spp.; lemon balm, *Melissa officinalis*; oregano, *Origanum* spp.; perilla, *Perilla frutescens*; rosemary, *Rosmarinus officinalis*; sage, *Salvia officinalis*; savory, *Satureja* spp.; and thyme, *Thymus* spp. Many members of the Lamiacaae family, some with the common name "mint," are native to Florida. Several of these are listed as endangered or threatened. Native calamints include Ashe's calamint, *Calamintha ashei*; Florida calamint, *Calamintha dentata*; Georgia calamint, *Calamintha georgiana*; and scarlet calamint, *Calamintha coccinea*. Native members of the genus *Dicerandra* include coastalplain balm, *Dicerandra linearifolia*; Robin's mint, *Dicerandra cornutissima*; scrub balm, *Dicerandra frutescens*; Lakela's mint, *Dicerandra immaculate*; Titusville balm, *Dicerandra thinicola*; and yellow scrub balm, *Dicerandra christmanii*. Native mountainmints include the Appalachian mountainmint, *Pycnanthemum flexuosum*; awned mountainmint, *Pycnanthemum setosum*; coastalplain mountainmint, *Pycnanthemum nudum*; Florida mountainmint, *Pycnanthemum floridanum*; southern mountainmint, *Pycnanthemum pycnanthemoides*; and whiteleaf moutainmint, *Pycnanthemum albescens*. The wild pennyroyal, *Piloblephis rigida*, is found throughout peninsular Florida.

CULTIVATION Most mints prefer partial shade, although some will tolerate full sun. Some varieties are difficult to maintain through the summer in south Florida and may decline or die in semitropical heat and moisture. Others show no ill effects. Most species of mint are not picky as to soil type and can withstand more dampness than most other herbs. Mints have limited drought tolerance and achieve their best growth with regular irrigation. Plants can become invasive if not kept in check. Some can be grown from seed, although others are sterile. They can also be propagated with cuttings and through root division.

HARVEST AND USE Leaves can be harvested at any time. They are best used fresh and have a short storage life. Dried mint loses much of its flavor. Various cocktails, especially mint juleps and mojitos, make use of mint as a flavoring agent and garnish. Mint can also be used to flavor tea, to make jelly, to flavor ice cream, and as a seasoning for lamb. It is a common ingredient in Middle Eastern cuisines. It is also used with good effect in the Thai warm beef salad, yam neua.

Miracle Fruit

SCIENTIFIC NAME: *Synsepalum dulcificum*
FAMILY: Sapotaceae
OTHER COMMON NAME: Fruta del Milagro

Woody Perennial; Evergreen Shrub

Characteristics

Overall Rating	★★
Ease of Care	★★
Utility	★
Landscape Value	★★★★
Salt Tolerance	★★★
Drought Tolerance	★★
Heat/Humidity Tolerance	★★★★★
Cold Tolerance	★
Shade Tolerance	★
Longevity	★★★★

The fruit of the miracle fruit resembles a jellybean in size and shape. It holds little food value, and the scant pulp is slimy and essentially tasteless. It does, however, harbor a noteworthy secret that justifies its inclusion within this book. When the miracle fruit is eaten prior to the consumption of sour or bitter foods, it causes such foods to taste sweet and pleasant.

Known Hazards

None

GEOGRAPHIC DISTRIBUTION The miracle fruit is native to tropical regions of West Africa. It is grown as a landscape specimen in coastal regions of south Florida and can be grown as a container plant throughout the state. It has also been widely distributed throughout Latin America. Attempts to harness the taste-twisting attributes of the miracle fruit for commercial purposes have met with only limited success.

Miracle fruit does well as a container plant. It requires acidic soil and fairs poorly in the limestone soils of south Florida.

PLANT DESCRIPTION The miracle fruit is a slow-growing evergreen shrub capable of attaining a height of more than 12 feet under ideal conditions. However, it rarely grows to a height of greater than 5 feet in Florida. The shrub is attractive and is densely foliated. The leaves are ovate, dark green, and shiny, measuring about 2 inches in length. Small white flowers precede the fruit. The fruit is a bright red oval berry containing a single seed.

FLAVOR AND SCENT Miracle fruit possesses no scent and little flavor. It causes the tongue to interpret bitter and sour flavors as sweet. The effect diminishes after about 30 minutes and fades altogether within an hour after consumption.

RELATIVES The giant miracle fruit, *Synsepalum subcordatum*, also from Africa, does not have the taste-altering attributes discussed here. The Sapotaceae family contains about 1,000 species. It is primarily known for its fruiting members, including the canistel, *Pouteria campechiana*; mamey sapote, *Pouteria sapota*; sapodilla, *Manilkara zapota*; and star apple, *Chrysophyllum cainito*. No other members of the family are described within these pages.

CULTIVATION Miracle fruit is tropical in habit, and must be protected against frost when grown outdoors. It may be seriously damaged at 30° F. The plant loves acidic soil and requires a pH of less than 6.5 for optimal growth. It fares poorly in the oolitic limestone soils of south Florida. The plant prefers full sun, although it can endure partial shade. It prefers well-drained soil and cannot tolerate wet feet. Miracle fruit can be grown from cuttings or seed. However, seed life is short and the germination rate is poor.

HARVEST AND USE The fruit is borne throughout the year, generally with two main crops. It is generally consumed fresh, often in conjunction with grapefruit, limes, lemons, or other acid-citrus fruit. The fruit also radically changes the flavor of items such as stout beer, radishes, strawberries, mustard, pickles, cheeses, and hot-pepper sauce. The consumption of several miracle fruit berries during the same sitting does not appear to enhance the effect. Cooking destroys the protein, miraculin, that is responsible for producing the effect.

Moujean Tea

SCIENTIFIC NAME: *Nashia inaguensis*
FAMILY: Verbenaceae
OTHER COMMON NAME: Bahama Berry,
   Pineapple Verbena

Woody Perennial; Evergreen Shrub

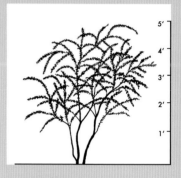

Characteristics

Overall Rating	★★★★
Ease of Care	★★★
Utility	★★★
Landscape Value	★★★★
Salt Tolerance	★★
Drought Tolerance	★
Heat/Humidity Tolerance	★★★★★
Cold Tolerance	★★
Shade Tolerance	★★
Longevity	★★★

Moujean tea is a little-known evergreen shrub that, in most respects, is well suited to growth in south Florida. The plant makes a delightful addition to the landscape and also serves as a superb scent plant. The tea produced from this plant is elegantly flavored and should be viewed as a product with commercial potential. Because of these attributes, moujean tea is being planted with increasing frequency in south Florida gardens.

Known Hazards

None. However, some caution is advised in that the health effects have probably not been adequately studied.

ORIGIN AND DISTRIBUTION Moujean tea is native to the eastern Caribbean, including Puerto Rico, the Bahamas, and Jamaica, although it is rare throughout much of its range. It is reportedly common on the islands of Inagua in the Bahamas. In Florida, growth is limited to the southern half of the peninsula and protected coastal locations as far north as Daytona Beach. It can be raised as a container plant in locations subject to more frequent winter freezes. The availability of this species in Florida is somewhat limited. However, when the supply is spotty, it can be obtained from mail-order nurseries.

PLANT DESCRIPTION Moujean tea is a small, spreading shrub reaching a maximum height of about 6 feet. The trunk may eventually attain a diameter of 3 or 4 inches. The habit of growth is somewhat unruly, with a spray of loose arching branches. The plant nevertheless makes a very attractive addition to the garden and can be substituted for an array of other shrubs. The dark-green leaves are tiny, measuring between a quarter-inch and a half-inch in length. They are elliptic in form and are glossy but slightly wrinkled in texture. Small cream-colored flowers form clusters around the leaf axils in the late summer. The flowers are tubular, with four petals and four stamens. They draw numerous insect pollinators. Orange berries ripen in the fall. These resemble tiny beads and measure only about 1/8 of an inch in diameter.

SCENT AND TASTE Moujean tea is highly aromatic, and the scent produced by this plant is one of the finest. The leaves, when bruised or crushed, emit a spicy fragrance, with hints of vanilla and pineapple. These same elements are reflected in the flavor of beverages brewed with the leaves. The flowers are intensely fragrant and emit a sweet, citrus-jasmine scent.

CULTIVARS No cultivars have been selected to date.

RELATIVES The Nashia genus is thought to contain 7 species, including *Nashia armata, Nashia cayensis, Nashia myrtifolia, Nashia nipensis, Nashia spinifera,* and *Nashia variifolia.* It is unclear whether any of these close relatives have potential as scent or tea plants. Other members of the Verbenaceae family covered within this book are lemon verbena, *Aloysia triphylla,* and Mexican oregano, *Lippia graveolens.*

CULTIVATION Moujean tea will grow in full sun or light, partial shade. The plant has moderate to high water needs. The soil surrounding the roots must never be permitted to dry out completely. At the same time, the plant prefers reasonably well-drained soil and cannot stand prolonged waterlogging. While it will tolerate a wide range of soils, it seems to prefer some organic content. Moujean tea thrives in the heat and humidity of the south Florida summer. It suffers when temperatures fall much below 40° F. It will recover from an occasional light frost, but is likely to succumb at about 28° F. Moujean tea has not shown susceptibility to any major diseases or insect pests in Florida. Mealybugs are an occasional, minor problem. The plant can be propagated from cuttings, which must be kept moist until they are well rooted. Moujean tea responds well to pruning and can be maintained as a semi-formal specimen. It can even be used as a topiary plant. The foliage will become dense and bushy if the branch tips are cut back frequently. Because of its miniaturized leaves, moujean tea has also become popular as a bonsai plant.

HARVEST AND USE Leaves, fruit, and flowers can all be harvested for use in tea. They can be used fresh or dried. The fresh leaves are leathery and tough, and they must be steeped in hot water for an extended period to produce a beverage of acceptable strength. Moujean tea can also be added to commercial tea to impart a unique vanilla-citrus flavor and aroma.

If new growth is periodically pruned, moujean tea will form a densely foliated shrub.

Mustard

SCIENTIFIC NAME: *Brassica* spp.
FAMILY: Brassicaceae
OTHER COMMON NAME: Mostaza (Spanish)

Herbaceous Annual

Planted in Spring

Planted in Winter

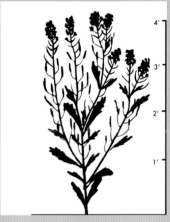

Characteristics

Overall Rating	★★
Ease of Care	★★★★
Utility	★★★
Landscape Value	★★
Salt Tolerance	★
Drought Tolerance	★★★
Heat/Humidity Tolerance	★★★
Cold Tolerance	★★
Shade Tolerance	★
Longevity	★

Known Hazards

The seed and pods may be toxic to grazing livestock if consumed in large quantities. While allergic reactions to mustard are relatively rare, they can be severe in persons affected. Mustard contains salicylates, and consumption may cause reactions in those who are intolerant of these compounds. Mustards tend to exude caustic oils when damaged. Although formerly used as a poultice ingredient, prolonged contact with the skin may cause burning and lesions. Mustard has invasive qualities.

Mustard refers to several species within the genus *Brassica*, cultivated for their seeds. Mustard is easy to grow, but requires some effort in harvesting and processing. The plant spreads by seed and has been classified as an invasive-exotic in some areas of the country.

GEOGRAPHIC DISTRIBUTION The mustards widely used as spice probably originated around the Mediterranean basin. However, as a result of cultivation and trading, they became extremely widespread at an early date. Their precise origins have been lost to time. Various mustard species have escaped cultivation and now grow wild over much of North America. Several are viewed as noxious weeds. Both black mustard and Indian mustard have invaded natural locations in Florida.

Mustard seedpods form in place of yellow flowers.

PLANT DESCRIPTION The mustard species that are typically used as spices are branching annuals. They reach a height of between 3 and 6 feet. The rate of growth is rapid. Leaves are variable. Lower leaves are lobed, while upper leaves tend to be entire or dentate. Yellow flowers, which appear in the spring, are borne in clusters on short pedicels. Spherical seeds develop in slender green pods.

FLAVOR AND SCENT Mustard seed has a spicy, hot, slightly bitter flavor and a pungent aroma. The flavor is derived from the essential oil, which is liberated by grinding the seed and by wetting the processed seed or combining it with vinegar. Black and brown mustard have a sharp flavor, while white mustard tends to be milder. Cooking diminishes the "bite" of black and brown mustard.

VARIETIES Black mustard, *Brassica nigra*, bears yellow flowers. It produces small, dark-brown seeds. These are ground and used as table mustard. Brown mustard, *Brassica juncea*, also bears yellow flowers. It produces larger, light-brown seeds. The leaves are harvested as mustard greens, while the seeds are used in table mustard. White mustard, *Brassica hirta* or *Brassica alba,* is also used as both a vegetable and a spice.

RELATIVES The Brassicaceae family consists of about 325 genera and 3,500 species. It contains numerous leafy green vegetables. Many of these cruciferous vegetables fall within the *Brassica* genus. The Indian mustard plant, *Brassica juncea*, is cultivated for use as mustard greens. This pungent vegetable is regarded as an important African American "soul" food. Other plants within the genus utilized as vegetables include Abyssinian cabbage, *Brassica carinata*; bok choy, *Brassica rapa chinensis*; broccoli, *Brassica oleracea italica*; Brussels sprouts, *Brassica oleracea gemmifera*; cabbage, *Brassica oleracea capitata*; cauliflower; *Brassica oleracea botrytis*; Chinese cabbage, *Brassica rapa pekinensis*; kale or collard greens, *Brassica oleracea acephala*; Mediterranean cabbage, *Brassica fruticulosa*; mustard spinach, *Brassica perviridis*; and rutabaga, *Brassica napus*. More distantly related are arugula, *Eruca vesicaria*; daikon, *Raphanus sativus longipinnatus*; and wasabi, *Wasabia japonica*. Members of the Brassicaceae family covered within this book include: horseradish, *Armoracia rusticana*; pepperweed, *Lepidium verginicum*; sea rocket, *Cakile edentula*; and watercress, *Nasturtium nasturtium-aquaticum*.

CULTIVATION Mustard is a low-maintenance plant that will grow throughout the state of Florida. The plant is tolerant of adverse conditions. It requires little water and prefers low to moderate rainfall. It prefers sandy soil, but will grow in various soil types with a wide pH range. In north Florida, seeds are sown in early spring. In south Florida, they are sown in the fall. If mustard is not harvested in a timely manner, it will self-sow and may rapidly take over the garden.

Mustard seeds are nearly round. They germinate within two weeks under ideal conditions.

HARVEST AND USE The seeds are ready for harvest about 6 weeks after flowering. If left on the plant too long, the pods will shatter and disburse their seeds. The tops of the plants are cut and dried. The seeds are then thrashed from the cuttings. Mustard is used to flavor a vast array of dishes. Traditional mustard paste is usually made of a combination of black and white mustard seeds. The seeds are ground and are combined with vinegar or olive oil or some combination of vinegar and olive oil.

Myrtle

SCIENTIFIC NAME: *Myrtus communis*
FAMILY: Myrtaceae
OTHER COMMON NAME: Mirto (Spanish)

Woody Perennial; Evergreen Shrub

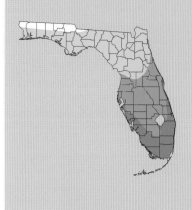

Characteristics

Overall Rating	★★★★
Ease of Care	★★★
Utility	★★★
Landscape Value	★★★★★
Salt Tolerance	★★
Drought Tolerance	★★★
Heat/Humidity Tolerance	★★★
Cold Tolerance	★★★
Shade Tolerance	★
Longevity	★★★★

This compact and attractive evergreen shrub is renowned for its scented foliage. The leaves are used as a flavoring agent, and the leaves and woods are used for smoking meats. Myrtle has been used in cooking since ancient times, and has a prominent plant in Greek mythology.

Known Hazards

None

132

GEOGRAPHIC DISTRIBUTION Members of the tiny *Myrtus* genus are indigenous to the Mediterranean region, including North Africa and southern Europe. The myrtle has been widely distributed and is grown as a hedge throughout the Middle East. It is also a popular plant in southern England and in California.

True myrtle (shown here) is a compact plant with small leaves. It should not be confused with crape myrtle, *Lagerstroemia* spp., which is an unrelated flowering shrub native to Southeast Asia. Crape myrtle is planted heavily as an ornamental in Florida.

PLANT DESCRIPTION Myrtle is a densely foliated evergreen shrub which is capable of attaining a height of 18 feet with an equal spread, but which is usually much smaller. The rate of growth is slow. As a result of its attractive form and slow growth, this plant is sometimes used in bonsai. Leaves are small, measuring 1 to 2 inches in length. The leaves are ovate to lanceolate, stiff, leathery, and sharply pointed. When crushed, they exude a pleasant scent. The fragrant flowers, which are white, appear during the late spring and summer. These have five rounded petals and a prominent spray of stamens. Insects appear to be the primary pollinating agents. The flowers are followed by small, blue-purple berries, which contain several seeds.

FLAVOR AND SCENT The scent of the foliage is pleasant and aromatic, resembling eucalyptus. The flavor is bitter, spicy, and somewhat resinous.

VARIETIES The species most often available in Florida is the common myrtle, *Myrtus communis*.

Saharan myrtle, *Myrtus nivellei*, is an endangered species indigenous to Algeria and Chad. A dwarf variety is sometimes available. A variegated type has been produced, but does not appear to be widely available.

RELATIVES Myrtaceae is an important family of flowering plants, containing numerous fruit-bearing species and spice-producing species. The *Myrtus* genus is tiny, consisting only of the two species mentioned above. It is closely associated with the *Eugenia* and *Syzygium* genera. The name myrtle is regularly applied to plants such as crepe myrtle and wax myrtle, which are not members of the myrtle genus.

CULTIVATION Myrtle prefers light shade to full sun. It is very drought tolerant and may become chlorotic during periods of high rainfall. The plant requires proper drainage. It does very well as a container plant. It can be propagated through hardwood and softwood cuttings. The plant responds well to tip pruning, and the size and shape can be easily managed. Myrtle is hardy to about 22° F and may be damaged by frost in north Florida.

HARVEST AND USE The leaves can be used fresh or can be dried. The leaves can be sprinkled over coals during the cooking process to impart a spicy flavor to meats and other food. The wood can also be used for smoking purposes. The leaves can be used in cooking as a substitute for bay leaves. The berries are edible and, when dried, can be used in a manner similar to black pepper. On the Mediterranean island of Sardinia, the berries and leaves are used in the production of "mirto," a popular local liqueur. The flowers are edible and can be used as a garnish or in salads.

A close-up of myrtle leaves

Nasturtium

SCIENTIFIC NAME: *Tropaeolum majus*
FAMILY: Tropaeolaceae
OTHER COMMON NAMES: Indian Cress, Capuchina \
  (Spanish)

Perennial; Semi-Evergreen Creeper

Planted in Spring

Planted in Fall

Characteristics

Overall Rating	★★★★
Ease of Care	★★★★
Utility	★★★
Landscape Value	★★★★★
Salt Tolerance	★
Drought Tolerance	★★
Heat/Humidity Tolerance	★★★★★
Cold Tolerance	★★★★
Shade Tolerance	★★★
Longevity	★★

All parts of this ornamental flowering plant are edible, including the flowers. In fact, nasturtium excels as an edible, lending its pleasant flavor to salads, garnishes, and dips. It grows well as an annual in north Florida and as a cool-weather annual in south Florida. The only caution with respect to this plant is that it has demonstrated some invasive tendencies.

Known Hazards

May have invasive tendencies

134

GEOGRAPHIC DISTRIBUTION The species is native to South America, and may have originated in the Andean region of Peru. It has been widely distributed around the world and is grown extensively in southern Europe. It has escaped cultivation in some locations. It will grow throughout Florida, although it is not frost tolerant.

Nasturtium flowers add a rich splash of color to the garden. However, excessive fertilization can cause the plants to cease flowering and to put out strictly vegetative growth.

PLANT DESCRIPTION Nasturtium is a perennial creeper. It has a sprawling, vinelike habit of growth. The pale-green leaves are near circular and form horizontal, umbrella-like plates atop vertical petioles. In this respect they somewhat resemble miniature lily pads or lotus leaves. Showy flowers appear from May through August. These are typically yellow or yellow-orange and have 5 petals. One of the sepals is modified into an elongated, nectar-bearing spur. The fruit is a three-part schizocarp, with each section containing a large seed.

FLAVOR AND SCENT The flavor is delicate and sweet, with tangy pepper and mustard undertones. It is reminiscent of watercress. The seedpods, and especially the seeds themselves, are hotter in flavor. The flowers are lightly fragrant.

VARIETIES The most frequently encountered species in Florida is *Tropaeolum majus*. Numerous cultivars have been selected, primarily for their flowering characteristics. Some are probably hybrids between *Tropaeolum majus* and *Tropaeolum peltophorum*. Some double-flowering varieties are 'Darjeeling Gold,' 'Double Gleam,' 'Hermine Grasshof,' and 'Margaret Long.' Other cultivars include 'Black Velvet,' 'Gleam Hybrid,' 'Jewel of Africa,' 'Ladybird,' 'Peach Melba,' 'Salmon Baby,' 'Tom Thumb,' 'Vesuvius,' and 'Whirlybird.'

RELATIVES Tropaeolaceae is a small family of three genera and about 100 species. Nasturtium is the only member of the family discussed within these pages. The genus *Tropaeolum* accounts for about 80 species. Ornamental species include the canary creeper, *Tropaeolum peregrinum*, and the flame creeper, *Tropaeolum speciosum*. The mashua or añu, *Tropaeolum tuberosum*, produces an underground tuber that is consumed as a food item in Columbia, Ecuador, Peru, and other Andean nations.

CULTIVATION While nasturtium can be perennial in warmer climates, it is not frost tolerant and is usually grown as an annual. In north Florida, seeds are planted after the danger of frost has passed. In south Florida, the plant is grown over the cooler months of the year, as it stops flowering and takes on a stressed appearance during the heat of summer. Nasturtium can withstand a broad range of soil types and prospers in sandy, nutrient-poor soils. Fewer flowers appear when the plant is grown in nitrogen-rich soils with a high organic content. Nasturtium is not drought tolerant and requires periodic irrigation. Snails, slugs, and aphids have an affinity for this plant and occasionally damage the foliage.

HARVEST AND USE The leaves and flowers can be harvested at any time. Young leaves have a milder flavor than older leaves, which may become slightly bitter. The leaves and flowers are used fresh, primarily as salad ingredients or as a garnish. They can be briefly refrigerated. The seedpods can be pickled and used as a caper substitute. The seeds can be ground and used as a pepper substitute. Hummingbirds sometimes visit the flowers.

New Jersey Tea

SCIENTIFIC NAME: *Ceanothus americanus*
FAMILY: Rhamnaceae
OTHER COMMON NAMES: Redroot, Indian Tea

Woody Perennial; Deciduous Shrub

Characteristics

Overall Rating	★★★
Ease of Care	★★★★
Utility	★★
Landscape Value	★★★★
Salt Tolerance	★★
Drought Tolerance	★★★★
Heat/Humidity Tolerance	★★★
Cold Tolerance	★★★★★
Shade Tolerance	★★
Longevity	★★★

New Jersey tea is perhaps the best of several indigenous tea substitutes. Native Americans made extensive use of this plant, both in making a beverage and for medicinal purposes. Following the Boston Tea Party of 1773 and the Greenwich Tea Burning of 1774, New Jersey tea became a popular beverage with those opposed to British tariffs. Over more recent times, the plant gradually faded into obscurity as an herbal tea, despite occasional use by hikers and survivalists. Native plant enthusiasts should reacquaint themselves with this versatile shrub.

Known Hazards

None

GEOGRAPHIC DISTRIBUTION New Jersey tea is native to nearly the entire eastern United States, ranging as far north as southern Canada and as far west as Texas and Wisconsin. It grows throughout north Florida and occurs naturally as far south as Highlands County. It occurs as an understory plant in open scrub pine or scrub oak habitats and also appears in mixed-grass prairies, disturbed areas, and pasture fringes. It is quick to colonize areas burned over by fire.

New Jersey tea is a common plant throughout much of the eastern United States. The tea from the dried leaves is similar to oriental tea in flavor.

PLANT DESCRIPTION New Jersey tea is a small deciduous shrub, attaining a maximum height of about 3 feet. While the lower trunk is woody, the terminal branches are herbaceous. Leaves are opposite, oblong-ovate, with serrated margins and prominent, curving veins. Small, white, 5-petalled flowers are borne in showy 2-inch, oval clusters. These typically appear from May through July. The fruit is a three-lobed capsule. The roots, which have red outer bark, consist of a strong taproot and extensive mats of support roots. The roots have nodules that house nitrogen-fixing fungi. This plant is long lived and may resprout from the roots if burned or mowed over.

FLAVOR AND SCENT The leaves and twigs have a mild, wintergreen scent if crushed. When brewed into a tea, the flavor is very similar to oriental tea—one of the world's most popular beverages. The flowers are fragrant and are attractive to bees, hummingbirds, and several species of butterflies.

VARIETIES Natural hybrids have occurred between New Jersey tea and other *Ceanothus* species. Most plants are grown from seed and special selections are not readily available.

RELATIVES New Jersey tea is a member of the Rhamnaceae or buckthorn family. This family consists of about 50 genera and 850 species. It contains a few species with edible fruit, such as the Chinese jujube, *Ziziphus zizyphus*, and the Japanese raisin tree, *Hovenia dulcis*. The *Ceanothus* genus contains about 50 species, many of which are native to western North America. Blue blossom or wild lilac, *Ceanothus thyrsiflorus*, is native to California and is popular with native plant enthusiasts in that state. The only other member of the genus native to Florida appears to be the littleleaf buckbrush, *Ceanothus microphyllus*.

CULTIVATION New Jersey tea is a tough, durable plant. It prospers in well-drained soils and is drought tolerant once established. It will take full sun to partial shade. New Jersey tea is difficult to transplant. However, It can be propagated through seed or from cuttings. Seed sown in the fall or winter will germinate the following spring. It has few serious pests, although scale insects and mealybugs occasionally invade the foliage.

HARVEST AND USE Tender new leaves are harvested in late spring or early summer, usually when the plant is in flower. They are then dried in the shade. When steeped in hot water, New Jersey tea produces a pleasant-tasting beverage. It can be served hot or chilled. The root has reported medicinal uses, although these are not covered here. The fresh flowers, if crushed and ground in warm water, form a lather that can be used as a shampoo or soap substitute.

Oregano

SCIENTIFIC NAME: *Origanum* spp.
FAMILY: Lamiaceae
OTHER COMMON NAMES: Wild Marjoram, Orégano
  (Spanish)

Herbaceous Perennial

Planted in Spring

Planted in Fall

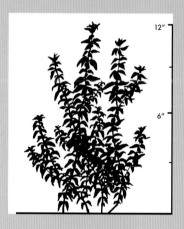

12"

6"

Characteristics

Overall Rating	★★★★
Ease of Care	★★★
Utility	★★★★★
Landscape Value	★★★
Salt Tolerance	★
Drought Tolerance	★★★
Heat/Humidity Tolerance	★★
Cold Tolerance	★★★
Shade Tolerance	★★
Longevity	★★

This book has already profiled two oregano substitutes—Cuban oregano and Mexican oregano. Here it presents true oregano, considered to be an essential spice in Italian cooking. Oregano has a long history of culinary and medicinal uses, dating back to the time of the ancient Greeks and earlier cultures. While oregano may prefer a drier, less humid climate than exists in Florida, it can nevertheless succeed admirably in most areas of the state.

Known Hazards

Oregano contains high levels of salicylates, and consumption may cause reactions in those who are intolerant of these compounds.

GEOGRAPHIC DISTRIBUTION Oregano is indigenous to the Mediterranean region.

PLANT DESCRIPTION Oregano is a short-lived perennial herb that is often treated as an annual. It is variable in form. Depending on the variety, it may grow to a height of between 6 inches and 2 feet. Lower stems are semi-woody. Newer growth is usually upright, although some types sprawl into a moundlike groundcover. The leaves are oval and entire, measuring between 1 and 1 1/2 inches in length. Tiny white or purple-white tubular flowers appear in the summer. These form among whorls of bracts that surround long spikes.

FLAVOR AND SCENT The flavor is warm, earthy, and slightly bitter. The scent is aromatic.

VARIETIES The contours of the *Origanum* genus are a source of taxonomic confusion. Common oregano, *Origanum vulgare*, is the plant most identified with the spice. It has given rise to various cultivar groups, including Italian oregano and Sicilian oregano. Cultivars include 'Aureum,' 'Aureum Crispum,' 'Compactum,' 'Heiderose,' 'Herrenhausen,' 'Rosenkuppel,' 'Thumble,' and 'Vidre.' Other species that fall within the genus and that are commonly referred to as oregano include Crete oregano, *Origanum dictamnus*; Greek oregano, *Origanum vulgare hirtum* (formerly *Origanum heracleoticum*); showy oregano, *Origanum pulchellum*; and Turkistan oregano, *Origanum tytthantum*.

RELATIVES Oregano is a member of the Lamiaceae or mint family. Species discussed within this book include basil, *Ocimum* spp.; bee balm, *Monarda didyma*; Cuban oregano, *Plectranthus amboinicus*; Jamaican mint, *Micromeria viminea*; lavender, *Lavandula* spp.; lemon balm, *Melissa officinalis*; mint, *Mentha* spp.; perilla, *Perilla frutescens*; rosemary, *Rosmarinus officinalis*; sage, *Salvia officinalis*; savory, *Satureja* spp.; and thyme, *Thymus* spp.

Marjoram, *Origanum majorana*, from southwest Asia, is closely related to oregano. It does not receive separate coverage here, because its habit of growth is so similar to that of oregano. However, the flavor is more delicate and less pungent than that of oregano. Egypt is the world's largest producer of marjoram.

CULTIVATION Oregano requires full sun and well-drained soil. It prefers neutral to slightly alkaline soils, although it will endure a wide pH range. Plants are usually started from seed, although the quality may be variable. In north Florida, seeds should be planted in the spring, after the threat of cold temperatures has passed. In south Florida, oregano is often grown as a cool-season herb.

If grown as a perennial, plants should be divided every two years through root division.

HARVEST AND USE Leaves can be harvested at any time for fresh use. However, they peak in flavor just before the plant goes to flower, as soon as the flower buds form. If the top portions of the plant are removed at that point in time, the plant will continue to put out new shoots, allowing for a second harvest. The leaves should be removed from the stems and dried in a shaded location with good air circulation. For reasons that are unknown, the flavors in dried oregano tend to be more concentrated than those in the fresh leaves. So that it will retain its aromatic flavor and essential character, oregano should be added toward the end of the cooking process. Oregano combines especially well with tomatoes and eggplant. It is often an ingredient in pizza.

From top to bottom: oregano cultivars 'Kents Beauty,' 'Variegated,' and Greek 'Kalitera'

Osage Orange

SCIENTIFIC NAME: *Maclura pomifera*
FAMILY: Moraceae
OTHER COMMON NAMES: Hedge Apple, Bowwood

Woody Perennial; Deciduous Tree

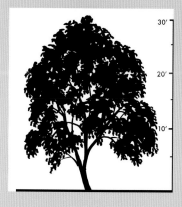

Characteristics

Overall Rating	★★
Ease of Care	★★★★★
Utility	★
Landscape Value	★★★
Salt Tolerance	★
Drought Tolerance	★★★★
Heat/Humidity Tolerance	★★★
Cold Tolerance	★★★★★
Shade Tolerance	★★★
Longevity	★★★★

The Osage orange produces a nonedible, woody fruit renowned for its scent characteristics and for its use as a bug repellent. The essential oil in the fruit contains the chemical 2,3,4,5-tetrahydroxystilbene, which has been shown to repel cockroaches. This attribute alone makes the species worth growing in Florida, where the cockroach is omnipresent.

Known Hazards

Sharp spines may cause mechanical injury. The fruit is inedible, and attempted consumption has been reported to cause vomiting.

GEOGRAPHIC DISTRIBUTION The Osage orange is indigenous to Texas, Oklahoma, Arkansas, Kansas, Missouri, and Louisiana. It has been widely planted in hedgerows throughout the Plains states, where it serves as a windbreak. It was formerly used as a thorny cattle barrier and living fence. The species has been introduced into many areas of the country, including north Florida. A large specimen is present on the grounds of Kanapaha Gardens in Gainesville. This species reportedly grows and fruits as far south as the Orlando area, although its southern limits are untested.

PLANT DESCRIPTION Osage orange is a small- to medium-size deciduous tree, typically growing to about 35 feet. It occasionally reaches a larger size. The trunk is short and the bark is deeply furrowed. The interior wood, which is yellow in color, is strong, dense, and flexible, and has been used in the manufacture of various items, including tool handles and hunting bows. It is impervious to rot and termites. The shiny, dark-green leaves are alternate, 4 or 5 inches in length, oblong-lanceolate in shape. Margins are smooth. The leaves turn yellow before they are shed in the fall. Spines are present at the leaf axils. Flowers, which usually emerge in May, are green and inconspicuous. The species is dioeceous, bearing male and female flowers on separate plants. The female trees appear to be capable of producing fruit even when no male pollinator is nearby. The compound fruit measures up to 5 inches in diameter. The interior is dense and somewhat woody. If damaged, the fruit exudes white latex.

SCENT The mature fruit emits a mild and pleasant orange-citrus scent. This scent is absent from the immature fruit and gradually fades from the mature fruit after it has been picked.

VARIETIES Several thornless, fruitless cultivars have been propagated through cuttings. These include 'Double O,' 'Park,' 'White Shield,' and 'Witchita.' However, the fruit lend visual interest and constitute the primary reason the plant is described within this book.

RELATIVES This species belongs to the Moraceae or mulberry family. This family contains about 40 genera and 1,000 species. Members include various fruiting species such as the fig, *Ficus carica*; red mulberry, *Morus rubra*; black mulberry, *Morus nigra*; and jackfruit, *Artocarpus heterophyllus*.

CULTIVATION The Osage orange is a durable plant and will grow on most soil types. No serious pests or diseases affect this species. It is drought resistant. The tree does require direct sun and will not tolerate significant shade. The species is cold hardy and may require some winter chill for proper development and fruiting.

HARVEST AND USE The fruit turns yellow-green when mature. The tree will often shed quantities of immature fruit over the late summer. The mature fruit can be placed throughout the home, especially in closets, in cabinets, laundry rooms, and other locations subject to invasion by cockroaches and other insect pests. When the fruit turns brown, it should be removed and discarded.

While it may resemble a citrus fruit in appearance, the fruit of the Osage orange is hard, woody, and inedible.

Pandanus

SCIENTIFIC NAME: *Pandanus* spp.
FAMILY: Pandanaceae
OTHER COMMON NAMES: Screwpine, Hala

Woody Perennial; Evergreen Monocot

Characteristics

Overall Rating	★★★
Ease of Care	★★★
Utility	★★★
Landscape Value	★★★★★
Salt Tolerance	★★★★
Drought Tolerance	★★★
Heat/Humidity Tolerance	★★★★★
Cold Tolerance	★★
Shade Tolerance	★★★
Longevity	★★★

The "screwpine" is grown as an ornamental in coastal areas of south Florida. The appearance is dramatic, giving an exotic, tropical feel to the landscape. However, few Floridians realize that other species from the same genus serve as a key flavoring agent in Malaysian, Thai, Indian, and Indonesian cooking. Types suitable for such uses tend to be more compact than those used for landscape purposes. However, they are equally attractive and easy to grow. Edible pandanus is available from a few south Florida nurseries.

Known Hazards

Some varieties of pandanus have sharp spines on the leaf petioles, although these are absent from most varieties used for culinary purposes.

142

GEOGRAPHIC DISTRIBUTION *Pandanus* species are widely distributed throughout Southeast Asia, Polynesia, and other tropical regions. The leaves have been used by various South Pacific cultures for making baskets and floor mats. Species suitable for use in cooking are raised as a minor commercial crop in Hawaii. Fresh and frozen leaves are shipped to Asian markets throughout the United States. In Southeast Asia, it is amost exclusively the leaves that are used for culinary purposes. In India and southern Asia, the male flowers are used in cooking. In Florida, pandanus will only grow in frost-free areas of the southern peninsula.

PLANT DESCRIPTION Pandanus is a palmlike evergreen that can achieve a height of 25 or 30 feet. The varieties that produce leaves used in cooking are more diminutive, rarely exceeding 5 feet in height. The leaves of these types have smooth margins. Varieties of pandanus that are grown for their leaves tend to be sterile, and rarely bear fruit. Pandanus is a monocot. The leaves are borne in a rosette pattern at the end of thick branches. As these drop away, they leave a pattern of spiral scars. Prop roots often extend from the main trunk to the ground. The plants are dioecious, bearing all male or all female flowers. The fruit of some species resembles a spiky pineapple. It is composed of woody sections called "keys."

FLAVOR AND SCENT The leaves give off a distinctive earthy, haylike, nutty fragrance. The flavor, when brought out through cooking, is somewhat reminiscent of roasted breadfruit. It is widely considered to be of the finest tastes of the Orient. The flowers of those species that are grown for their flowers exude a fragrance remininscent of roses, but with a pleasant fruity or resinous element.

VARIETIES The fragrant pandanus, *Pandanus amaryllifolius,* is the species most frequently used in Southeast Asian cooking. It is reproduced from cuttings. The kewra, *Pandanus odoratissimus,* is also used in cooking. The male flower adds its flavor and distrinctive aroma to various Indian dishes.

RELATIVES The Pandanaceae family is composed of about 600 species, which differ in size, leaf color, and fruit characteristics. The common screw pine, *Pandanus utilis,* is widely used as a landscape plant in Florida. It is thought to be endemic to Madagascar and Mauritius. The leaves are stiff, tough, and sword-like. Ribbon-plant, *Pandanus veitchii,* has white-banded, spiny leaves and does not produce fruit. No members of this family are native to Florida or North America.

CULTIVATION The primary factor limiting growth of pandanus in Florida is temperature. Even a brief frost may prove fatal. Regular watering will assist in establishment. However, once it is established, the plant is drought tolerant and resilient. Pandanus will grow in full sun or partial shade.

HARVEST AND USE Leaves are harvested as needed. Before they are added to the cooking pot, they may be torn into strips and knotted for easy retrieval. The leaves can be simmered in coconut milk to impart a unique flavor to curries. The leaves are also used in place of jasmine to flavor rice. To maximize the flavor, remaining liquid should be wrung from the cooked leaves before they are discarded. The leaves lose their flavor and fragrance if they are permitted to dry out. Kewra oil and water are produced from male flowers of the Kewra. The flowers are harvested as soon as they fully emerge, and the aromas are captured and concentrated through distilling.

Several types of pandanus are planted as ornamentals in Florida. These cannot be substituted for the edible species, which can be difficult to find.

Parsley

SCIENTIFIC NAME: *Petroselinum crispum*
FAMILY: Apiaceae
OTHER COMMON NAME: Perejil (Spanish)

Herbaceous Biennial

Planted in Spring

Planted in Fall

10"

5"

Characteristics

Overall Rating	★★★
Ease of Care	★★★
Utility	★★★★
Landscape Value	★★★★
Salt Tolerance	★
Drought Tolerance	★★★
Heat/Humidity Tolerance	★★★
Cold Tolerance	★★★★
Shade Tolerance	★★
Longevity	★★

Known Hazards

Consumption of parsley should be curtailed or limited during pregnancy, as the plant oil is considered a uterine stimulant. This herb should also be avoided while nursing. Parsley contains minute amounts of estragole, which some have identified as a mild carcinogen. Parsley should be avoided by those with kidney and rheumatic ailments.

This familiar relative of the carrot has a mild flavor and is amenable to many uses. It is far more than a garnish. From a nutritional standpoint, it rivals spinach, providing significant protein, alpha and omega oils, iron, and vitamins. Its deep green, ruffled leaves add visual interest to the garden. It is easy to understand why parsley is one of the world's most popular herbs.

144

GEOGRAPHIC DISTRIBUTION Parsley is native to southern Europe and the eastern Mediterranean region. It may have originated in Iran. Parsley is grown on a small scale as a commercial crop in Florida.

Some chefs prefer flat-leaf parsley over curly-leaf parsley because they consider it more flavorful.

PLANT DESCRIPTION Parsley is a low, clumping, biennial herb, reaching a maximum height of about 18 inches. Leaves are compound, usually with 3 or 5 leaflets. The leaflets are deeply lobed and finely cut. During the second year of growth, flower stalks appear, bearing loose umbels of small off-white to yellow flowers.

FLAVOR AND SCENT Parsley has a fresh, slightly bitter, slightly resinous taste.

VARIETIES Three subspecies are recognized. Flat-leaved or Italian parsley, *Petroselinum crispum neapolitanum,* has extremely flavorful leaves and includes numerous cultivars used for culinary purposes. Curly-leaved parsley, *Petroselinum crispum crispum,* has attractive leaves and may be used as a garnish or as a flavoring agent. Turnip-rooted parsley, *Petroselinum crispum tuberosum,* includes cultivars grown as a root crop, especially in Germany.

RELATIVES Other species within the Apiaceae family described within this book include: anise, *Pimpinella anisum;* caraway, *Carum carvi;* chervil, *Anthriscus cerefolium;* cilantro, *Coriandrum sativum;* culantro, *Eryngium foetidum;* cumin, *Cuminum cyminum;* dill, *Anethum graveolens;* fennel, *Foeniculum vulgare;* and lovage, *Levisticum officinale.*

CULTIVATION Parsley will grow in various soils, but prefers slightly acidic to neutral soil. It benefits from regular irrigation, although it also exhibits some drought tolerance. Parsley is grown from seed. Seeds are normally sown in spring in north Florida, and in the fall in frost-free areas of the state. While the seeds may germinate in as little as two weeks, the seeds of some varieties require more than a month to germinate. The germination rate is often poor. Soaking the seeds overnight promotes germination. In south Florida, parsley typically declines or expires during the summer. Parsley is often grown as an annual because the flavor of the leaves is said to decline in the second year of growth. Parsley has a deep taproot and is difficult to transplant.

HARVEST AND USE Parsley can be harvested when needed, with sprigs clipped from the outer fringes of the plant. Parsley loses flavor if dried, so should be used fresh or should be refrigerated or frozen for storage. It will last up to two weeks in the refrigerator. Parsley also loses flavor rapidly with cooking and is best as a fresh ingredient. Its uses as an herb and spice are similar to those of cilantro. Parsley can also be consumed as a vegetable. It is a primary ingredient in tabbouleh, which is very popular in the Middle East, especially Lebanon. Finally, it serves as a breath freshener, effective against garlic. Parsley is an important ingredient in the cuisines of Italy, Turkey, Syria, Lebanon, Jordan, Iran, and the Republic of Georgia. Parsley contains oxalic acid and may be contraindicated for people with kidney and rheumatic ailments. Pregnant women should avoid this herb, as it may stimulate pre-term labor.

Curly-leaf parsley makes an attractive garnish

Dried parsley will do in a pinch, but it is not the equivalent of the fresh herb.

Pepperweed

SCIENTIFIC NAME: *Lepidium virginicum*
FAMILY: Brassicaceae
OTHER COMMON NAMES: Virginia Pepperweed,
   Peppergrass

Herbaceous Annual or Biennial

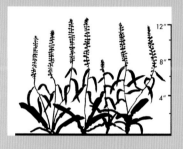

Characteristics

Overall Rating	★
Ease of Care	★★★★★
Utility	★★★
Landscape Value	★
Salt Tolerance	★
Drought Tolerance	★★★★★
Heat/Humidity Tolerance	★★★★★
Cold Tolerance	★★★★
Shade Tolerance	★★★
Longevity	★

Pepperweed is a common native plant. It is rarely, if ever, purposely cultivated. It is easily overlooked and is often considered a nuisance weed. Nevertheless, this mustard relative is a useful herb and spice plant. In fact, its flavor rivals that of black pepper, for which it may be substituted.

Known Hazards

This native plant can invade gardens and lawns. During harvest, care should be taken to avoid areas that have been sprayed with herbicides or other chemicals. Pepperweed may be a contact irritant for hypersensitive individuals.

146

GEOGRAPHIC DISTRIBUTION Pepperweed is found across North America, from Florida to Maine to Oregon. It is present in every county in Florida and is usually considered a nuisance weed. It is common in waste sites, along roadsides, pastures, embankments, and as a garden weed. It thrives in dry, loose soil.

The minute flowers of pepperweed are produced near the growing tip. The hot, peppery flavor of this native spice is concentrated in the seedpods.

PLANT DESCRIPTION This annual or biennial plant typically attains a height of between 8 and 20 inches. The plant initially develops as a low basal rosette, but eventually produces vertical flowering stems. It forms a lengthy taproot, from which the plant will regenerate if partially pulled or mowed over. Flowering occurs over lengthy periods during the growing season. Flowers are small and white to greenish white, with 4 petals. Flat, oval seedpods are borne in great quantity on short racemes surrounding the vertical stem. The seedpods eventually dry out and drop from the plant over the winter.

FLAVOR AND SCENT All parts of the plant have a peppery, somewhat hot taste, although this flavor is concentrated in the young seedpods.

VARIETIES No varieties have been selected.

RELATIVES Pepperweed is a member of the Brassicaceae or mustard family. This family consists of about 325 genera and 3,500 species. Other members covered within this book include horseradish, *Armoracia rusticana*; mustard, *Brassica* spp.; sea rocket, *Cakile edentula*; and watercress, *Nasturtium nasturtium-aquaticum*. The *Lepidium* genus is widely distributed around the world and contains about 170 species, including various cresses. Field pepperwort, *Lepidium campestre*, is native to Europe but is present in many areas of western North America and in at least one location in Florida. It is considered an invasive exotic. Despite the ecological threat posed by this plant, it can be used for culinary purposes in the same manner as native pepperweed. Maca, *Lepidium peruvianum*, is a member of the genus used as a root vegetable. It is native to Peru.

CULTIVATION This book does not recommend planting pepperweed, as the plant is virtually impossible to eliminate once established. It is a tough plant, capable of withstanding drought, poor soil, and other unfavorable conditions. It prefers direct sun but can tolerate some shade. In light of its abundance and wide distribution, pepperweed can be readily gathered, usually within a short distance from home.

HARVEST AND USE Despite its status as a weed, this species has several uses. The young leaves serve as a cooked herb. If boiled until tender, they can be added to stews and salads. The seedpods make an acceptable substitute for black pepper. They are best if used when green. The dried pods are papery and retain little flavor.

If not controlled, pepperweed can quickly take over portions of the garden.

Perilla

SCIENTIFIC NAME: *Perilla frutescens*
FAMILY: Lamiaceae
OTHER COMMON NAMES: Shiso, Beefsteak Plant

Herbaceous Annual

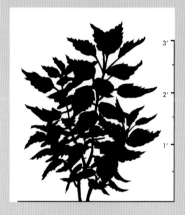

Characteristics

Overall Rating	★★★
Ease of Care	★★★★★
Utility	★★★★
Landscape Value	★★★★
Salt Tolerance	★
Drought Tolerance	★★★
Heat/Humidity Tolerance	★★★★
Cold Tolerance	★★★
Shade Tolerance	★★
Longevity	★★

This member of the mint family is a familiar herb in the Orient. It is, however, with some reluctance that perilla is presented as an herb for Florida homeowners. It is an invasive exotic and is difficult to eradicate once established. At the same time, it is easy to grow, ornamental, flavorful, and nutritious. It resembles a large-leafed basil or coleus in appearance. Its uses are similar to those of basil.

Known Hazards

While generally considered safe for human consumption, perilla has been implicated in livestock poisonings, especially when consumed in large quantities during flowering. Pregnant women should avoid perilla, as its safety under such circumstances has not been adequately assessed. Perilla is also classified as an invasive exotic.

GEOGRAPHIC DISTRIBUTION Perilla is native to eastern Asia. South Korea is a major producer and exporter. Perilla seed has been used in oil production. Prior to World War II, the United States imported significant quantities of perilla seed oil. Perilla has escaped cultivation in various nations and is considered a nuisance plant in some. It was introduced into the United States as an ornamental. Perilla has become naturalized across much of the eastern United States, including portions of the Florida Panhandle.

PLANT DESCRIPTION Perilla is an annual herb that can grow to a height of about 4 feet. The rate of growth is rapid. The stem is herbaceous and is square in cross section. Some varieties have purple- or burgundy-tinted stems and leaves. When grown in full sun, some types develop bright-purple foliage. The opposite leaves are ovate, with serrated edges. The leaf surface is wrinkled, especially near the edges. The leaves measure between 4 and 6 inches in diameter and are nearly as broad as they are long. Flowering occurs toward the end of summer, usually in August. Erect flower spikes arise from the leaf axils and branch tips. Tiny purple flowers form in whorls. These are followed by small nutlets.

FLAVOR AND SCENT The leaves have a pleasant, sweet flavor with hints of anise, mint, and cinnamon. All parts of the plant exude a pungent, mintlike aroma.

VARIETIES Within the *Perilla* genus, the main species of commercial import is *Perilla frutescens* var. *japonica*. Not all types are suitable for culinary use. Consequently, those who seek to raise this plant as a food item should obtain seeds of a selected cultivar from a reputable source. Cultivars suitable for culinary use include 'Aka Shiso,' 'Ao Shiso,' 'Bronze,' 'Crispa,' 'Green Zizu,' 'Lemon,' 'Purple Zizu,' and 'Shiso Noha.' Varieties with red or purple leaves tend to have a milder flavor than those with green leaves.

RELATIVES Perilla, like a multitude of other herbs, belongs to the Lamiaceae or mint family. Species discussed within this book include basil, *Ocimum* spp.; bee balm, *Monarda didyma*; Cuban oregano, *Plectranthus amboinicus*; Jamaican mint, *Micromeria viminea*; lavender, *Lavandula* spp.; lemon balm, *Melissa officinalis*; mint, *Mentha* spp.; oregano, *Origanum* spp.; rosemary, *Rosmarinus officinalis*; sage, *Salvia officinalis*; savory, *Satureja* spp.; and thyme, *Thymus* spp.

CULTIVATION Perilla is an extremely low-maintenance plant. It is easy to start and easy to grow. It prefers full sun and well-drained soil. It is generally grown from seed. However, the seed must be fresh, as it tends to lose viability over the course of several months. The gardener should consider the invasive potential of this plant when making planting decisions. Keeping the plant in a container and harvesting the plant before it goes to seed might serve to limit its spread.

HARVEST AND USE The leaves can be harvested as needed. Leaves can be frozen for extended storage. The seeds are harvested at the end of the season, before they have an opportunity to disperse. Perilla can be substituted for basil in most recipes that call for basil. It can be stewed as a potherb, added to stir-fry dishes, used as a salad ingredient, and employed as a spice. In terms of usage, it lies midway between a leafy green vegetable and a spicy potherb. Perilla is used extensively in the cuisines of eastern Asia. It is especially popular in Japan, where it is referred to as shiso. There, it is often combined with fish, eaten with sashimi, or used as an ingredient in noodle dishes. It is also popular in Korea. The leaves are pickled to create a dish referred to as kkaennip (perilla leaf kimchi). In both Japan and Korea, the seeds are used as a seasoning in numerous recipes. Perilla also serves as an occasional ingredient in Indonesian, Indian, Vietnamese, and Chinese cooking.

Red Bay

SCIENTIFIC NAME: *Persea borbonia*
FAMILY: Lauraceae

Woody Perennial; Evergreen Tree

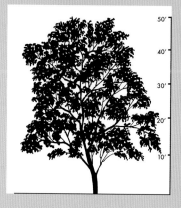

Characteristics

Overall Rating	★★★
Ease of Care	★★
Utility	★★★
Landscape Value	★★★★★
Salt Tolerance	★★★★
Drought Tolerance	★★★
Heat/Humidity Tolerance	★★★★
Cold Tolerance	★★★★
Shade Tolerance	★★★
Longevity	★★★★

Red bay is a native tree that can be substituted for the Mediterranean bay as a culinary spice. This graceful tree makes an outstanding landscape specimen and is available from nurseries specializing in native plants. Once it is established, it requires little or no care. The red bay matures into a beautiful shade tree.

Known Hazards

As with Mediterranean bay, the dried leaves may present a choking hazard unless they are removed from food before it is served.

150

GEOGRAPHIC DISTRIBUTION Red bay is indigenous to the southeastern United States, ranging as far north as Maryland and Delaware. Along the Gulf coast, it can be found as far west as eastern Texas. It grows throughout Florida, including extreme south Florida. It is a bottomland tree, most often associated with swamp margins and river floodplains. However, it has also been found in coastal habitats, such as barrier islands and hammocks immediately behind dunes and coastal scrub.

PLANT DESCRIPTION The red bay is a large evergreen tree capable of attaining a height of over 60 feet and a trunk diameter of 3 feet. A large specimen in Hamilton County, Florida, has attained a height of 77 feet. The bark is brown and deeply furrowed. The canopy is dense and semi-pyramidal in form, although the species can assume a more shrublike form in some instances. The alternate leaves are oblong, pointed, shiny, entire, and measure 3 to 5 inches in length. Inconspicuous yellow flowers appear in late spring. The fruit, which is borne toward the end of summer, is a small, blue-black drupe. The rate of growth is moderate.

FLAVOR AND SCENT The leaves are highly aromatic, with overtones of balsam and menthol. In flavor, they closely resemble those of the bay laurel.

VARIETIES A subspecies, the scrub bay or silk bay, *Persea borbonia humilis*, is native to central Florida and portions of south Florida. It has lower water requirements than red bay, is more shrublike in its habit of growth, and attains a slightly smaller size.

RELATIVES The Lauraceae family, which consists of about 2,000 species, is widely distributed throughout the world's tropical, subtropical, and warm-temperate regions. The *Persea* genus contains about 120 species. Swamp bay, *Persea palustris*, is an indigenous tree found throughout the state. It tends to grow in damper locations and has higher water needs than red bay. More distant relatives native to Florida include the endangered Florida licaria, *Licaria triandra*, of Miami-Dade County; and lancewood, *Ocotea coriacea*, from costal areas of the southeastern peninsula. Another distant relative is the avocado, *Persea americana*. Four other relatives—the bay laurel, *Laurus nobilis*; cinnamon, *Cinnamomum verum*; sassafras, *Sassafras albidumare*; and spicebush, *Lindera benzoin*—are covered in separate sections of this book.

CULTIVATION Red bay is a tough tree and is well adapted to Florida growing conditions. It has good drought and salt tolerances. However, it requires some irrigation during establishment. It will also tolerate some shade. Red bay prefers slightly acidic soil, but can endure a broad range of soil types. The wood is strong, but somewhat brittle and the tree tends to break up in hurricane-force winds. Propagation is by seed. This plant has historically been free of any serious pests or diseases. However, a fungus similar to Dutch elm disease has caused the death of some trees in northeast Florida and Georgia. A non-native ambrosia beetle functions as the vector, spreading the disease from one tree to another. In addition, galls sometimes deform the leaves.

HARVEST AND USE The leaves of the red bay can be harvested at any time of year. They are used in the same manner as those of the bay laurel. Like bay laurel, red bay functions as a key ingredient in crab and shrimp boils, and in conch and clam chowders. It can also be used to impart a unique flavor to rice. Leaves should be removed from food before serving as they present a choking hazard. Red bay is an important tree for wildlife. Various songbirds consume the drupes. It is also a host plant to the palamedes swallowtail butterfly.

The avocado, a relative of the red bay, is perhaps the best-known food plant within the Lauraceae family.

Root Beer Plant

SCIENTIFIC NAME: *Piper auritum*
FAMILY: Piperaceae
OTHER COMMON NAMES: Mexican Pepperleaf,
    Hoja Santa (Spanish)

Perennial; Semi-Woody Shrub

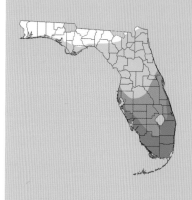

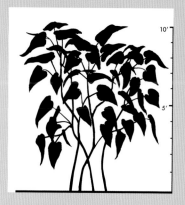

Characteristics

Overall Rating	★
Ease of Care	★★★★
Utility	★
Landscape Value	★★★
Salt Tolerance	★
Drought Tolerance	★★
Heat/Humidity Tolerance	★★★★★
Cold Tolerance	★★★
Shade Tolerance	★★★★★
Longevity	★★★

Known Hazards

Root beer plant has invasive tendencies and is considered an invasive exotic in some locations. The plant contains significant quantities of safrole, which is considered to be a mild carcinogen. Consumption is therefore discouraged.

This attractive, large-leafed member of the black pepper family emits a pleasant fragrance resembling that of root beer. It is introduced within this book strictly as a scent plant. Although it is regularly used in Mexican cooking, its safety as a culinary ingredient is in doubt.

GEOGRAPHIC DISTRIBUTION The root beer plant is native to Central America, ranging from southern Mexico through northern Columbia. The root beer plant will grow in protected areas of north Florida. It may be killed back as a result of winter cold, but will usually regenerate from the roots. Consistent year-round growth is relegated to the southern half of the peninsula. This plant has invaded natural areas on various Pacific Islands. It has also escaped cultivation in Miami-Dade and Broward counties.

PLANT DESCRIPTION The root beer plant is a shrublike perennial capable of attaining a height of about 15 feet. The habit of growth is open and somewhat sprawling. Heart-shaped leaves measure between 8 and 12 inches in length. Minute flowers are borne on elongated spikes. This plant can produce large stands or thickets by sending up suckers from subsurface rhizomes.

SCENT The leaves are aromatic, giving off the scent of root beer spiced with anise and eucalyptus.

VARIETIES No selections have been made of this species.

RELATIVES The family Piperaceae contains about 1,000 species of herbs, shrubs, and understory plants. The *Piper* genus contains the important spice black pepper, *Piper nigrum*, previously described within these pages. Other species of interest within the genus include betel, *Piper betle*, and kava, *Piper methysticum*. The betel leaf has been used as a stimulant for hundreds of years in southern Asia, where it is chewed in conjunction with lime and the areca nut. This practice has been linked with cancers of the mouth and digestive system. Kava is a root crop grown throughout the south Pacific.

CULTIVATION The root beer plant grows best in partially shaded locations. It requires irrigation during periods of low rainfall. It wilts and droops during periods of water stress. However, it will usually spring back to life if supplied with water. The plant can be propagated by separating and replanting new shoots growing from underground rhizomes. Because the root beer plant has displayed invasive tendencies in some locations, the gardener should carefully weigh the impact of planting this species. It should never be located near the margins of natural areas.

HARVEST AND USE The leaves can be used as a strewing herb or can simply be enjoyed in the garden. Root beer plant is sometimes used in cooking, especially in Mexico and the Dominican Republic. When the leaves are used as a wrap, they readily impart their distinctive flavor to pork, chicken, and seafood. The plant has also been used as an ingredient in mole verde and as a flavoring agent for cheese, beverages, and various dishes. However, the safety of this plant for culinary applications is in doubt. Like sassafras, this plant contains safrole, which the United States Food and Drug Administration has banned as a result of its carcinogenic properties.

The root beer plant, a black pepper relative, produces aromatic leaves that can measure over 12 inches in length.

Rose

SCIENTIFIC NAME: *Rosa* spp.
FAMILY: Rosaceae
OTHER COMMON NAME: Rosal (Spanish)

Woody Perennial; Deciduous Shrub

Characteristics

Overall Rating	★★★★
Ease of Care	★★★
Utility	★★
Landscape Value	★★★★★
Salt Tolerance	★★★★
Drought Tolerance	★★★
Heat/Humidity Tolerance	★★★★
Cold Tolerance	★★★★★
Shade Tolerance	★★
Longevity	★★★★

In the United States, the rose is grown as an ornamental and for its pleasant fragrance within the garden. However, the rose has culinary applications in other regions of the world. Rose hips have a high vitamin C content. They may be gathered and consumed as a fruit or, as is more common, processed into syrup. Rose petals lend their scent to rose water, which is one of the primary uses discussed here. They are also dried and used as flavor and aroma agents in Indian cooking.

Known Hazards

Roses have sharp thorns that may cause mechanical injury.

GEOGRAPHIC DISTRIBUTION Wild roses are distributed throughout subtropical and temperate regions of the northern hemisphere.

PLANT DESCRIPTION The rose is a deciduous, climbing shrub, with most species reaching a height of between 2 and 10 feet. Young branches are flexible, somewhat canelike, and armed with sharp prickles. The leaves are compound, with an odd number of leaflets, usually between 3 and 9. Leaflets typically measure from 1 to 3 inches in length. The margins are serrated. The flowers of most non-hybridized species have five petals and five sepals. Following bloom, the ovary swells into a berrylike structure called a rose hip. This has a tough outer layer and soft interior tissue lined with fine hairs and pockets of seeds.

Thousands of cultivars of roses have been bred and selected, primarily for the appearance of their blooms. Most ornamental roses are double-flowered. Wild roses and a few older selections are single-flowered. The flowers have five petals, and each petal has two lobes.

FLAVOR AND SCENT The bouquet of the rose is sweet, pleasant, and familiar. The flavor closely duplicates the smell. The flavor of dried rose petals is delicate and can be overwhelmed by other strong flavors and spices.

VARIETIES Roses with high scent content are favored for culinary purposes. The Damask rose, thought to be a hybrid of *Rosa gallica*, is the primary rose used for the production of rose oil for the perfume industry and for the production of rose water. The cultivar 'Trigintipetala' is considered the premier selection for such purposes. Other cultivars include 'Celsiana,' 'Ispahan,' 'Leda,' 'Quatre Saisons,' and 'Rose de Resht.' Damasks with an extended bloom (perpetual Damasks) include the cultivars 'Cartier,' 'Comte de Chambord,' 'Marbree,' and 'Portland.' Rose-de-mai, *Rosa centifolia*, is also used for culinary and perfume applications. In India, gulab roses from northern regions of the country are favored for culinary purposes. Hybrid teas and other modern roses often bloom over an extended period, but vary in the level of scent they produce.

RELATIVES The Rosaceae is very large family of flowering plants, consisting of more than 100 genera and more than 3,000 species. It contains many important fruiting plants, such as the apple, pear, peach, strawberry, blackberry, raspberry, cherry, quince, and plum. The *Rosa* genus contains over 100 species. Species native to Florida include the Carolina rose, *Rosa carolina*; climbing rose, *Rosa setigera*; and swamp rose, *Rosa palustris*. The only other member of the Rosaceae family covered within this book is the burnet, *Sanguisorba minor*.

CULTIVATION Roses prefer slightly acidic soil. While they will tolerate a wider pH range, they achieve optimal growth on soils with a pH of 6.0 to 6.5. Roses have some salt tolerance and can be grown on barrier islands. Roses are periodically pruned to remove older canes and damaged wood. It should be noted, however, that flowers generally form on canes that are at least 2 years old. Older varieties require less pruning than modern hybrids.

HARVEST AND USE Rose petals can be sun dried and can then be used whole or powdered. Rose water is produced through steam distillation of rose petals. The flowers are harvested as soon as they fully open. They should be quickly used after they are gathered. To make rose water, the flowers are covered with a thin layer of boiling water, and the steam is collected through condensation. The process requires a commercial or homemade still. About 2 quarts of rose petals are required to make a pint of rose water. If the distillation process is carried on for more than an hour with any one batch of flowers, the flavor will be dulled and diluted. If sealed in an airtight container, rose water can be stored in the refrigerator for several weeks. Rose water is an important ingredient in the cuisines of Iran, Bulgaria, Greece, Morocco, India, Lebanon, Syria, and Turkey. It is used in small amounts to flavor yogurt, teas, sweets, pastries, and various beverages. A liqueur known as Gulab is produced from roses in the Udaipur region of India. If the culinary uses of the rose hold no appeal, the gardener can simply use the rose as a scent herb.

Some rose hips are tough, sour, and barely edible, while others provide a worthwhile food source. The hips of a few varieties are pressed to make syrup or oil. Others are used to make jam or rose-hip tea. Rose hips have a high Vitamin C content.

Roselle

SCIENTIFIC NAME: *Hibiscus sabdariffa*
FAMILY: Malvaceae
OTHER COMMON NAMES: Indian Sorrel, Flor de
    Jamaica (Spanish)

Herbaceous Annual

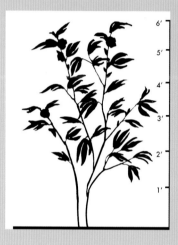

Characteristics

Overall Rating	★★★
Ease of Care	★★★
Utility	★★★
Landscape Value	★★★★
Salt Tolerance	★★
Drought Tolerance	★★
Heat/Humidity Tolerance	★★★★★
Cold Tolerance	★★
Shade Tolerance	★★
Longevity	★★

This hibiscus is grown for its fleshy calyx, which is used to produce syrups and jellies, to flavor beverages, and as a general flavoring and coloring agent. It has found its way into diverse cuisines, such as those of Senegal, Thailand, Trinidad, Jamaica, Egypt, the Philippines, Mexico, China, Panama, and Germany. Roselle is an attractive plant and is particularly well suited to growth in south Florida.

Known Hazards
None

156

GEOGRAPHIC DISTRIBUTION Roselle is native to India, Bangladesh, Myanmar, Thailand, and Malaysia. It was transported to Africa at an early date and may have been introduced into the Americas by African slaves. Today, Thailand and China are the world's largest producers. Quantities are currently imported into the United States for use in herbal teas. Roselle is frost sensitive and requires a long growing season. This species has been grown commercially in Florida. Other Gulf coast states have produced experimental crops. While it can be grown as an annual throughout Florida, roselle is best suited to growth in central and southern portions of the state.

PLANT DESCRIPTION Roselle is an herbaceous annual, reaching a height of between 4 and 7 feet. It is bushy in form. Stems are smooth and are usually tinged with red. Leaves, measuring from 3 to 6 inches, are alternate, with toothed margins and red veins. Leaves are deeply lobed, palmately veined, and somewhat maple-like. Margins may be irregularly serrated or may be relatively smooth. Showy flowers are borne in the leaf axils. These are typically yellow with a maroon spot and measure up to 5 inches in diameter. A red calyx, measuring between 1 1/2 and 2 inches in length, forms at the base. This is divided into five valves, each containing several light brown seeds.

FLAVOR AND SCENT The flavor is somewhat acidic but pleasant and resembles a sweetened cranberry.

VARIETIES Several subspecies have been identified, not all of which are suitable for use as a food item. *Hibiscus sabdariffa altissima* is an erect plant, cultivated for the fiber in its stems. The subspecies discussed here is *Hibiscus sabdariffa* var. *sabdariffa*, which is a bushy herb. Several races exist, with the race Ruber best adapted for culinary use. Cultivars include: 'Archer,' 'F141,' 'Louisiana Red,' 'Louisiana White,' 'Thai Red,' and 'Victor.'

RELATIVES The Malvaceae or mallow family is made up of more than 100 genera and over 1,000 species of flowering plants. Within this family, cotton, *Gossypium* spp., and okra, *Abelmoschus esculentus*, produce crops of commercial import. The *Hibiscus* genus contains about 200 species. Several members are grown as landscape shrubs and ornamentals in Florida. These include the common garden hibiscus, *Hibiscus syriacus*, the red-leaf hibiscus, *Hibiscus acetosella*, and the widely grown Chinese hibiscus, *Hibiscus rosa-sinensis*. Apart from roselle, the only other member of the Malvaceae family covered within this book is cacao, *Theobroma cacao*.

CULTIVATION Roselle is generally grown from seed and the various strains and cultivars come true to seed. Seeds are sown in May in south and central Florida. Competing weeds must be eliminated until the plants are established.

HARVEST AND USE The calyxes mature from late September through January. They can simply be broken off once they have swollen to full size. Harvesting the calyxes stimulates additional flowering. The green leaves are also edible, and can be used as a spinach substitute.

The emerging flower buds of roselle will soon open into showy blooms.

Rosemary

SCIENTIFIC NAME: *Rosmarinus officinalis*
FAMILY: Lamiaceae
OTHER COMMON NAME: Romero (Spanish)

Woody-Perennial; Evergreen Sub-shrub

Characteristics

Overall Rating	★★★★★
Ease of Care	★★★★★
Utility	★★★★★
Landscape Value	★★★★★
Salt Tolerance	★★★★
Drought Tolerance	★★★★
Heat/Humidity Tolerance	★★★★
Cold Tolerance	★★★★★
Shade Tolerance	★★
Longevity	★★★★

Known Hazards

Rosemary oil can be poisonous if ingested in large quantities. While use of rosemary as a spice is considered safe, there are some counter indications against consumption during pregnancy. The plant contains salicylates, and consumption may cause reactions in those who are intolerant of these compounds.

Rosemary is unquestionably one of the easiest, toughest, most attractive, and most rewarding herbs that can be grown in Florida. It deserves to be planted in every home garden. The name is derived from the Latin *rosmarinus*, meaning "dew of the sea." In former times, this plant was used to symbolize remembrance. It is widely used as a seasoning in Italian, Greek, French, Spanish, and some Middle Eastern cuisines. The International Herb Association designated rosemary as the Herb of the Year in 2000.

GEOGRAPHIC DISTRIBUTION Rosemary is native to the Mediterranean region, occurring in scrubland, open woods, hilly terrain, and other habitats. It prefers a mild, relatively dry climate. Rosemary will grow as a perennial throughout Florida. It is not damaged by a light frost. However, in north Florida and the Panhandle it may suffer setbacks as a result of winter cold. Various cultivars are hardy to between 25° F and 10° F.

Rosemary is slow-growing, but eventually fills in to form an attractive specimen. It can be substituted within the landscape in place of other less useful ornamental shrubs.

PLANT DESCRIPTION Rosemary is a perennial shrub or subshrub. Depending on the form and cultivar, the plant may grow to only a few inches in height or may rise to a height of 7 feet. The bark is gray and scaly. Leaves are narrow and needlelike. They are dark green above, light green to white and somewhat cottony below. They range from 1 to 2 inches in length. Small tubular flowers appear in late winter and spring. These are about 1/2 of an inch in length, and vary in color depending on the cultivar. Rosemary can live for more than 60 years.

FLAVOR AND SCENT Rosemary is highly fragrant. The scent is earthy, piney, and pungent. The flavor is warm and pleasant, with a slight hint of camphor.

VARIETIES At least 100 cultivars have been selected over time. These include the following:

'Albus' – This variety has white flowers. It is considered somewhat cold hardy and is capable of surviving north Florida winters outdoors.

'Arp' – This variety, selected in Arp, Texas, is considered one of the most cold-hardy types of rosemary. It has an upright form, light green leaves, and pale blue flowers, which appear in late spring and early summer.

'Aureus' – This cultivar has speckled yellow leaves.

'Beneden Blue' – This cultivar, also known as 'Pine Scented,' is an upright form with very narrow, dark green leaves. Deep blue flowers appear during the summer. This variety is moderately cold hardy.

'Blue Boy' – 'Blue Boy' is a dwarf variety. It is not cold hardy.

'Blue Lady' – This cultivar has narrow leaves and bears blue-violet flowers during the summer.

'Blue Spires' – 'Blue Spires' is an attractive variety that sweeps outward to form tall vertical branches. Flowers are blue.

'Collingwood Ingram' – This cultivar has a creeping habit of growth. It is not especially cold tolerant.

'Golden Rain' – 'Golden Rain' has yellow streaks along the leaf margins. It has an upright habit of growth.

'Herb Cottage' – This is an upright, compact, broad-leaved variety. It is moderately cold hardy.

'Hill Hardy' – This upright variety, alternately known as 'Madeline Hill,' has thin, needlelike foliage. It is cold hardy throughout Florida, in all but the coldest winters.

'Irene' – 'Irene' is a trailing variety with an attractive, mounding habit of growth. The violet flowers are borne in the spring.

'Logee Blue' – This upright cultivar is vigorous and densely foliated. The foliage is blue-green.

'Majorica Pink' – This is a cascading form with pink flowers. It is not cold hardy.

'Miss Jessup' – This variety is tall and has an erect habit of growth. It is considered moderately cold hardy.

'Prostratus' – 'Prostratus' is a mounding variety, capable of spreading over several square feet. Flowers are pale lavender-blue.

'Rex' – 'Rex' is an upright variety with dark green foliage. It produces blue flowers during the summer.

'Russian River' – This variety is considered somewhat cold hardy.

'Salem' – This is an upright, deep green cultivar with good cold tolerance. Flowers are violet-blue.

'Santa Barbara' – This is a low growing cultivar that produces dark blue flowers. It is not cold tolerant.

'Sawyer's Selection' – This is one of the tallest forms of rosemary, capable of reaching up 7 feet in height.

'Severn Sea' – 'Severn Sea' is a semi-prostrate variety. Flowers are violet.

'Spice Islands' – This is an erect, thickly

Dried rosemary leaves will gradually lose their flavor unless they are stored in a dark location and in an airtight container.

foliated cultivar that bears dark blue flowers in late winter.

'Tuscan Blue' – 'Tuscan Blue' is an upright cultivar that produces heavy blooms of blue flowers during the late summer.

RELATIVES Rosemary is a member of the Lamiaceae or mint family. This family contains about 7,000 species. Among these are numerous herbs with culinary applications. Those discussed within this book include basil, *Ocimum* spp.; bee balm, *Monarda didyma*; Cuban oregano, *Plectranthus amboinicus*; Jamaican mint, *Micromeria viminea*; lavender, *Lavandula* spp.; lemon balm, *Melissa officinalis*; mint, *Mentha* spp.; oregano, *Origanum* spp.; perilla, *Perilla frutescens*; sage, *Salvia officinalis*; savory, *Satureja* spp.; and thyme, *Thymus* spp. The genus *Rosmarinus* contains just two species. The second species, *Rosmarinus eriocalyx*, is a diminutive herb native

to North Africa and Spain.

Several species that belong to closely related genera are native to Florida. Some are aromatic and resemble rosemary in pertinent respects. These so-called "scrub mints" include Apalachicola rosemary, *Conradina glabra*; Etonia false rosemary, *Conradina etonia*; large-flowered rosemary, *Conradina grandiflora*; and wild rosemary, *Conradina canescens*. Several of these plants are threatened or endangered and should not be gathered from the wild. Some are available from nurseries. Florida rosemary, *Ceratiola ericoides*, is a fairly common plant. It grows throughout the state on old dune lines, frequently burned-over sites, and infertile coastal areas. The plant produces a pleasant, honeylike fragrance during the warmer months. A few native plant enthusiasts have substituted wild rosemary for rosemary in cooking, although the safety of this practice is uncertain.

The cultivar 'Tuscan Blue' is robust in its habit of grown and can attain a height of up to 6 feet. It bears ornamental, bright blue flowers.

While it resembles rosemary, the plant shown in this photograph is false rosemary, *Conradina canescens*. This attractive species is native to the Florida Panhandle, occurring in scrub habitat. The entire plant is aromatic, and its scent resembles that of rosemary.

'Prostratus' has a creeping habit of growth, and tends to spread out horizontally. Prostrate rosemary can be used as a groundcover or as a foundation planting.

The flowers come in a variety of colors and are attractive to bees.

CULTIVATION Rosemary is resistant to extreme heat and is moderately resistant to drought. It also has moderate salt tolerance and can be grown in barrier-island gardens. Rosemary does not like wet feet and can be killed by over-watering. While rosemary can withstand an hour or two of shade, it requires several hours of direct sun each day. Plants grown in heavily shaded areas become leggy and achieve poor growth. Throughout the peninsula, rosemary can be left outdoors during the winter. Several cultivars will survive the winter as far north as the Alabama border. More tender varieties should be brought indoors to avoid the hard freezes that visit that region. Rosemary makes an excellent border planting or foundation planting. It can also be trained as a topiary or grown as bonsai. It can be grown from seed, although germination rates are disappointing. In addition, named cultivars do not always come true to seed. Rosemary is easily propagated from cuttings. A 6-inch sprig is removed from the parent plant, stripped of leaves along its base, dipped in rooting hormone, and planted in moist medium. The plant can also be propagated by ground layering.

HARVEST AND USE Rosemary can be harvested at any time by snipping sprigs from the plant. In fact, the plant will take on a thicker, bushier form if cut back on a frequent basis. No more than 15 percent of the plant should be removed at any one time. Rosemary is at its best when fresh. However, it can also be dried and frozen. Rosemary enhances the flavor of lamb, chicken, pork, and fish. It is a superb roasting and grilling herb. It can be added directly to hot coals to produce a smoky fragrance. It can also be used to flavor olive oil, added to various pickles, steeped as a flavoring for beverages and teas, and included in potpourri mixes.

Rue

SCIENTIFIC NAME: *Ruta graveolens*
FAMILY: Rutaceae
OTHER COMMON NAME: Ruda (Spanish)

Semi-Woody Perennial; Evergreen Sub-shrub

Characteristics

Overall Rating	★★
Ease of Care	★★★★
Utility	★
Landscape Value	★★★★
Salt Tolerance	★
Drought Tolerance	★★★★
Heat/Humidity Tolerance	★★★
Cold Tolerance	★★★★
Shade Tolerance	★★★
Longevity	★★★

Rue was a common spice and herbal medicine from ancient times until the early 1900s. It is still planted with some frequency as an ornamental herb. However, it has fallen into disfavor for culinary purposes. Modern attitudes toward this herb stem, in part, from the fact that it is toxic if consumed in large quantities.

Known Hazards

Consumption of rue should be avoided by those who are pregnant or nursing. Rue is considered a uterine stimulant and abortifacient. Contact with the flowers and foliage of this plant may cause burning, itching, and the formation of vesicles on the skin of sensitive individuals. The effects may be accentuated by exposure to sunlight.

162

GEOGRAPHIC DISTRIBUTION Rue is native to southern Europe. It often grows in rocky, poor, alkaline soils. It is used sparingly in the cuisines of several Mediterranean countries, including Italy. It is an important ingredient in the cuisine of Ethiopia. Rue is well suited to growth in Florida and is widely available.

PLANT DESCRIPTION Rue is a perennial herb. This short-lived evergreen shrub can attain a height of about 30 inches. The lower stem is woody. The foliage is gray-blue. The symbol for the suit of clubs in a card deck may have been modeled on a rue leaf. The tripinnate leaves are borne alternately. They are an important food of the caterpillar of the black swallowtail butterfly. In the late summer, small greenish-yellow flowers form on terminal panicles.

FLAVOR AND SCENT The scent is aromatic, but not altogether pleasant. The taste is sharp and startlingly bitter. The chemical compound responsible for the bitter taste is rutin.

VARIETIES Several cultivars have been selected, including 'Blue Beauty,' 'Curly Girl,' 'Jackman's Blue,' and 'Variegata.'

RELATIVES Rue is a member of the Rutaceae or citrus family, which is made up of about 900 species. It is distantly related to such fruiting plants as the sweet orange and grapefruit. Members of the Rutaceae family described within this book include calamondin, *Citrus mitis*; curry leaf tree, *Muraya koenigii*; kaffir lime, *Citrus hystrix*; lemon, *Citrus limon*; and lime, *Citrus* spp. The *Ruta* genus contains between 8 and 20 species. No members of the genus are endemic to Florida. Other species include Corsican rue, *Ruta corsica*; Egyptian rue, *Ruta angustifolia*; fringed rue, *Ruta chalepensis*; mountain rue, *Ruta montana*, and white-flowered rue, *Ruta albiflora*.

CULTIVATION Rue is not demanding in its cultural requirements. It prefers full sun. It is drought tolerant, once established. It will succeed on nearly any soil type, as long as drainage is adequate. Rue can be grown from seed or cuttings.

HARVEST AND USE Rue may be added to various dishes, but should be used in very small quantities. It can quickly overpower other flavors. The leaves can be added to meat sauce, eggs, cheese, cream cheese, salads, and other foods that might benefit from a hint of bitterness. It can be used to offset the acidity of tomato-based sauces. Fresh leaves are preferred, as the dried herb loses much of its fragrance but none of its bitterness. Rue should not be used to excess. While it would be difficult to consume sufficient quantities to pose any danger, large amounts have been known to cause vomiting and other symptoms. Pregnant women should not consume this herb as it may function as an abortifacient. In addition, some find the sap to be a skin irritant. Consequently, gloves should be worn when harvesting rue. Some individuals are highly allergic to rue. Following exposure or ingestion, such persons may experience photosensitivity and severe dermatitis. Yet, even with these drawbacks and potential dangers, rue is worth growing for the beauty of its foliage and as an occasional culinary herb.

Rue, sometimes referred to as the "herb of grace," is distantly related to citrus, although it bears little outward resemblance.

Rumberry

SCIENTIFIC NAME: *Myrciaria floribunda*
FAMILY: Myrtaceae
OTHER COMMON NAMES: Guavaberry, Guayabito
   (Spanish)

Woody Perennial; Evergreen Shrub

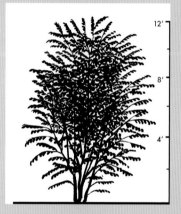

Characteristics

Overall Rating	★★★
Ease of Care	★★★★★
Utility	★★
Landscape Value	★★★★★
Salt Tolerance	★★
Drought Tolerance	★★★
Heat/Humidity Tolerance	★★★★★
Cold Tolerance	★★
Shade Tolerance	★★
Longevity	★★★★

The rumberry is a beautiful landscape specimen. It is resistant to hurricanes and drought. It flowers prolifically and bears prodigious crops of berries. The berries are small, scant-fleshed, and sour until fully ripe. They are only marginally appealing when eaten out of hand. However, when sweetened and used as a flavoring agent, the berries become a source of delight.

Known Hazards

None

GEOGRAPHIC DISTRIBUTION Rumberry is native to the Caribbean and coastal areas of Central America and northern South America. It is common in the Virgin Islands, Cuba, the Antilles, Puerto Rico, Trinidad, and Jamaica. Guavaberry liqueur is popular in St. Maarten and nearby islands. A Christmas punch made from rumberry is traditionally consumed in the Virgin Islands. In Florida, growth is relegated to southern parts of the peninsula. The tree is capable of tolerating a light frost.

PLANT DESCRIPTION Rumberry is a large evergreen shrub or small, multitrunked tree. It can reach a height of over 30 feet, but rarely grows to this size in Florida. As with many other members of the Myrtaceae family, the bark flakes off in patches, giving the trunk a mottled appearance. Leaves are opposite, oblong-lanceolate, and measure 2 to 3 inches in length. They are arranged at even intervals along terminal branches. Flowers are delicate, white, and tufted, appearing at leaf nodes on new growth. The fruit, which usually contains a single seed, but which occasionally contains two hemispheric seeds, measures about 1/2 of an inch in diameter. It may be yellow, red, dark purple, or black.

FLAVOR The berries are highly aromatic, spicy, and bittersweet. They may be intensely sour if they are consumed before they ripen.

VARIETIES A yellow-fruited variety exists, but is not regularly available in Florida.

RELATIVES The family Myrtaceae is extremely rich in fruiting plants. It includes members such as the cherry of the Rio Grande, *Eugenia aggregata*; feijoa, *Feijoa sellowiana*; grumichama, *Eugenia braziliensis*; and guava, *Psidium guajava*. The *Myrciaria* genus contains about 70 species, primarily from tropical America. The most renowned member is the jaboticaba, *Myrciaria* spp., of Brazil and neighboring countries. The blue grape, *Myrciaria vexator*, also bears a fruit of good quality. In the literature, the rumberry is often confused with the closely related camu-camu, *Myrciaria dubia*, of the Amazon region. However, the camu-camu bears a larger, thick-skinned fruit that is extremely sour and acidic.

CULTIVATION The rumberry is reasonably well suited to growth in south Florida. It will grow on poor soil, but requires irrigation until it is established. Thereafter, it is fairly drought tolerant, although new flushes of leaves tend to wilt in extremely dry weather. Plants in Florida are grown from seed. No significant pest problems or diseases affect this plant.

HARVEST AND USE In Florida, flowers appear in several treewide flushes over the warmer months. The berries ripen sporadically, with the peak of production occurring during late summer and early fall. Berries should not be harvested until they have achieved full color. The berries are picked by hand, which can be a laborious task given the small size of the fruit, the prolific numbers in which it appears, and its tendency to ripen unevenly. Rumberry can be used in beverages, tarts, pies, ice cream, and jellies. The strained pulp is combined with rum and cane sugar, then aged and fermented, to produce the famed guavaberry liqueur of the West Indies.

Rumberry flowers are attractive and numerous. A tree in bloom may look as if it is caked with snow. However, the flowers are short-lived and begin to wither and turn brown the day after they emerge.

Sage

SCIENTIFIC NAME: *Salvia officinalis*
FAMILY: Lamiaceae
OTHER COMMON NAMES: Garden Sage, Common Sage

Herbaceous Perennial; Evergreen Sub-shrub

Characteristics

Overall Rating	★★★
Ease of Care	★★★★
Utility	★★★
Landscape Value	★★★
Salt Tolerance	★★★
Drought Tolerance	★★★★
Heat/Humidity Tolerance	★★★
Cold Tolerance	★★★
Shade Tolerance	★★
Longevity	★★

Known Hazards

On rare occasions, this plant has been known to cause inflammation of the lips of sensitive individuals. Sage is considered a uterine stimulant, and consumption should be avoided or severely restricted during pregnancy. The plant contains salicylates, and consumption may cause reactions in those who are intolerant to these compounds.

In the past, sage was associated with longevity. Today, it is a popular cooking herb and marinade ingredient. The velvety, gray-green foliage provides an understated accent to the garden. The fact that sage is somewhat drought tolerant, heat tolerant, and easy to grow makes it an outstanding choice for Florida yards. The International Herb Association designated sage as the Herb of the Year in 2001.

GEOGRAPHIC DISTRIBUTION Sage is native to southern Europe and north Africa.

PLANT DESCRIPTION Sage is a short-lived perennial. This evergreen subshrub may grow to a height of about 2 1/2 feet with an equal spread. Lower stems are woody. The foliage is gray-green. Leaf surfaces are somewhat downy and may also be rough in texture. The opposite leaves are spadelike, lanceolate to ovate. They generally measure between 3 and 7 inches in length, depending on the cultivar. Flowers, borne on axillary racemes, come in various tints, but are usually blue, purple, or white.

'Tricolor' sage is a cultivar of *Salvia officinalis*. It is decorative, makes a unique garnish, and is virtually indistinguishable in taste from other culinary sages.

FLAVOR AND SCENT The flavor is mild, slightly peppery. The scent is similar to that of rosemary.

VARIETIES While the common name "sage" can be applied to many species from the genus *Salvia*, the primary species used as a culinary herb is common sage, *Salvia officinalis*. Numerous cultivars have been selected, which include 'Alba,' a white flowered variety; 'Aurea' a small cultivar with yellow leaves; 'Berggarten,' a large-leaved variety; 'Holt's Mammoth,' a large-leaved variety that does not flower; 'Icterina,' a cultivar with variegated leaves; 'Lavandulaefolia' a small-leaved cultivar; 'Purpurascens,' a variety that produces purple-tinged leaves; and 'Tricolor,' a cultivar with white, purple, and green variegated leaves. Another culinary sage that does well in Florida is pineapple sage, *Salvia elegans*.

The gray-green leaf has a rough, pebbly texture above and has a downy, felt-like underside.

RELATIVES The Lamiaceae or mint family contains several important herbs and spices. Species discussed within this book include basil, *Ocimum* spp.; bee balm, *Monarda didyma*; Cuban oregano, *Plectranthus amboinicus*; Jamaican mint, *Micromeria viminea*; lavender, *Lavandula* spp.; lemon balm, *Melissa officinalis*; mint, *Mentha* spp.; oregano, *Origanum* spp.; perilla, *Perilla frutescens*; rosemary, *Rosmarinus officinalis*; savory, *Satureja* spp.; and thyme, *Thymus* spp. Salvia is a very large genus and may contain upwards of 900 species. Other species that are planted in the United States include: blue Brazilian sage, *Salvia guaranitica*; blue oak sage, *Salvia chamaedryoides*; cedar sage, *Salvia roemeriana*; fragrant sage, *Salvia clevelandii*; fruit-scented sage, *Salvia dorisiana*; Guatemalan blue vine sage, *Salvia cacaliaefolia*; Mexican bush sage, *Salvia leucantha*; Mexican sage, *Salvia mexicana*; Mexican purple sage, *Salvia purpurea*; mountain sage, *Salvia regla*; painted salvia, *Salvia viridis*; roseleaf sage, *Salvia involucrata*; scarlet sage, *Salvia coccinea*; silver sage, *Salvia argentea*; snowflake sage, *Salvia chionophylla*; and Texas sage, *Salvia greggii*. Many of the foregoing sages are not edible and are grown purely for ornamental purposes. Diviner's sage, *Salvia divinorum*, is a Mexican species that is the source of a psychedelic drug. Florida criminalized possession of this plant in 2008. Several species within the genus are native to Florida, including azure sage, *Salvia azurea*, of central and north Florida; Florida Keys sage, *Salvia riparia*, of south Florida; tropical sage, *Salvia coccinea*, from scattered locations around the state; lyre leaf sage, *Salvia lyrata*, widely distributed throughout the state; river sage, *Salvia misella*, of peninsular Florida; West Indian sage, *Salvia occidentalis*, of south Florida; and Yucatan sage, *Salvia micrantha*, of extreme south Florida.

CULTIVATION Sage performs best in full sun, but will tolerate some early morning or late afternoon shade. It requires well-drained soil and prefers slightly alkaline soils. It rarely requires irrigation, except during periods of establishment and very dry conditions. Mildew can become a problem under persistently wet conditions. Sage will not succeed if planted in low, damp areas. Sage is somewhat salt tolerant and can be grown on barrier islands if not exposed to volumes of salt spray.

HARVEST AND USE Sage should be cut back and harvested frequently to encourage new growth. Sage can be used fresh, or it can be dried without substantial loss in flavor. Sage is an important ingredient in many European cuisines. It is used in poultry, pork, and lamb dishes, as well as in various stews and sauces. It is used in marinades too. Sage can also be added to omelets, added to stuffing, deep-fried, or can be battered and sautéed.

Sassafras

SCIENTIFIC NAME: *Sassafras albidum*
FAMILY: Lauraceae
OTHER COMMON NAMES: White Sassafras, Sasafrás
   (Spanish)

Woody Perennial; Deciduous Shrub

Characteristics

Overall Rating	★★
Ease of Care	★★★
Utility	★
Landscape Value	★★★
Salt Tolerance	★
Drought Tolerance	★★★★
Heat/Humidity Tolerance	★★★
Cold Tolerance	★★★★★
Shade Tolerance	★★★★
Longevity	★★★★

Native Americans employed this plant for a wide range of purposes. Early settlers also brewed sassafras into various concoctions and home remedies. Sassafras lends its distinctive flavor to the popular soft drink root beer. The main component of the oil derived from the plant, safrole, is a suspected carcinogen. Consequently, sassafras is no longer widely used as a flavoring agent. The leaves, which do not contain significant amounts of safrole, are used in the preparation of filé powder (pronounced FEE-lay), an essential Cajun flavoring and thickening agent. Sassafras brings spectacular fall color to the garden. Its leaves turn red, purple, and orange.

Known Hazards

The entire plant is considered mildly carcinogenic. Concentrated and prolonged doses have been shown to cause liver cancer in laboratory animals. Consumption should be avoided except as specified.

GEOGRAPHIC DISTRIBUTION Sassafras is native to most of the eastern United States, ranging from Maine to Florida, and west to Michigan and Texas. It is also present in southern Canada. It is found throughout north Florida and in scattered locations of peninsular Florida as far south as the Tampa Bay area.

PLANT DESCRIPTION Sassafras is a deciduous shrub or small tree. Under certain conditions, it has been known to achieve a height of 50 feet, although specimens more than 15 feet tall are rare in Florida. Suckers sometimes grow from the roots, and the plant occasionally forms lose thickets. The alternate leaves have from 1 to 3 lobes. The same tree may contain all three basic leaf shapes. Leaves measure up to 7 inches in length. They are of soft texture, with smooth and somewhat rounded margins. In the fall, the leaves turn bright colors before they are shed. The bark of mature trees is brown and furrowed. The wood of young branches is week and pliable. Small yellow-green flowers appear in the spring. These are dioecious. The fruit is an oval, blue-black drupe, measuring less than 1/2 of an inch in length.

FLAVOR AND SCENT All parts of the plant are aromatic when bruised or crushed. The leaves, small twigs, and roots, in particular, give off a distinctive spicy, root-beer scent.

RELATIVES The family Lauraceae contains about 50 genera and as many as 2,000 species. Most members are evergreen. The most important member of the family used for food purposes is the avocado, *Persea americana*, native to Mexico and Central America. The *Sassafras* genus consists of only 2 species. The other species, Chinese sassafras, *Sassafras tzumu*, is native to China. Other members of the Lauraceae family included in this book are the bay laurel, *Laurus nobilis*; cinnamon, *Cinnamomum verum*; red bay, *Persea borbonia*; and spicebush, *Lindera benzoin*.

CULTIVATION Sassafras can be harvested from wild stands or can be brought into the home garden and planted in natural areas. Because it is a pioneering, native species, it requires little care once it has been established. It will grow on sandy, nutrient-poor soils. It is said to prefer full sun, but is frequently seen growing as an understory plant. The rate of growth is fast.

HARVEST AND USE In former times, the root and inner bark of the plant were employed as flavoring for sassafras tea and root beer. In 1976, the Food and Drug Administration banned safrole and sassafras-containing safrole as food additives. Sassafras is still used as the main ingredient in filé powder. The Choctaw Tribe of the Gulf coast first made use of this ingredient. Displaced Acadians in Louisiana later adopted it. Small branches are lopped from the plant in late summer or early fall and dried. The leaves are removed, ground into a fine powder, sifted, and stored for later use. Filé is used at the end of the cooking process or at the table. It is employed sparingly as a thickening agent in gumbo and other dishes. While sassafras reputedly acts as an insect repellent, this property has not been established with scientific certainty.

Sassafras leaves can be oval, mitten-shaped, or can have three lobes. Many animals browse on the foliage, including white-tailed deer, black bears, and rabbits.

Savory

SCIENTIFIC NAME: *Satureja* spp.
FAMILY: Lamiaceae
OTHER COMMON NAME: Tomillo (Spanish)

Herbaceous Annual or Perennial

Planted in Spring

Planted in Fall

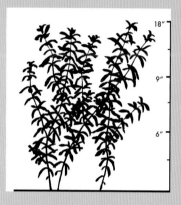

Characteristics

Overall Rating	★★★
Ease of Care	★★★★
Utility	★★★★
Landscape Value	★★★
Salt Tolerance	★
Drought Tolerance	★★★
Heat/Humidity Tolerance	★★★
Cold Tolerance	★★★★
Shade Tolerance	★
Longevity	★★

Savory is a member of the mint family. It was one of the strongest flavoring agents used in European cooking prior to initiation of the spice trade with India. It continues to be important in Italian, Romanian, and Bulgarian cuisines. It is also valued as a landscape specimen.

Known Hazards

None

170

GEOGRAPHIC DISTRIBUTION Savory is native to southern Europe and, possibly, southwestern Asia. It is thought that British colonists first introduced savory to North America. Several relatives are native to Florida. Savory can be grown throughout Florida, and winter savory is cold hardy in all areas of the state.

PLANT DESCRIPTION Savory is a low, annual herb or short-lived perennial capable of reaching a height of about 18 inches. Leaves are lanceolate, medium green and shiny, and typically measure about 1 inch in length. Flowering occurs in late summer. Flowers are lavender, pink, or white.

FLAVOR AND SCENT The flavor is strong, spicy, aromatic, slightly bitter, and slightly peppery. Summer savory is said to have a more delicate flavor than winter savory, although the two types are almost indistinguishable. Savory resembles thyme, in taste and especially in aroma, and lends itself to similar uses.

VARIETIES Summer savory, *Satureja hortensis*, is an annual that is widely used as a culinary ingredient. Winter savory, *Satureja montana*, is a woody perennial that usually grows for about 3 years before it begins to decline.

RELATIVES Savory is a member of the Lamiaceae or mint family. Other family members discussed within this book include basil, *Ocimum* spp.; bee balm, *Monarda didyma*; Cuban oregano, *Plectranthus amboinicus*; Jamaican mint, *Micromeria viminea*; lavender, *Lavandula* spp.; lemon balm, *Melissa officinalis*; mint, *Mentha* spp.; oregano, *Origanum* spp.; perilla, *Perilla frutescens*; rosemary, *Rosmarinus officinalis*; sage, *Salvia officinalis*; and thyme, *Thymus* spp. The genus *Satureja* is composed of about 40 species. Other members of the genus used for culinary purposes include the Chilean shrub mint, *Satureja multiflora*; lemon savory, *Satureja biflora*, from Africa; Oregon tea, *Satureja douglasii*, native to western parts of North America; and thyme-leaved savory, *Satureja thymbra*, native to the Mediterranean and Middle East. Other species, grown primarily as ornamentals, include Alpine calamint, *Satureja alpine*, and calamint, *Satureja calamintha*. At least 6 species that are placed by some authorities within the *Satureja* genus are native to Florida. These include Ashe's calamint, *Satureja ashei*, of central Florida; Brown's savory, *Satureja brownei*, from scattered locations throughout the state; Florida catamint, *Satureja dentata*, from the central Panhandle; Georgia catamint, *Satureja georgiana*, from a few Panhandle locations; scarlet catamint, *Satureja macrocalyx*, with separate populations in the Panhandle and central Florida; and wild pennyroyal, *Satureja rigida*, of peninsular Florida.

CULTIVATION In north Florida, seed should be sown as soon as the danger of frost has passed. Like many other temperate herbs, savory fares poorly in the heat and humidity of summer in peninsular Florida. Gardeners within subtropical areas of the state should start this herb in the fall. They can attempt to coax this plant through summer conditions by providing afternoon shade and perfect drainage, or they can treat it as an annual. Seeds germinate in 2 or 3 weeks. The plant prefers well-drained soil. Winter savory should be trimmed back in early spring to promote vegetative growth. Summer savory self sows. Unless this effect is sought, the plant should cut down before it bolts.

HARVEST AND USE Leaves are harvested as needed. Young leaves of winter savory are more tender than older leaves. Savory can be used fresh as an ingredient in tomato-based sauces and to flavor dishes containing beans, lentils, pork, poultry, eggs, cabbage, and potatoes. Savory is sometimes used to flavor sausages and salami. Leaves can be dried, in which case whole branches are hung upside down in a dark location with good air circulation. The flavor weakens with cooking and is very nearly extinguished through prolonged stewing. Consequently, savory should be added toward the end of the cooking process.

Winter savory, while perhaps not as popular as summer savory, has the advantage of being a perennial herb. The flavor is slightly stronger than that of summer savory.

Sea Rocket

SCIENTIFIC NAME: *Cakile edentula*
FAMILY: Brassicaceae
OTHER COMMON NAME: American Sea Rocket

Herbaceous Perennial; Succulant

Characteristics

Overall Rating	★★
Ease of Care	★★★
Utility	★★★
Landscape Value	★★★
Salt Tolerance	★★★★★
Drought Tolerance	★★★★
Heat/Humidity Tolerance	★★★
Cold Tolerance	★★★★
Shade Tolerance	★
Longevity	★★

Sea rocket is a native plant with several desirable qualities. Most notably, it will grow in nutrient-poor sand on the coast and barrier islands, where few other plants will survive. While sea rocket may not rank within the upper echelon of herbs in terms of flavor, it provides the savvy grower with opportunity in a challenging environment.

Known Hazards

Regulations should be consulted before gathering any part of this plant from wild settings. Sea rocket helps prevent beach erosion.

172

GEOGRAPHIC DISTRIBUTION This species ranges from Florida up the eastern seaboard to Newfoundland and as far west as Wisconsin. It is also found along the Gulf coast as far west as Louisiana. It is primarily an inhabitant of beaches and barrier islands. While it can tolerate some salt, it typically grows well above the high-tide mark and is also found along freshwater beaches. This plant is relatively common in Florida and appears to be secure throughout its range, although populations often shift with the dunes. It plays an important role in checking beach erosion, so state and local regulations should be consulted before harvesting plant material from the wild.

PLANT DESCRIPTION This low, sprawling, succulent plant reaches a height of 5 to 18 inches. It is an annual throughout most of its range. The white, hermaphroditic flowers measure less than 1/2 of an inch in diameter. They have four petals and are in evidence from June through September. Insects pollinate the flowers. Two-segmented fruit ripen from August through October. These may be dispersed by waves. Curiously, recent studies suggest that the sea rocket can "recognize" other sea rockets growing nearby. While a sea rocket plant will readily send out roots to compete with other species, it refrains from sending out roots to compete directly with other sea rockets.

FLAVOR The leaves and young stems have a distinctive, horseradish-like flavor, but become somewhat bitter with age.

VARIETIES At least one subspecies has been recognized: Harper's sea rocket, *Cakile edentula harperi*. In addition, several unnamed strains or varieties have been observed.

RELATIVES The Brassicacea family, which is made up of about 3,500 species, includes a number of important spices, herbs, and leafy vegetables. Other members of the Brassicaceae family covered within this book include horseradish, *Armoracia rusticana*; mustard, *brassica* spp.; pepperweed, *Lepidium verginicum*; and watercress, *Nasturtium nasturtium-aquaticum*. The *Cakile* genus consists of about seven species. The sea rocket is closely related to *Cakile maritima*, native to Europe, which is also edible.

CULTIVATION This plant can be readily established in the home garden. Seeds may not be readily available from seed supply companies, but can sometimes be obtained from the wild. They are planted in the spring. Germination is typically rapid. The plant requires loose, sandy soil and full sun.

HARVEST AND USE Although sea rocket has sometimes been described as a "survival" food, young leaves are tender, mild, and can be quite flavorful. Unlike some native plants, they are not just edible, but are actually worth eating. The young leaves can be consumed raw and can be added to salads. Older leaves become somewhat stronger-tasting and are best prepared as a potherb. The seedpods and flowers are also edible. The root, while certainly not the most desirable fare, can be ground into a powder and combined with other flours to make bread.

Sesame

SCIENTIFIC NAME: *Sesamum indicum*
FAMILY: Pedaliaceae
OTHER COMMON NAME: Sésamo (Spanish)

Herbaceous Annual

Characteristics

Overall Rating	★★
Ease of Care	★★★
Utility	★★
Landscape Value	★★
Salt Tolerance	★
Drought Tolerance	★★★★
Heat/Humidity Tolerance	★★★
Cold Tolerance	★★
Shade Tolerance	★
Longevity	★

Sesame is an important seed crop. It is cultivated for use as a condiment and mild spice. It is also used in nutritive pastes and for use in the production of sesame oil. The plant itself is attractive, with showy, bell-shaped flowers and an erect habit of growth. The primary obstacle to growing sesame in Florida is the fact that sesame is a dry-weather crop and that summers in Florida are wet

Known Hazards
None

174

GEOGRAPHIC DISTRIBUTION Sesame is thought to be the world's oldest oil-seed crop. Although its precise origin is uncertain, sesame is thought to have first been cultivated in India. Close relatives are indigenous to southern Asia and Africa. It was grown in ancient Assyria over 4,000 years ago. It is thought that African slaves first brought the seeds to North America. Thomas Jefferson experimented with sesame in his gardens at Monticello. Today, the world's largest producer is India. Significant production also occurs in China, Turkey, Africa, and Latin America, especially Mexico. Some commercial production occurs in the southwestern United States, primarily Texas. Sesame requires a long growing season and is not suitable for growth in northern regions.

PLANT DESCRIPTION Sesame is an annual herb, erect in form, capable of attaining a height of 4 feet, but usually topping out at about 2 feet. The stem is lightly pubescent. Leaves are medium green and opposite, measuring 3 to 6 inches in length. They are lanceolate to ovate-oblong. Leaves toward the top of the stem are narrow. Those toward the base are thicker and may be lobed. Flowers are white to rose. Grooved seedpods follow the flowers. Each may contain more than 100 seeds. Upon maturity, the seedpods burst open, dispelling their contents.

FLAVOR AND SCENT The flavor is nutty, warm, and rich. The fragrance is light and earthy.

VARIETIES Sesame is variable, and various lines have been selected for commercial production. Germplasm banks have been established in the United States and in Japan. Cultivars include, 'Aceitera,' 'Arawaca,' 'Blanco,' 'Cal Beauty,' 'Dulce,' 'Inamar,' 'Llano,' 'Maporal,' 'Margo,' 'Oro,' 'Piritu,' 'S25,' 'S26,' 'S28,' 'S29,' and 'Turen.'

RELATIVES The family Pedaliaceae contains about 15 genera and 75 species. Members are characterized by leaf and stem surfaces coated with mucilaginous hairs, prominent flowers, and hooked or barbed seed capsules. No other species belonging to this family is reviewed with these pages. The genus *Sesamum* consists of about 20 species, most of which are native to Africa.

CULTIVATION Sesame is a tough plant and is drought resistant. However, those cultivars that have shown the highest drought resistance have faired poorly in the moist conditions prevalent in the southeastern United States. Sesame should be planted in full sun. It is almost universally grown from seed. The plants sprout, flower, and produce seed over the course of about 5 months.

HARVEST AND USE The seeds are ready for harvest when the top parts of the stalk dry out. During harvest, care must be taken not to shatter the pod and lose the seed. A paste, tahini, is made from crushed sesame seeds. It is an important ingredient in various Middle Eastern cuisines. The popular spread hummus, depending on the recipe, may be a mixture of tahini, ground chickpeas, olive oil, and other ingredients. The Greek dessert pasteli is made from a combination of sesame seeds and honey. In Japan, sesame is often added to the outer layer of sushi rolls. In the United States, sesame is most frequently encountered on hamburger rolls, bagels, and as a topping on various breads. About 50 percent of the seed weight is made up of oil. The oil is widely used in cooking in Korea, Japan, and China.

Oil-rich sesame seeds have a long history of culinary use. Their presence on hamburger buns is the main way by which many American's become acquainted with this condiment.

Sorrel

SCIENTIFIC NAME: *Rumex acetosa*
FAMILY: Polygonaceae
OTHER COMMON NAMES: Spinach Dock, Alazán
  (Spanish)

Herbaceous Perennial

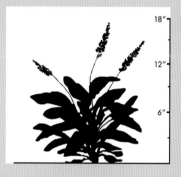

Characteristics

Overall Rating	★★★
Ease of Care	★★★
Utility	★★
Landscape Value	★
Salt Tolerance	★
Drought Tolerance	★★★
Heat/Humidity Tolerance	★★★
Cold Tolerance	★★★
Shade Tolerance	★★
Longevity	★★

Sorrel is an herb that is considered important in France and a few other parts of Europe, but that has fallen into disuse in the United States. It should not be confused with West Indian sorrel, nor should it be confused with various native "sorrels" within the family Oxalidaceae. Sorrel is tough, productive, and requires little care. This under-appreciated plant deserves a prominent place in the Florida herb garden.

Known Hazards

May have some invasive potential. Also, contains oxalic acid. should be avoided by those with kidney stones, kidney disease, and gout.

176

GEOGRAPHIC DISTRIBUTION Sorrel is native to Europe and Asia. It has escaped cultivation in the northeast, in the Great Lakes region, and across much of southern Canada.

PLANT DESCRIPTION Sorrel is a perennial herb that can live for as long as 10 years. The rate of growth is rapid. This erect plant forms clumps that measure up to 2 feet in height. A woody root anchors the base. The plant has oblong leaves with wavy margins that narrow toward the tips. Leaves measure from 3 to 12 inches in length. Spikes of reddish-purple flowers appear during the summer.

FLAVOR AND SCENT The flavor is sour and tangy, but agreeable. The leaves have no discernable scent.

VARIETIES Several cultivars have been selected. 'Belleville' is commonly available in the United States. The cultivar 'Profusion' reportedly does not produce seeds. 'Large de Lyon' is widely planted in Europe. Other cultivars include 'Blond de Lyon,' 'Nobel,' and 'Pallagi Nagylevel.'

RELATIVES The Polygonaceae or smartweed family consists of about 45 genera and 1,100 species. Vietnamese mint, *Persicaria odorata*, covered separately within these pages, is a member of the Polygonaceae family. The seagrape, *Coccoloba uvifera*, is a native fruiting plant that falls within this family. Rhubarb, *Rheum x hybridum*, is also a member of the Polygonaceae family. The genus *Rumex*, which consists of sorrels and docks, contains about 200 species. French sorrel, *Rumex scutatus*, native to Europe, is used in a manner similar to common sorrel. 'Silver Sword' is a well-regarded cultivar. Several members of the *Rumex* genus are native to Florida, including heartwing dock, *Rumex hastatulus*, and swamp dock, *Rumex verticillatus*. However, most species present in Florida have been introduced from elsewhere. Curly dock, *Rumex crispus*; fiddle dock, *Rumex pulcher*; sheep sorrel, *Rumex acetosella*; and tropical dock, *Rumex obovatus*, are exotic species that grow as weeds in Florida.

CULTIVATION Sorrel is a low-maintenance plant. It can be started from seed, from cuttings, or by division. It benefits from enriched soil, but will grow in most soils that are well drained. In Florida it does best in partial shade. The plant has a tendency to go to seed in summer heat. Flower heads should be removed to encourage vegetative growth. Even if the plant dies back during the summer, it is likely to resume growth from the roots once conditions are more to its liking. Sorrel may require irrigation during periods of drought. No significant pests or diseases bother this species. It is hardy to USDA zone 6.

French sorrel, *Rumex scutatus,* like common sorrel, can be used as a fresh herb or as a potherb. The flavor is similar.

HARVEST AND USE Leaves can be removed from the plant as needed. When considered in terms of use, sorrel falls somewhere between an herb and a vegetable. It can be prepared as a potherb, like spinach, or can be used fresh in salads. The French use sorrel in omelets, fish sauce, and various soups. Sorrel leaves contain oxalic acid. This compound is not harmful if consumed in small quantities by those in good health. However, those with kidney stones, kidney disease, gout, or rheumatic ailments should avoid this herb.

Spicebush

SCIENTIFIC NAME: *Lindera benzoin*
FAMILY: Lauraceae

Woody Perennial; Deciduous Shrub

Characteristics

Overall Rating	★★★
Ease of Care	★★★★
Utility	★★★
Landscape Value	★★★
Salt Tolerance	★★
Drought Tolerance	★★★
Heat/Humidity Tolerance	★★
Cold Tolerance	★★★★★
Shade Tolerance	★★★★
Longevity	★★★

This native plant was widely used by the Creeks and other Native Americans as a medicinal plant and as a flavoring agent for teas and beverages. Spicebush makes an attractive addition to a naturalized garden. It and can be grown throughout north and central Florida.

Known Hazards

None

GEOGRAPHIC DISTRIBUTION Spicebush is distributed throughout the eastern United States, from Maine south to Florida and west to Texas. It occurs naturally in the Florida Panhandle and in central Florida as far south as Indian River County. It is an understory plant, often associated with streams and bottomlands.

PLANT DESCRIPTION Spicebush is a deciduous shrub that attains a maximum height of about 12 feet. Several trunks support a rounded, but somewhat open canopy of medium texture. The rate of grow is moderate. The alternate leaves measure from 3 to 6 inches in length. They are elliptical, entire, and light green in color. They turn golden yellow before they are shed in the fall. Small yellow flowers appear in clumps along the branches in March immediately before the leaves emerge. The species is dioeceous, meaning that male and female flowers are borne on separate plants. The male flowers are larger and more attractive. A male pollinator is required for fruit set. The fruit is a red, ovoid drupe, measuring about 1/2 of an inch in length. The fruit persists into the winter after the leaves have dropped.

FLAVOR AND SCENT The foliage and twigs emit a spicy, somewhat lemony scent when crushed. The fruit resembles allspice in flavor, but has a peppery component.

VARIETIES Several selections have been made. These include 'Green Gold' and 'Rubra,' which do not bear fruit. 'Xanthocarpa' bears orange fruit.

RELATIVES The family Lauraceae contains about 50 genera and as many as 2,000 species. The avocado, *Persea americana*, is a prominent fruiting member. Relatives native to Florida include the endangered Florida licaria, *Licaria triandra*, of Miami-Dade County; and lancewood, *Ocotea coriacea*, from coastal areas of the southeastern peninsula. Four other relatives—the bay, *Laurus nobilis*; cinnamon, *Cinnamomum verum*; red bay, *Persea borbonia*; and sassafras, *Sassafras albidumare*—are covered in separate sections of this book.

CULTIVATION Spicebush will grow in partial shade. However, it tends to become leggy in heavily shaded locations. It prefers moist but reasonably well-drained soil. Although it naturally occurs near wetlands, spicebush has a fair degree of drought tolerance. No serious diseases affect the species. It can be grown from seed, sown directly into the ground during the fall, or cold stratified for planting in the spring.

HARVEST AND USE Tea is produced by steeping the leaves or berries in hot water. The flavor is pleasant, but is enhanced with the addition of a sweetener. The leaves lose their flavor when dried, so must be used fresh. The ripe fruit can also be used as a food seasoning. It can be substituted for allspice in most recipes that call for allspice. The fruit will not keep for more than a few days in the refrigerator, but can be frozen for extended storage. The seed is removed before use. Birds consume the fruit. Spicebush is a host plant for the caterpillar of the spicebush swallowtail butterfly.

Spicebush is an attractive addition to the home garden. Its small yellow flowers appear in late winter or early spring. By late summer or early fall, the showy red fruits provide additional ornamentation and serve to attract wildlife.

Star Anise

SCIENTIFIC NAME: *Illicium verum*
FAMILY: Illiciaceae
OTHER COMMON NAME: Anís de Estrella (Spanish)

Woody Perennial; Evergreen Shrub

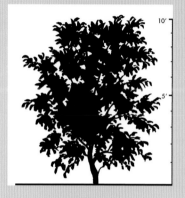

Characteristics

Overall Rating	★★★
Ease of Care	★★★
Utility	★★★
Landscape Value	★★★★
Salt Tolerance	★
Drought Tolerance	★★★
Heat/Humidity Tolerance	★★★★
Cold Tolerance	★★★
Shade Tolerance	★★★★
Longevity	★★★

Although star anise is similar in flavor to anise, the two species are not closely related, nor are they similar in their habits of growth. While anise is an herbaceous annual, star anise is an ornamental, evergreen shrub. Star anise is an attractive, low-maintenance species and makes a valuable addition to the garden in south Florida, central Florida, and in protected locations in north Florida.

Known Hazards

The essential oil from this plant contains minute quantities of safrole, which is considered a mild carcinogen. Only true star anise should be used as a spice and condiment. The closely allied Japanese anise and other related species are poisonous and must not be consumed.

GEOGRAPHIC DISTRIBUTION Star anise is native to southern China. It is grown commercially in India, China, and Indonesia. Star anise can be grown throughout Florida, although it is susceptible to damage from cold winter temperatures in north Florida.

The leaves of star anise closely resemble those of other species within the *Illicium* genus.

PLANT DESCRIPTION Star anise is an evergreen shrub or small evergreen tree capable of living for more than 100 years. Leaves are leathery, dark green, and pointed. The tree has a somewhat magnolialike habit of growth. During the summer, it produces showy, star-shaped, cream-colored flowers. The fruit is a star-shaped, woody, periocarp, with 8 pointed segments. These contain rounded, medium-brown seeds.

FLAVOR AND SCENT The flavor is similar to that of true anise. It is licoricelike, sweet, and aromatic.

VARIETIES No known cultivars exist.

RELATIVES Authorities classify star anise within either the family Illiciacea or the family Schisandraceae, depending on the system of taxonomy employed. The family Schisandraceae consists of about 60 species. The *Illicium* genus contains about 35 species. Star anise is the only plant within the genus used for culinary purposes. Yellow anise, *Illicium parviflorum*, native to Florida and covered in a separate section of this book, is toxic. It is presented within these pages solely for use as a scent agent and strewing herb. Florida anise, *Illicium floridanum*, another native plant covered within these pages, is similarly toxic and has no culinary uses. Japanese star anise, *Illicium anisatum*, is also toxic and has been implicated in serious human poisonings. It is often

planted as an ornamental at Buddhist shrines and is sometimes burned as incense. Due to similarities in appearance, it is virtually impossible to differentiate dried Japanese star anise from its edible counterpart.

CULTIVATION Star anise is well suited to growth in Florida and is not demanding in its cultural requirements. It will take full sun or partial shade, but should be planted in a protected location. It prefers acidic, well-drained soil. It is hardy to about 20° F, but may require winter protection in areas of the state from Ocala northward. Star anise can be grown from seed and can also be started from semi-hardwood cuttings.

HARVEST AND USE Fruiting begins when the tree is about 5 years old. Star anise can be used as a flavoring for tea. It is also sometimes employed as an ingredient in incense. In India, it is used in garam masala seasoning. In China it is used in five-spice powder. Thus, star anise has been used on a broad scale as a food plant and is generally regarded as safe. However, in 2003, the Food and Drug Administration issued a health advisory regarding teas brewed with star anise, based on the inability of authorities to distinguish them from teas brewed with or adulterated by poisonous Japanese star anise. Gardeners who intend to harvest spice for culinary use should make absolutely certain they are planting *Illicium verum*, as most other species within the *Illicium* genus are poisonous or are suspected to be poisonous.

Star anise pods typically have 8 rays. This potent spice is important in Chinese and other cuisines.

Stevia

SCIENTIFIC NAME: *Stevia rebaudiana*
FAMILY: Asteraceae
OTHER COMMON NAMES: Sweet Leaf, Hierba Dulce
(Spanish)

Herbaceous Perennial

Characteristics

Overall Rating	★★
Ease of Care	★★★
Utility	★★★
Landscape Value	★★
Salt Tolerance	★
Drought Tolerance	★★
Heat/Humidity Tolerance	★★★
Cold Tolerance	★
Shade Tolerance	★★
Longevity	★

Stevia is a natural plant sweetener. It has virtually no calories and is several times sweeter than table sugar. At the same time, stevia is not an especially vigorous plant, nor is it especially attractive. However, because stevia shows immense promise as a sweetening agent, it makes a novel addition to the home garden.

Known Hazards

Should not be consumed during pregnancy, as its effects have not been adequately investigated. A few individuals have reported digestive upset following consumption.

GEOGRAPHIC DISTRIBUTION Stevia is native to hilly regions of Brazil and Paraguay. China is the world's largest commercial producer and exporter. Stevia has been used extensively as a sweetener in Japan since the 1970s. While it is available in the United States as a dietary supplement, it has not been approved as a sweetener or food additive. The Food and Drug Administration has taken the position that additional testing is needed before stevia is deemed safe for general consumption. Various food and beverage companies are working to gain approval of stevia-sweetened products.

The use of stevia as a sweetener is rising. However, the flavor is not identical to that of cane sugar.

PLANT DESCRIPTION Apart from its role as a natural sweetener, stevia is an undistinguished plant. It is a perennial subtropical herb in south Florida, but grows as an annual in north Florida. It reaches about 20 inches in height.

FLAVOR AND SCENT The taste is intensely sweet, but is not identical to that of refined sugar. Unlike refined sugar—which rapidly dissolves and disappears in the mouth—the sweetness of stevia lingers on the palate for several minutes after consumption. A very faint licorice note or bitterness may be detectable in the aftertaste, although this does not detract from the overall appeal. The degree of sweetness is determined by the amount of stevioside and rebaudiocide in the leaves of the plant.

VARIETIES Stevia plants vary greatly in terms of the degree of sweetness produced. Major food companies have made use of patented plants in their research. About 100 varieties have been developed worldwide, although few of these are available to recreational gardeners.

RELATIVES Stevia is a member of the Asteraceae or aster family. This is generally recognized as the largest family of flowering plants, containing more than 24,000 species. This book covers several members, including chamomile, *Chamaemilum nobile* and *Matricaria recutita*; chicory, *Cichorium intybus*; goldenrod, *Solidago* spp.; Mexican tarragon, *Tagetes lucida*; and tarragon, *Artemisia dracunculus*.

CULTIVATION Stevia is reasonably easy to grow and can succeed throughout Florida. It prefers sandy, acidic soil, but will adapt to most soil types. The plant is frost tender. Because seedlings are of variable sweetness, stevia should be grown from starter plants or cuttings. Cuttings are easy to root. In south Florida, the species grows as a perennial. However, the plants should be severely cut back upon the advent of cool weather. Plants should be replaced every two years, as they tend to decline in the third year. In north Florida, cuttings should be harvested prior to the onset of cold weather. These may be rooted and grown indoors over the winter and planted out again in the spring. Stevia prefers some midday shade, especially during the summer. The use of shade cloth may be beneficial in some locations. Mulch is also recommended. Stevia requires regular watering, and soil surrounding the plants must not be allowed to completely dry out. At the same time, proper drainage is crucial.

HARVEST AND USE The sweetness within the leaves increases toward fall, shortly before the plants enter their reproductive phase. Plants intended for harvest should not be allowed to flower, as the content of stevioside falls dramatically. Plants harvested during the morning are reportedly sweeter than those harvested later in the day. Branches are severed and hung upside down to dry in a dark, well-ventilated location. The leaves are then separated from the stems and crushed or ground. A tablespoon of crushed leaves is roughly equivalent to a cup of sugar.

Sugarcane

SCIENTIFIC NAME: *Saccharum officinarum*
FAMILY: Poaceae
OTHER COMMON NAME: Caña de Azúcar (Spanish)

Perennial Monocot

Characteristics

Overall Rating	★★★★
Ease of Care	★★★
Utility	★★
Landscape Value	★★
Salt Tolerance	★★
Drought Tolerance	★★
Heat/Humidity Tolerance	★★★★★
Cold Tolerance	★★
Shade Tolerance	★★
Longevity	★★

Known Hazards

Sugarcane is considered a mild allergen. The fibrous consistency of raw chewing cane may present a choking hazard to children and others.

Sugarcane is the last of four sweetening agents covered within this book. It is also, by far, the most commercially important. About 75 percent of the world's sugar is derived from sugarcane. Most of the remainder is derived from sugar beets. Sugarcane can be grown as a backyard crop throughout Florida.

GEOGRAPHIC DISTRIBUTION Sugarcane is native to southern Asia or, possibly, the island of New Guinea. It is primarily a crop of humid, tropical lowlands and has been widely distributed throughout the world's tropical and subtropical regions. It was grown in the Canary Islands prior to 1500. The Spanish probably transported this crop to the West Indies. Prior to the Civil War, several large sugarcane plantations existed in Florida. Today, commercial production continues in areas around the southern rim of Lake Okeechobee, especially in Palm Beach, Hendry, and Glades counties. Florida accounts for about half of the production of cane sugar within the United States. Louisiana, Hawaii, and Texas also have some commercial production. Brazil ranks as the world's largest producer of cane sugar.

Sugarcane is a stout, perennial grass. Most modern cultivars are hybrids of two or more species.

PLANT DESCRIPTION Sugarcane is a robust, somewhat coarse, perennial grass. The stalk, which measures between 1 and 2 inches in diameter, is made up of segments and joints. The space between the nodes varies with the cultivar. The interior of the stalk, which contains the xylem and phloem, is spongy and is laced with vertical fibers and bundles. Leaves form on opposite sides of the nodes. About 10 are usually present on the stalk at any given time. The leaf is composed of a sheath and the blade itself. Blades are swordlike, with sharp edges. Once the cane reaches physical maturity, it produces an inflorescence that may accommodate more than 100,000 tiny flowers. Seeds are numerous and minute.

FLAVOR Sugarcane juice is intensely sweet, and yields about 10 percent sugar by weight when processed.

VARIETIES Sugarcane varieties are developed from multi-species hybrids. Species that may have contributed characteristics to modern cultivars

include *Saccharum robustum*, *Saccharum barberi*, and *Saccharum spontaneum*. Generally, sugarcane is classified as chewing cane, crystal cane, or syrup cane, depending on its intended use. Most home growers and small-scale growers plant chewing cane or syrup cane. Chewing cane varieties include 'CP 57-603,' 'CP 80-1837,' 'CP 80-1907,' 'Florida Red,' 'Georgia Yellow Gal,' 'Java Green,' and 'White Transparent.' Syrup cane varieties include 'Cayana,' 'CP 36-111,' 'CP 52-48,' 'CP 67-500,' and 'Louisiana Ribbon.'

RELATIVES The family Poaceae is composed of the true grasses. It consists of about 600 genera and as many as 10,000 species. It contains many species with economic import, such as bamboo, rice, wheat, oats, barley, corn, and others. The genus *Saccharum* consists of about 20 species. The other grass covered within this book is lemon grass, *Cymbopogon citratus*, used extensively in Asian cooking.

CULTIVATION Sugarcane prefers fertile soil and warm temperatures. Temperatures below 40° F can damage young plants. In south Florida, sugarcane is planted over the winter, and the stalks mature about 12 months after planting. After the stalks are harvested, they are allowed to regrow several times before the old plants are removed and new plants are started. Commercial sugarcane fields are replanted every 3 years, on average. Sugarcane is started from cuttings. It will not come true to seed, since the plant is a multi-species hybrid. Rabbits and roof rats are serious pests, and physical barriers or other controls may prove necessary. Insect pests include the sugarcane borer, *Diatraea saccharalis*; lesser cornstalk borer, *Elasmopalpus lignosellus*; and wire worm, *Melanotus communis*.

HARVEST AND USE In south Florida, sugarcane is typically harvested throughout the winter. Sugar yields increase as the plant matures. While commercial sugarcane is mechanically harvested, the hobbyist can used a machete, cane knife, or lopping shears to fell the cane. The top several nodes can be discarded, as the sugar content is usually low. Commercial operations use heavy rollers to crush the cane and extract the juice.

Freshly cut sugar cane awaiting processing in Turrialba, Costa Rica

Sumac

SCIENTIFIC NAMES: *Rhus copallinum* and *Rhus glabra*
FAMILY: Anacardiaceae
OTHER COMMON NAME: Zumaque (Spanish)

Woody Perennial; Deciduous Shrub

Characteristics

Overall Rating	★★★
Ease of Care	★★★★
Utility	★★★
Landscape Value	★★
Salt Tolerance	★★★★
Drought Tolerance	★★★★
Heat/Humidity Tolerance	★★★★
Cold Tolerance	★★★★★
Shade Tolerance	★★★
Longevity	★★★★

To some, the name "sumac" conjures up visions of anti-itch lotions and ruined summers. However, poison sumac—the plant responsible for such misery—is somewhat scarce. The sumacs addressed here are useful plants that are indigenous to Florida and other areas of eastern North America. Native Americans used sumac for medicinal purposes and for dye. The primary use discussed here is as a flavoring agent. Sumac makes a refreshing lemonade-like beverage or tea.

Known Hazards

Poison sumac can cause severe dermatitis and should be avoided. Other forms of sumac may be mildly allergenic.

GEOGRAPHIC DISTRIBUTION Various sumacs are native to North America and Asia. However, the center of diversity is Africa, where more than 100 species exist. The species described within this section are native to Florida.

PLANT DESCRIPTION Sumac is a deciduous shrub typically reaching a height of 8 to 15 feet. It has an open habit of growth. Leaves are pinnately compound, with between 11 and 31 leaflets. These average about 3 inches in length. Tiny greenish-white or yellowish-white 5-petaled flowers form in the summer. These are borne on erect, many-branched panicles or flower spikes that emerge from the branch tips. Plants are dioecious, bearing all male or all female flowers. The female flowers mature into dense groups of red or reddish-brown berries. Each berry, actually a tiny drupe, measures about 1/4 of an inch in diameter and contains a single hard stone. Growth is rapid, and the life span of an individual plant ranges from 10 to 25 years. Thickets may live on indefinitely. In the fall, the leaves turn bright scarlet and are one of the most visible signs of the change of seasons.

FLAVOR The flavor is sour, with a tart fruitiness. It is aromatic and pleasant.

Winged sumac is found throughout the state of Florida and likely occurs in every county.

VARIETIES Winged sumac, *Rhus copallinum*, is common throughout the state and is present in nearly every county. The leaf stem is winged between the leaflets. Leaflets have smooth margins. The reddish berries are borne in large pendant clusters. Smooth sumac, *Rhus glabra*, is found in the Panhandle. No wings are present, and the leaflets have serrated margins. Reddish berries are borne in upright clusters. These may become pendant as they mature. The berries of both species are well suited to use as a flavoring agent. Staghorn sumac, *Rhus hirta*, the most common sumac in many parts of the country, does not occur naturally as far south as Florida.

RELATIVES The family Anacardiaceae contains about 80 genera. The *Rhus* genus contains about 250 species. Fragrant sumac, *Rhus aromatica*, is scarce in Florida and is found only in the Panhandle. False poison sumac, *Rhus michauxii*, is an endangered species, found only in north-central Florida. Poison sumac, *Toxicodendron vernix*, is an inhabitant of wetlands and is relatively rare. It nevertheless is present in several central and north Florida counties, and was encountered by workers building the Disney theme parks. The plant produces pendant groups of small white berries. Other rash-producing relatives include poisonwood, *Metopium toxiferum*, and poison ivy, *Toxicodendron radicans*. The notorious invasive exotic Brazilian pepper, *Schinus terebinthifolius*, is a member of the Anacardiaceae family. Fruiting plants belonging to the family include the mango, *Mangifera indica*; red mombin, *Spondias purpurea*; yellow mombin, *Spondias mombin*; and ambarella, *Spondias dulcis*. Nut-producing plants include the cashew, *Anacardium occidentale*, and pistachio, *Pistacia vera*.

CULTIVATION The species of sumac discussed here are pioneering species that spring up along roadsides, railroad tracks, abandoned fields, and on other disturbed sites. Indeed, those who are not familiar with its attributes may view sumac as an aggressive weed. This plant is easy to grow. It can withstand poor soil and drought, and prefers dry, sandy soil. Sumac can be reproduced by seed or by separating root suckers from the base of the plant. Unless suckers are removed, the plant may form a thicket. Sumac is nevertheless an attractive plant and makes a suitable addition to any naturalized garden.

HARVEST AND USE Spikes of berries, called bobs, are clipped from the plant when ripe—that is, when the berries are coated with fine red hairs. Berries ripen during the fall and may remain on the plant throughout the winter months. Harvest can therefore be staggered to some degree. However, rains will eventually leach all flavor from the bobs. The berries are rubbed loose from the bunch and steeped in hot water until the water turns a deep red. Beverages made with sumac may be sweetened with honey, sugar, or a sugar substitute. Caution must be exercised not to confuse the sumacs identified here with poison sumac.

Pictured here is a mature bob of staghorn sumac, ready to be clipped from the branch and made into tea. This species, although common in northern states, is not found as far south as Florida.

Tamarind

SCIENTIFIC NAME: *Tamarindus indica*
FAMILY: Fabaceae
OTHER COMMON NAME: Tamarindo (Spanish)

Woody Perennial; Semi-Evergreen Tree

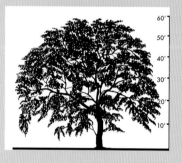

Characteristics

Overall Rating	★★★★
Ease of Care	★★★★
Utility	★★★
Landscape Value	★★★★
Salt Tolerance	★★★★
Drought Tolerance	★★★★★
Heat/Humidity Tolerance	★★★★★
Cold Tolerance	★★★
Shade Tolerance	★★
Longevity	★★★★★

In terms of usage, tamarind lies midway between a fruit and a spice. The fruit, a swollen pod filled with tangy, sour-sweet pulp, is borne in great profusion. The pulp is an important ingredient in Indian cooking and has many uses. The tree is tough, wind resistant, and adaptable. It succeeds admirably in south Florida, where it deserves to be planted on a more frequent basis.

Known Hazards

None

188

GEOGRAPHIC DISTRIBUTION The tamarind is native to tropical regions of eastern Africa. It is grown in many tropical areas of the globe. India, Indonesia, the Philippines, and Thailand are major exporters.

PLANT DESCRIPTION The tamarind is a large evergreen to semi-deciduous tree that may grow to 80 feet. Leaves are alternate, pinnately compound, and made up of between 10 and 26 leaflets arranged in pairs. The leaflets are light green, usually less than an inch in length. They fold closed during cold weather, after sunset, or when the tree is subjected to stress. The trunk is straight and stout, covered in scabrous, dark-gray bark. Most branches are horizontal. The habit of growth is slow to moderate. The tree is long lived and has been known to bear fruit for more than 150 years. Pale, 1-inch flowers are borne on short racemes that emerge from new wood. In Florida, flowering usually occurs in early summer. The fruit is a brown pod, measuring between 3 and 10 inches in length. The pod swells with maturity. Inside, it contains brown pulp surrounding several flat, brown seeds. A few strands of fiber run through the pulp from the base of the pod to the apex. The pulp is thick, sticky, and pasty. As the pod ripens, the pulp shrinks and dehydrates, and the skin becomes brittle.

Tamarind flowers are small and relatively inconspicuous. However, a close inspection shows them to be ornate and attractive.

FLAVOR The flavor is sweet, sour, and tangy.

VARIETIES The tamarind is sometimes grouped into two types. East Indian types have long pods containing 6 to 12 seeds. West Indian types have shorter pods containing 3 to 5 seeds. Superior cultivars, when they can be obtained, include 'Markham,' 'Manilla Sweet,' and 'See Tong.' Several sweet or semi-sweet varieties of tamarind are available in Florida, although these are often reproduced from seed.

RELATIVES The tamarind is a member of the Fabaceae family (formerly Leguminosae). This immense family, estimated to contain between 10,000 and 19,000 species, contains numerous species of economic import. Members of the Fabaceae family described within this book include carob, *Ceratonia siliqua*, and fenugreek, *Trigonella foenum-graecum*.

CULTIVATION The tamarind requires a tropical or subtropical climate. Foliage is damaged at about 28° F. The tree may be severely injured at temperatures of 25° F. The tamarind will grow on various soil types, including poor soils and oolitic limestone. Like most fruit trees, it requires proper drainage. It is somewhat tolerant of salt spray. It will establish readily in windy sites and can withstand hurricane-force winds. The tamarind should be planted in full sun. The tamarind is highly drought tolerant and does not require irrigation. However, some irrigation should be provided to newly planted trees until they become established. Periodic applications of a balanced fertilizer will speed growth. In Florida, few pests and diseases affect the tree. Scales, mealybugs, aphids, and thrips are sometimes present in small numbers, but rarely require treatment. The tamarind is most often grown from seed. Seeds remain viable for up to a year and germinate readily, often within a week. The tree can also be propagated through grafting and air layering.

HARVEST AND USE In Florida, the tamarind usually ripens during the late fall and winter. The tamarind is harvested by hand, by clipping or pulling the pods from the branch. The pods can be stored on the tree for several weeks after they ripen. Once harvested, the pods can be refrigerated and stored for extended periods. A single tree may produce upwards of 250 pounds of pods. The pulp can be used in sauces, gravies, and chutneys. It can be used as a flavoring in drinks and can be combined with sugar to make a delicious candy.

Emerging foliage of the tamarind is tinged with red.

Tarragon

SCIENTIFIC NAME: *Artemisia dracunculus*
FAMILY: Asteraceae
OTHER COMMON NAMES: Dragon's Wort, Estragón
 (Spanish)

Herbaceous Perennial

Planted in Spring

Planted in Fall

Characteristics

Overall Rating	★★★★
Ease of Care	★★★
Utility	★★★★★
Landscape Value	★★★
Salt Tolerance	★
Drought Tolerance	★★★★
Heat/Humidity Tolerance	★★★★
Cold Tolerance	★★★
Shade Tolerance	★★
Longevity	★★★

This herb, frequently employed in the cuisines of southern Europe, is valued for its aromatic leaves. The name "tarragon" is derived from the French, *estragon*, meaning "little dragon." Tarragon can be a difficult herb in peninsular Florida, especially during the summer. However, the superb flavor and handsome growth habit of this herb make it well worth planting in every region of the state.

Known Hazards

A few individuals are severely allergic to this herb. Tarragon contains salicylates, and consumption may cause reactions in those who are intolerant of these compounds. The herb also contains minute amounts of estragole, which some have identified as a carcinogen. Tarragon is considered safe if consumed in moderation.

GEOGRAPHIC DISTRIBUTION Tarragon is indigenous to Europe and Asia. It may also be native to western North America or may have been introduced through early migrations. In Europe, it was not widely used in cooking until the 1500s. Today, it is raised commercially in France and California.

PLANT DESCRIPTION Tarragon is a perennial herb, shrublike in form, attaining a height of 1 to 4 feet. Stems are erect and branching. Leaves are lanceolate and dark green, measuring from 1 to 3 inches in length. Flowers are yellow-green. Plants tend to decline after 3 or 4 years and are periodically replaced.

Tarragon is graceful in habit, as can be seen in this photograph of the slender growth tip.

FLAVOR AND SCENT The flavor is strong, earthy, and warm. It resembles anise and has a distinct licorice component. The scent is mildly pungent.

VARIETIES French tarragon is aromatic and highly flavored, and is preferred for culinary applications. Russian tarragon is a larger, hardier, more aggressive selection, but has a weaker flavor and aroma. It is considered inferior in many respects. Mexican tarragon, *Tagetes lucida*, which is only tangentially related to tarragon, has a flavor and aroma similar to that of French tarragon. Mexican tarragon has better tolerance than tarragon for summer conditions in Florida. It is a worthy substitute in locations where true tarragon struggles.

RELATIVES The genus *Artemisia* contains about 300 species and includes several noteworthy herbs and ornamentals. In the past, wormwood, *Artemisia absinthium*, was used extensively as an ingredient in alcoholic drinks such as vermouth, wormwood beer, and absinthe; however, this usage is less common today. This book describes several other members of the Asteraceae family, including chamomile, *Chamaemilum nobile* and *Matricaria recutita*; chicory, *Cichorium intybus*; goldenrod, *Solidago* spp.; Mexican tarragon, *Tagetes lucida*; and stevia, *Stevia rebaudiana*.

CULTIVATION Tarragon is planted in north Florida after the threat of frost has passed. In south Florida it is often planted in the fall. As noted above, it is difficult to maintain this species through the heat and humidity of the south Florida summer. Providing partial shade, especially during the hottest parts of the day, may help this plant cope with summer conditions. The species is somewhat drought tolerant. Tarragon prefers slightly acidic soil, but will grow in soils with a pH of from 5 to 7.8. Good drainage is a requirement. Tarragon is rarely reproduced from seed, and the plant rarely produces viable seed. It can be established through root division or from cuttings.

HARVEST AND USE Tarragon is often harvested twice during the growing season. However, leaves can be snipped from the plant at any time. This herb is at its best when used fresh. Leaves intended for future use are dried in partial shade. Tarragon, in combination with chervil, chives, and parsley, is an ingredient in the French seasoning *fines herbes*. It is used in Béarnaise sauce, Dijon mustard, tarter sauce, and as an ingredient in flavored vinegars.

Dried tarragon, while not as potent as the fresh herb, nevertheless retains the essential flavor.

Tea

SCIENTIFIC NAME: *Camellia sinensis*
FAMILY: Theaceae
OTHER COMMON NAME: Té (Spanish)

Woody Perennial; Evergreen Shrub

Characteristics

Overall Rating	★★★
Ease of Care	★★★
Utility	★★★
Landscape Value	★★★★
Salt Tolerance	★
Drought Tolerance	★★★★
Heat/Humidity Tolerance	★★★
Cold Tolerance	★★★★
Shade Tolerance	★★★★
Longevity	★★★

Known Hazards

Tea contains caffeine. Excessive consumption can cause nervousness, anxiety, muscle twitches, insomnia, headaches, heart palpitations, and other health disorders. Some studies suggest that pregnant women should limit their intake of caffeine. In addition, caffeine can raise intraocular pressure, and consumption is therefore contraindicated for those with certain forms of glaucoma.

Tea may be the most consumed beverage on earth next to water. It has been a staple drink in China for 3,000 years and has been cultivated in Japan for at least 1,200 years. An ancient Chinese expression holds, "It is better to be deprived of food for three days than to be without tea for one." Tea is a stimulant and health tonic. Social connotations are attached to its use. Given its popularity, adaptability, and beauty, it is incomprehensible why so few people within the United States raise this plant.

GEOGRAPHIC DISTRIBUTION Tea is native to southern China, northern Myanmar, and northeastern India. The word "tea" is reportedly derived from the old Chinese word for the plant. High-quality teas are grown in China, Sri Lanka, Japan, Indonesia, Taiwan, and elsewhere. India is the world's largest producer. In the United States, tea will grow as far north as USDA hardiness zone 7, and will succeed throughout Florida.

PLANT DESCRIPTION Tea is an attractive, upright evergreen shrub or small tree. It can reach a height of up to 16 feet or more if not pruned. The leaves, arranged alternately, measure from 2 to 6 inches in length. The shape is lanceolate and margins are serrate. The fragrant flowers are about an inch and a half in diameter, with 7 or 8 white petals and a spray of yellow stamens. Blooms appear in the fall. The fruit is a dry capsule. The growth rate is moderate.

Tea is an ornamental plant and deserves to be more widely planted in Florida and other warm regions of the United States.

FLAVOR AND SCENT The flavor is mild, slightly astringent, and agreeable. The aroma is light but aromatic, and instantly recognizable.

VARIETIES Tea is often grouped within two subspecies. Chinese tea or small-leaved tea, *Camellia sinensis sinensis*, has a shrublike growth habit with multiple stems. Assam tea or large-leaved tea, *Camellia sinensis assamica*, is treelike in form, with a single trunk. Various hybrids exist between these two subspecies. The Cambodian variety, *Camellia sinensis parvifolia*, is thought to be a hybrid between these two subspecies. The common categories of commercial tea—white tea, green tea, Oolong tea, and black tea—result from different picking and curing techniques, and have nothing to do with the plant variety.

RELATIVES The family Theaceae consists of small trees and bushes, many of which are native to eastern Asia. The *Camellia* genus consists of about 150 species. Many species are highly decorative and produce showy flowers. The most widely planted ornamental species, *Camellia japonica*, has given rise to over 2,000 cultivars.

CULTIVATION Tea requires a tropical or subtropical climate. The plant will briefly endure temperatures as low as 20° F without serious harm. However, a hard freeze, with temperatures dipping into the teens, may prove fatal. Plants grown at higher elevations are said to be of better quality, perhaps as a result of slower growth. Tea generally requires at least 50 inches of rainfall a year, although it will grow in drier climates with supplemental irrigation. The plant is generally kept at a height of about 4 feet to facilitate harvest. Tea is reasonably well suited to Florida's climate, as it prefers hot, humid summers and mild, dry winters. Tea prefers acidic soil, requiring a pH of between 4.8 and 7.0. The soil should be consistently moist, but well drained. Adding peat to the soil is advantageous. The plant should be grown in partial shade and should be shielded from the midday sun, especially when young. Shade cloth may be deployed in open areas. Tea can be grown from seed. However, seeds require between 90 and 120 days to germinate and must be kept moist throughout this period. Tea can also be reproduced through cuttings and by air layering.

HARVEST AND USE Harvesting and curing tea is a complex and somewhat demanding process. It takes about 3 years before the plant matures sufficiently to provide consistent harvests. Only the top 2 inches of recent growth is plucked from the plant—usually the first 2 or 3 leaves. The tea plant will put out new flushes every few weeks over the warmer months, allowing for repeated harvests. Quality is better if no rain has occurred for two weeks prior to harvest. White tea is made from only the bud and the very youngest leaf immediately below the bud, before it has fully opened. White tea undergoes little processing and no fermentation. The bud and leaf are dried in the shade for a few hours, then steamed or roasted for a minute or two before being dried in an oven for 20 minutes at 250° F. Green tea can be processed in the same fashion, but is made with the top two or three leaves. Oolong tee undergoes some oxidation or fermentation. It can be processed by sun drying the leaves for about an hour, shade drying the leaves for several additional hours, then finishing the drying process in an oven for 20 minutes at 250° F. Black tea undergoes significant oxidation or fermentation. To make black tea, the leaves should be crushed and rolled between the hands, shade dried for 2 or 3 days, then dried in the oven for 20 minutes at 250° F. Various health benefits have been attributed to moderate consumption of tea. Tea has antibacterial properties and serves as an antioxidant. However, tea also contains caffeine and over-consumption can lead to nervousness, insomnia, and other conditions.

Thyme

SCIENTIFIC NAME: *Thymus* spp.
FAMILY: Lamiaceae
OTHER COMMON NAME: Tomillo (Spanish)

Semi-Woody Perennial; Evergreen Sub-shrub

Characteristics

Overall Rating	★★★★
Ease of Care	★★★
Utility	★★★★★
Landscape Value	★★★★
Salt Tolerance	★
Drought Tolerance	★★★★
Heat/Humidity Tolerance	★★★
Cold Tolerance	★★★★★
Shade Tolerance	★★★
Longevity	★★★

Thyme (pronounced "time") is a familiar cottage herb that has been revered since ancient times. It is decorative, relatively easy to grow, and functional. Selections of this diminutive subshrub can bring a diverse mix of textures and colors into the garden. Although it is considered a temperate-climate herb, thyme will succeed in all regions of Florida. While the flavor is distinctive, thyme blends well with other herbs and has a wide range of uses. Thyme ranks as a "must have" for serious herb gardeners.

Known Hazards

Thyme oil is poisonous in large doses and should not be ingested. There are some counter indications against ingestion of thyme during pregnancy, as it may act as a uterine stimulant. Thyme contains salicylates. Consumption may cause reactions in those who are intolerant of these compounds.

194

GEOGRAPHIC DISTRIBUTION Most thyme species are indigenous to Eurasia. Use of this herb has been traced back to ancient Egypt. Thyme has escaped cultivation in some areas of the northeastern United States. It has not exhibited invasive tendencies in Florida.

PLANT DESCRIPTION Thyme is a perennial evergreen, usually assuming the form of a creeping groundcover, rarely assuming a clumping or upright form and attaining the dimensions of a low sub-shrub. The creeping forms rarely reach a height of greater than few inches. Lower stems become woody and tough over time, and the branches can become somewhat wiry. The opposite leaves are dark green or gray-green and tiny. They measure from 1/4 of an inch to just under an inch in length. Flowers occur in terminal heads, and may be white, pink, bluish-lavender, or purple.

Creeping thyme is a low groundcover that is versatile, hardy, and easy to grow.

FLAVOR AND SCENT Thyme is highly aromatic, spicy, and slightly astringent. Some varieties have a pronounced lemon or citrus note. The fragrance is pungent, pleasant, and somewhat minty.

VARIETIES The *Thymus* genus consists of about 200 species, many of which are well suited to culinary use. Among these, common thyme, *Thymus vulgaris*, also called garden thyme, is most widely planted. It has given rise to many cultivars. More than 100 species and cultivars of thyme are regularly grown as culinary herbs, including: 'Caraway Thyme,' *Thymus herba-barona*, a vigorous culinary thyme; 'Citrus Thyme,' *Thymus citriodorus*, which has a pleasant citrus scent; 'Creeping Lemon Thyme,' a cultivar that produces pink flowers and which rarely exceeds 5 inches in height; 'Elfin Thyme,' a creeping variety that is one of the smallest; 'Lemon Thyme,' a lemon-scented variety that has some tolerance for summer conditions in south Florida; 'Orange Thyme,' a low ground-hugging variety that smells of orange; 'Silver Thyme,' an ornamental cultivar not highly valued for culinary use; 'Spicy Orange Thyme,' a creeping variety that produces pink flowers; 'Summer Thyme,' a strongly flavored thyme; and 'Wooly Thyme,' a variety that attains a height of about 6 inches.

RELATIVES The Lamiaceae or mint family contains several important herbs and spices. Species discussed within this book include basil, *Ocimum* spp.; bee balm, *Monarda didyma*; Cuban oregano, *Plectranthus amboinicus*; Jamaican mint, *Micromeria viminea*; lavender, *Lavandula* spp.; lemon balm, *Melissa officinalis*; mint, *Mentha* spp.; oregano, *Origanum* spp.; perilla, *Perilla frutescens*; rosemary, *Rosmarinus officinalis*; sage, *Salvia officinalis*; and savory, *Satureja* spp. No members of the *Thymus* genus are native to Florida. Brown's savory, *Micromeria brownei*, is a native member of the Lamiaceae family that bears an outward resemblance to thyme. It is found in scattered locations throughout Florida.

CULTIVATION Thyme flourishes in full sun. Unlike many herbs, it prefers slightly alkaline soil. It prospers in oolitic limestone and rock beds. Because this species is prone to root rot in wet soils, proper drainage is critical. Thyme will grow outdoors as far north as USDA zone 6. It is not frost tender in north Florida. In peninsular Florida, thyme struggles during the summer. If it can be kept alive, it will quickly rebound upon the return of cooler, drier weather.

HARVEST AND USE The leaves can be harvested at any time by snipping springs from the plant. No more than a third of the foliage should be removed at any given time. This herb is often at its best during or immediately before flowering. Fresh thyme can be stored in the refrigerator for about a week if wrapped in damp paper towels. It can also be dried in a warm, dry location. Dried thyme will keep for about 6 months if stored in an airtight container. The leaves should be removed from the stems with a fork or other device and crushed before use. Unlike many herbs, thyme retains its flavor through long cooking and is thus suitable for use in stews and crock-pot recipes. Thyme is used to flavor various meats, especially lamb, and is also widely employed in poultry dishes and soups. It is one of the signature flavors of French cuisine.

This close-up photograph of a shoot shows the transformation that occurs with age. While new growth is soft and green, older growth becomes woody and wiry.

195

Turmeric

SCIENTIFIC NAME: *Curcuma longa*
FAMILY: Zingiberaceae
OTHER COMMON NAME: Cúrcuma (Spanish)

Herbaceous Perennial

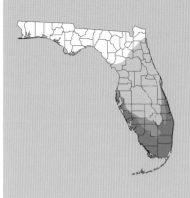

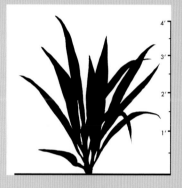

Characteristics

Overall Rating	★★★
Ease of Care	★★★
Utility	★★
Landscape Value	★★★★
Salt Tolerance	★
Drought Tolerance	★★
Heat/Humidity Tolerance	★★★★★
Cold Tolerance	★★
Shade Tolerance	★★★
Longevity	★★

Known Hazards

While turmeric is considered safe for human consumption, persons predisposed to kidney stones and gallstones should consult with a physician before use. Excessive use may cause stomach upset in some individuals. Some authorities discourage use during pregnancy. Turmeric contains salicylates, and consumption may cause reactions in those who are intolerant of these compounds.

This member of the ginger family has been used as a spice since at least 600 B.C. It is considered a sacred spice in parts of India and is used in religious ceremonies. Like many members of the ginger family, it makes an outstanding ornamental.

196

GEOGRAPHIC DISTRIBUTION Turmeric is native to southern Asia. India is the world's largest producer. The Indian city of Sangli is a major trading center and worldwide distribution point for turmeric. China, Myanmar, Taiwan, Vietnam, Australia, Peru, and Indonesia are also engaged in commercial production.

PLANT DESCRIPTION Turmeric is a perennial herb that can reach a height of 4 feet. The leaf sheaths form a short pseudo-stem, crowned by 5 to 12 lanceolate leaves. Yellow or cream-colored flowers are borne in a central spike during the summer. The plant tends to go dormant over the winter. Rhizomes, consisting of a "mother" rhizome and various fingers, provide support for the pseudostems.

FLAVOR AND SCENT Turmeric has a warm, earthy, peppery flavor with hints of citrus and mustard. It is mildly aromatic

VARIETIES Few varieties are available in Florida. Recognized commercial varieties, grown in India, include 'Armur,' 'Duggirala,' 'Kesar,' 'Kodur,' 'Mydukuru,' 'Rajapuri,' 'Salem,' 'Sugandham,' and 'Tekurpet.'

RELATIVES Turmeric is a member of the Zingiberaceae or ginger family. The section of this book covering ginger, *Zingiber officinale*, describes other important members of the Zingiberaceae family. *Curcuma*, sometimes referred to as the "hidden ginger" genus, contains about 90 species. *Curcuma aromatica* is widely grown in India and is used as a turmeric substitute. Temulawak, *Curcuma xanthorrhiza*, native to Indonesia, is sometimes used as a spice. Mango ginger, *Curcuma mangga*, native to India, is used as a flavoring agent and pickle. Zedoary, *Curcuma zedoaria*, also native to India, is occasionally used as a spice and vegetable.

CULTIVATION Turmeric prefers lightly acidic, well-drained soil. It cannot withstand wet feet, and waterlogged soil may prove fatal. The plant is typically grown from whole or split "mother" rhizomes. Fresh rhizomes, suitable for planting, may sometimes be obtained from Asian markets.

During the growing season, the rhizomes swell and form clusters of fingers or secondary rhizomes. Turmeric prefers a hot, moist climate. The plant ceases growth when temperatures drop below 60 degrees. It is harmed by near-freezing temperatures and may be killed back by a light frost. It can be grown in containers or moved indoors in areas prone to winter cold. Pests include nematodes and various scale insects. Rhizome rot is a prominent fungal disease.

HARVEST AND USE The spice is derived from the rhizomes, which are harvested from 8 to 11 months after planting. Maturity is indicated when the leaves turn yellow and experience some die back. The rhizomes, which are coated with gray-brown outer skin, are carefully cleaned of dirt. The flesh inside is bright orange. After removal, the flesh is boiled until white froth appears. It is then dried in the sun for about 2 weeks, and kept whole for storage or ground into a powder for immediate use. Turmeric is used as the base of numerous curries. It is also used as a dye, although its bright yellow color tends to fade over time. The yellow sap from the roots can stain fingers and clothing. The leaves of turmeric are also used in cooking, although they do not resemble the spice in flavor.

Turmeric resembles other members of the ginger family in its form of growth. The spice comes from the underground rhizomes.

Vanilla

SCIENTIFIC NAME: *Vanilla planifolia*
FAMILY: Orchidaceae
OTHER COMMON NAME: Vainilla (Spanish)

Herbaceous Evergreen Vine

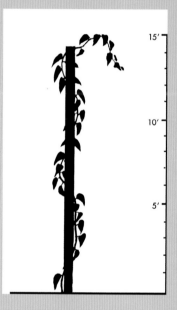

Characteristics

Overall Rating	★★
Ease of Care	★★
Utility	★
Landscape Value	★★★★
Salt Tolerance	★
Drought Tolerance	★★
Heat/Humidity Tolerance	★★★★
Cold Tolerance	★
Shade Tolerance	★★★★
Longevity	★★★

Known Hazards

None

For the motivated gardener in south Florida, vanilla can make a fascinating addition to the home garden. The vanilla orchid is an attractive plant that yields the valuable spice. Much of the "vanilla" found at the supermarket is actually a synthetic substitute. Real vanilla is expensive and has a superior flavor. Vanilla is the only member of the orchid family used in food and commerce. The Aztecs employed this plant as a flavoring agent. The name vanilla is derived from the Spanish *vainilla*, meaning sheath.

198

GEOGRAPHIC DISTRIBUTION The vanilla orchid of commerce is native to Mexico, the Caribbean, and, possibly, south Florida. Commercial production occurs in Madagascar, Guadeloupe, the Seychelles, Papua New Guinea, Tahiti, the Philippines, Mexico, Guatemala, and Indonesia. In Florida, growth is limited to coastal areas of the southern peninsula and the Keys. It can be grown in a greenhouse in more northerly locations.

PLANT DESCRIPTION Vanilla is a climbing vine that can ultimately reach a length of 50 or 60 feet. The alternate leaves are elliptic, lanceolate, leathery, and dark green. Aerial roots grow from each node. The trumpet-shaped flowers, borne on short peduncles, are large, showy, and fragrant. They are cream or light green in color. Each flower opens only over the course of a single day. If the flower is not pollinated, it will desiccate and drop from the vine. If the flower is pollinated, it will develop into an elongated pod, the "vanilla bean." The pod may be from 4 to 9 inches in length.

A dried vanilla bean alongside a fresh vanilla bean

FLAVOR AND SCENT Vanilla is nearly inedible unless diluted with other flavors. It has a rich, smooth, but somewhat volatile taste. No flavor is more basic. No flavor is more distinctive. The aroma is lightly floral.

VARIETIES In addition to *Vanilla plantifolia*, the species *Vanilla pompana*, and *Vanilla tahitensis* are also used for commercial production in some locations. Only *Vanilla plantifolia* is widely available in Florida.

RELATIVES Vanilla is a member of the Orchidaceae or orchid family. This immense family, the second-largest family of flowering plants following the Asteraceae or sunflower family, consists of more than 750 genera and 20,000 species. The *Vanilla* genus consists of about 100 vinelike species. These are native to various tropical and subtropical regions around the globe. Other members of the genus include Antilles vanilla, *Vanilla pompana*; Chamisso's vanilla, *Vanilla chamissonis*; Edwall's vanilla, *Vanilla edwalli*; green withe, *Vanilla claviculata*; inflated vanilla, *Vanilla odorata*; leafless vanilla, *Vanilla aphylla*; Mexican vanilla, *Vanilla mexicana*; Tahitian vanilla, *Vanilla tahitensis*; and Thai vanilla, *Vanilla siamensis*. At least four members of the *Vanilla* genus are

native to Florida, including worm vine orchid, *Vanilla barbellata*; leafy vanilla, *Vanilla phaeantha*; scentless vanilla, *Vanilla inodora*; and Dillon's vanilla, *Vanilla dilloniana*. *Vanilla planifolia* grows wild in some south Florida locations. It is unclear whether *vanilla planifolia* is truly indigenous or whether native peoples brought the species to Florida at an early date.

CULTIVATION Vanilla is cold sensitive. Temperatures below 40° F will result in growth setbacks. A light frost may prove fatal. The vanilla orchid prefers humid conditions. A trellis or other structure must be provided to support the vine. The base should be planted in a mix of sphagnum moss and soil with a high organic content. The roots should be kept moist, but must not become waterlogged. Most commercial orchid fertilizers provide good results. Some light shade is beneficial, as leaves and stems can scorch if consistently exposed to the midday sun. The plant can attain a length of over 6 feet in its first season of growth. Most commercial vanilla is pollinated by hand, with pollen transferred by brush to the stigma of each flower. Absent hand pollination, only a small percentage of flowers develop into pods.

HARVEST AND USE The vine typically needs to grow to 8 or 10 feet before it begins to flower. The part of the plant used as a spice is the vanilla bean. The bean ripens about 7 to 9 months after the flower appears. The pod itself, rather than the seeds within, contains the primary flavoring agents. However, the pods are usually harvested whole. They are picked when they turn from green to yellow. The pods are set out in the sun to dry for 5 or 6 hours. They are then wrapped in cloth and placed in airtight boxes to ferment. The process is repeated several times until the pods turn black. The pods are then preserved in glass vials or ground. Vanilla is an important flavoring for ice cream, pudding, confections, and baked goods.

Vanilla should be provided with a trellis or other object upon which it can climb.

199

Vietnamese Mint

SCIENTIFIC NAME: *Persicaria odorata*
FAMILY: Polygonaceae
OTHER COMMON NAMES: Hot Mint, Laksa Leaf

Herbaceous Perennial; Evergreen Creeper

Characteristics

Overall Rating	★★★
Ease of Care	★★★
Utility	★★★★
Landscape Value	★★★
Salt Tolerance	★
Drought Tolerance	★★
Heat/Humidity Tolerance	★★★★
Cold Tolerance	★★
Shade Tolerance	★★
Longevity	★★★

Notwithstanding its common name, this species does not belong to the mint family, nor does its flavor bear a strong resemblance to that of most mints. The leaves are flavorful and are used in various Southeast Asian recipes. The popularity of Vietnamese mint within the United States is increasing in conjunction with a growing appreciation for Asian cuisines. This plant is vigorous and is easy to grow.

Known Hazards

May pose some risk as an invasive species in light of its aggressive, spreading habit of growth.

200

GEOGRAPHIC DISTRIBUTION Vietnamese mint is native to Vietnam, Cambodia, and surrounding regions. It is frost sensitive but can be moved indoors during the winter in north Florida. This plant is a commercial crop in south Florida. It is typically grown in greenhouses using hydroponics. It is then shipped to Asian markets nationwide.

PLANT DESCRIPTION Vietnamese mint is a perennial herb with a sprawling habit of growth. It reaches a height of about 15 inches. Leaves are simple, lanceolate, drawing to an elongated point. Leaves exposed to direct sun often develop a dark v-shaped blotch at the center. The stems, which may have a reddish tint, are thickly jointed. This plant bears clusters of small, white to light pink flowers.

FLAVOR AND SCENT The taste and scent is reminiscent of coriander, with a lemony-citrus note and hot-pepper-like heat.

RELATIVES Notwithstanding its common name, this herb is not closely related to the mints. It falls within the Polygonaceae or smartweed family. This family consists of about 45 genera and 1,100 species. Some members have jointed stems with raised nodes. Relatives of economic import include rhubarb and buckwheat. The genus *Persicaria* consists of about 200 species. It contains the water pepper, *Persicaria hydropiper*, which is used as a vegetable, herb, and spice in Southeast Asia and Japan. The flavor resembles a mix of hot pepper and cilantro. The seeds of this plant are sometimes used in Wasabi. Water pepper has escaped cultivation in many regions of the United States and is considered an invasive plant. Various knotweeds and smartweeds, within the family Polygonaceae, are native to Florida, including bog smartweed, *Polygonum setaceum*; denseflower knotweed, *Polygonum glabrum*; dotted smartweed, *Polygonum punctatum*; glaucous knotweed, *Polygonum glaucum*; hairy smartweed, *Polygonum hirsutum*; mild water pepper, *Polygonum hydropiperoides*; and Pennsylvania smartweed, *Polygonum pensylvanicum*.

CULTIVATION Vietnamese mint is not carried by many nurseries and may be difficult to find. However, the fresh herb is sometimes available from oriental markets. New plants can be started by dipping stems in rooting hormone and by placing them in water or moist medium. Seeds are available from a few catalogue sources and can be collected from established plants once they have flowered. The plant is tropical in habit and thrives in warm, humid conditions. It is killed back by freezing temperatures, but usually reemerges the following season. Vietnamese mint has high water needs and is not drought tolerant. In peninsular Florida, irrigation is required during the dry season, from November to May. This plant self-sows freely and may have invasive tendencies. The gardener should refrain from planting this species along the edges of waterways, irrigation ditches, wetlands, or other natural areas.

HARVEST AND USE The leaves of Vietnamese mint are a key component of laksa, a spicy soup popular in Malaysia and Singapore. In Vietnam, this herb is also used in various noodle soups, stir-fried meat preparations, and other dishes. In various regions of Southeast Asia it is used as a salad ingredient and garnish.

Watercress

SCIENTIFIC NAME: *Nasturtium nasturtium-aquaticum*
FAMILY: Brassicaceae
OTHER COMMON NAME: Berro (Spanish)

Herbaceous Perennial

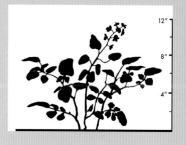

Characteristics

Overall Rating	★★
Ease of Care	★★★
Utility	★★★★
Landscape Value	★★
Salt Tolerance	★
Drought Tolerance	★★
Heat/Humidity Tolerance	★★★★★
Cold Tolerance	★★★★
Shade Tolerance	★★★
Longevity	★★

Known Hazards

This plant has invasive tendencies. Cultivation should be relegated to container gardens and other controlled situations where escape is unlikely or impossible. Care should be taken when harvesting the plant from any location where water quality is suspect. Watercress should be thoroughly cooked if taken from a location draining areas where livestock is present, as it could harbor parasites.

In use, watercress lies somewhere between an herb and a vegetable. It is flavorful and is packed with vitamins and minerals. Apart from its culinary applications, the distinctive characteristic of watercress is that it will succeed in places that are too damp for most other herbs.

202

GEOGRAPHIC DISTRIBUTION Watercress is native to Europe and Asia. It is considered an invasive exotic in many areas of the United States. In Florida, watercress has escaped cultivation and grows wild in many locations, including various springheads and tributaries leading to the St. Johns River.

PLANT DESCRIPTION Watercress is a semi-aquatic, trailing perennial. Stems are succulent and float on the water's surface. Leaves are alternate. They are pinnately compound and contain 3 to 9 oval leaflets, which measure about an inch in diameter. Small white flowers with 4 petals appear during late spring and early summer. The rate of growth is rapid.

FLAVOR AND SCENT The flavor is somewhat peppery and tangy. The aroma is mildly pungent.

RELATIVES The Brassicaceae or cabbage family is composed of about 325 genera and 3,500 species. It contains a number of edible plants, including various green vegetables. Various relatives are covered under the section devoted to mustard, *Brassica* spp. Other Brassicaceae species covered in this book are horseradish, *Armoracia rusticana*; pepperweed, *Lepidium verginicum*; and sea rocket, *Cakile edentula*. The *Nasturtium* genus contains 7 species, one of which is native to Florida. Florida watercress, *Nasturtium floridanum*, grows in scattered north Florida locations and throughout the peninsula. More distantly related "cresses" that are native to Florida include lakecress, *Neobeckia aquatica*; southern marsh yellowcress, *Rorippa teres*; Virginia winged rockcress, *Sibara virginica*; Pennsylvania bittercress, *Cardamine pennsylvanica*; sand bittercress, *Cardamine parviflora*; and wideleaf pinelandcress, *Warea amplexifolia*.

CULTIVATION Watercress is well suited to hydroponic gardening. To achieve optimal growth, the water should be slightly alkaline. Watercress can be grown in association with most water features, but prefers clean, flowing water. If no flowing water is available, watercress can be grown in soil that is kept consistently moist. It is readily grown from seeds, which should be sown in pots that are partially immersed in water. Seeds germinate after about 10 days. Watercress can also be grown from cuttings. Because watercress has displayed invasive tendencies, it should not be planted near any wetlands or watercourses where it is not already present.

HARVEST AND USE Young foliage should be cut from the plant. The flavor tends to be best over the cooler months. The leaves become slightly bitter once the plant begins flowering. Watercress can often be found growing in the wild. Watercress gathered from around springheads is usually safe for human consumption. However, caution should be exercised when harvesting watercress from less pristine waterways. Watercress gathered from streams that receive runoff from cattle operations or other infusions of waste may be infected with *E. coli*, liver flukes, and other harmful organisms. Watercress gathered from any questionable source should be thoroughly washed and cooked prior to consumption. Watercress is excellent as a salad ingredient, garnish, sandwich topping, or spinachlike potherb.

Watercress can survive crowding and is often prolific in its habit of growth.

Wax Myrtle

SCIENTIFIC NAME: *Myrica cerifera*
FAMILY: Myricaceae
OTHER COMMON NAMES: Southern Bayberry,
  Candleberry

Woody Perennial; Semi-Deciduous

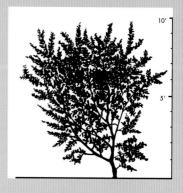

Characteristics

Overall Rating	★★
Ease of Care	★★★★★
Utility	★
Landscape Value	★★★★
Salt Tolerance	★★★★
Drought Tolerance	★★★★
Heat/Humidity Tolerance	★★★★
Cold Tolerance	★★★★★
Shade Tolerance	★★★
Longevity	★★★

This native plant is hardy and attractive, and is included within this book as a result of the pleasant scent of the foliage and berries. It is widely planted as a landscape shrub throughout the southeastern United States. The berries attract wildlife to the garden, especially warblers, cardinals, white-eyed vireos, and others.

Known Hazards

While wax myrtle has been brewed into a tea for medicinal purposes, its safety has not been adequately assessed.

GEOGRAPHIC DISTRIBUTION This species ranges from New Jersey south along the eastern seaboard and west to Texas along the gulf coast. It is common in bogs, pine barrens, and open woods. It forms thickets in the Everglades and along riverbanks and estuaries.

PLANT DESCRIPTION Wax myrtle is a shrub or small tree and typically reaches a height of 10 or 12 feet. Multiple trunks are common. Growth is fast. The plant is evergreen in south and central Florida, and is semideciduous in portions of the Panhandle and north Florida. Leaves are narrow, ranging from 2 to 5 inches in length and often have curled or wavy edges. Blooms appear in late winter. Plants are dioecious, bearing all male or all female flowers. Male flowers form on short, green catkins. Female flowers, which are inconspicuous, mature into small, blue-gray berries. These are borne in tight formation directly on the branches. Only the female plant bears fruit. Each berry contains a single seed, and is covered with wax.

FLAVOR AND SCENT Leaves are aromatic, emitting a sweet, resinous, balsamic fragrance when crushed. The leaf surface is coated with hundreds of minute glands. The berries, although more or less inedible, are highly scented.

VARIETIES Dwarf varieties 'Georgia Gem' and 'Pumilla' are sometimes available. Other named cultivars include 'Don's Dwarf,' 'Fairfax,' 'Jamaica Road,' and 'Myda.'

RELATIVES The small family Myricaceae is composed of 3 genera. The genus *Myrica* is composed of about 40 species. The northern bayberry, *Myrica pennsylvanica*, inhabits the eastern coastal plain from Canada south to North Carolina, where its range overlaps with that of the southern wax myrtle. The red bayberry, *Myrica rubra*, is cultivated in China for its edible berries. *Myrica faya*, native to the Azores and Canary Islands, produces edible berries. It has been introduced to Hawaii, where it is considered an invasive species.

CULTIVATION Wax myrtle is a tough native plant and is easy to grow. It can withstand a wide range of soil types. In fact, it readily grows on poor, sandy soil as a result of the fact that nodules within its roots house nitrogen-fixing bacteria. It is salt tolerant, often growing on the banks of brackish waterways, and can withstand both drought and flooding. In the home garden, suckers should be removed from around the base to prevent the plant from forming a thicket. It can be pruned and trained into various shapes. Wax myrtle is often reproduced by separating suckers from the rest of a colony, or by digging up sections of the root mat, from which new sprouts are formed.

HARVEST AND USE Cut branches can be brought indoors to provide a pleasant aroma. The leaves can be used as a substitute for bay leaves in cooking. The wax coating on the berries can be used to make scented candles. The berries are immersed in boiling water and the surface is periodically skimmed to remove the wax. Some products marketed as bayberry wax are merely commercial waxes scented with bayberry. Real bayberry wax is expensive and is somewhat brittle, but represents a unique local product. The wax can be used in the manufacture of scented soaps and candles.

Wax myrtle is a familiar native shrub that is frequently used in home and commercial landscapes.

Wild Cinnamon

SCIENTIFIC NAME: *Canella winterana*
FAMILY: Canellaceae
OTHER COMMON NAME: Cinnamon Bark

Woody Perennial; Evergreen Tree

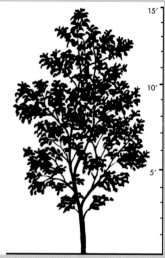

Characteristics

Overall Rating	★★★
Ease of Care	★★★★
Utility	★
Landscape Value	★★★★★
Salt Tolerance	★★★★
Drought Tolerance	★★★
Heat/Humidity Tolerance	★★★★★
Cold Tolerance	★★
Shade Tolerance	★★★
Longevity	★★★★

Known Hazards

This plant is endangered and must not be removed or harvested from natural locations. While the inner bark has been used as a spice and condiment without any known adverse reactions, its safety has not been adequately accessed. There are unconfirmed reports that oils derived from the leaves of this species caused dermatitis in a few sensitive individuals. The leaves may be toxic and should not be ingested.

Wild cinnamon is not a close relative of cinnamon, source of the familiar spice. Wild cinnamon is a native plant that is attractive in form and foliage. It deserves wider planting in the home landscape in south Florida. The species is considered endangered in the wild in Florida. A few nurseries that specialize in native plants sell wild cinnamon. The inner bark has been used to flavor drinks and as a spice. The berries have also been used for culinary purposes.

GEOGRAPHIC DISTRIBUTION Wild cinnamon is native to the Caribbean, the Bahamas, and Florida. In the Bahamas, the bark has been harvested and exported as a spice and condiment. This species is present in Cuba, the Dominican Republic, Jamaica, the northern Antilles, and Puerto Rico. In Florida, it occurs naturally in Collier, Miami-Dade, and Monroe counties, including the Keys. It is frost sensitive and growth is relegated to southern parts of the peninsula. It should probably not be attempted north of Cape Coral on the west coast and Martin County on the east coast.

Wild cinnamon is an attractive small tree with a columnar habit of growth.

PLANT DESCRIPTION Wild cinnamon is a large evergreen shrub or small evergreen tree capable of attaining a height of about 25 feet. It is somewhat columnar in form, showing little horizontal spread. The wood is dense and close-grained. The rate of growth is slow to moderate. The opposite leaves are leathery. They are entire and ovate, borne on short petioles, and measure from 4 to 7 inches in length. Small flowers appear in dense terminal clusters in summer. These are deep red, with 5 petals. Small, oblong, green berries follow the flowers. These are slow to mature and persist over the winter. They turn bright red upon ripening.

FLAVOR AND SCENT The leaves are aromatic and emit a clovelike scent when crushed or bruised. The dried inner bark has a pungent, cinnamonlike odor, and the taste is bitter. The berries are somewhat hot and resemble black pepper in flavor.

RELATIVES The family Canallaceae is composed of about 15 species of trees in 5 genera. The *Canella* genus is thought to be composed of just 2 species. The other species, *Canella axillaris*, is native to Brazil.

CULTIVATION Wild cinnamon is a tough plant, with good drought tolerance and low water needs once established. It will grow in a wide range of soils. It will tolerate alkaline soils. It has moderate salt tolerance. No serious pest or disease problems affect this plant.

HARVEST AND USE When pruning this shrub for use in the home landscape, limbs can be removed and prepared in a manner similar to cinnamon. The yellow inner bark, stripped of its corky layer, is dried. The resulting "quills" can be used to flavor beverages. The berries are dried, crushed, and used as a substitute for black pepper in some locations, although the safety of this practice is uncertain. Leaf extracts have reportedly been used as a fish poison, and the leaves should be regarded as poisonous. Some individuals may be allergic to this plant and may develop a skin rash following contact. The leaves can be used as a strewing herb.

The flower buds give way to small, brilliant red flowers.

Witch Hazel

SCIENTIFIC NAME: *Hamamelis virginiana*
FAMILY: Hamamelidaceae
OTHER COMMON NAME: American Witch Hazel

Woody Perennial; Deciduous Shrub

Characteristics

Overall Rating	★★
Ease of Care	★★★★
Utility	★
Landscape Value	★★★
Salt Tolerance	★
Drought Tolerance	★★★
Heat/Humidity Tolerance	★★
Cold Tolerance	★★★★★
Shade Tolerance	★★★
Longevity	★★★★

Known Hazards

Unless contained in products approved by the FDA for internal consumption, witch hazel should only be used externally. Generally considered safe to use as an astringent and as an aroma agent.

Native Americans valued witch hazel for medicinal purposes. In modern times, this species has been used as an astringent, as an ingredient in salves for pain relief, and as the source of distilled oil used for scent and in rubs. Because it blooms in the late fall and winter, witch hazel has the advantage of bringing late color to the home garden.

GEOGRAPHIC DISTRIBUTION Witch hazel is native over much of the eastern United States. Northern witch hazel ranges as far north as southern Canada. In Florida, it grows throughout the Panhandle and as far south as Highland County. It is found in various habitats, but is most prominent along forest edges, along ravines and streams, and as an understory plant.

PLANT DESCRIPTION Witch hazel is a deciduous shrub or small tree. It can reach a height of 30 feet, but is usually less than 10 feet in height. The rate of growth is moderate. Witch hazel typically has a short trunk and an open crown supported by irregular, zigzagging branches. Leaves are alternate, broadly elliptic, with toothed margins. They are rough and lightly pubescent in texture and measure from 3 to 6 inches in length. After the tree has shed its leaves for the winter, clusters of flowers emerge from the leaf scars. These are yellow, somewhat spidery in appearance, with elongate petals. Brown, hairy capsules develop following flowering. These contain small black seeds. The capsules mature over the following growing season and eventually burst open with an audible pop, spraying the seeds over a wide area.

SCENT Witch hazel is a highly aromatic plant. The aroma is pervasive. It has a pleasant, somewhat spicy character.

VARIETIES Some authorities treat southern witchhazel, *Hamamelis macrophylla*, as a separate species. A few hybrids and selections have been distributed by nurseries, including 'Angelly,' 'Arnold's Promise,' 'Antoine Kort,' 'Barmstedt Gold,' 'Birgit,' 'Diane,' 'Georges,' 'Orange Beauty,' 'Pallida,' 'Ruby Glow,' and 'Sarah.' It is uncertain which of these would succeed in Florida's climate, as most were bred in more northerly locations.

RELATIVES The family Hamamelidaceae is composed of about 26 genera and 100 species. Most are found in Asia. The fringe flower, *Loropetalum chinense*, from Japan and southern China is sometimes planted as an ornamental in the southern United States. Plants within the family that are native to North America include Ozark witch hazel, *Hamamelis vernalis*; witch alder, *Fothergilla major*; Dwarf witch alder, *Fothergilla gardenii*; and sweetgum, *Liquidambar styraciflua*.

CULTIVATION Witch hazel is not especially demanding in its cultural requirements, but it is not tolerant of extended drought. It will tolerate light shade. It is not particular as to soil type and will grow in sandy soil, clay soil, and soil with a pH of 5.5 to 7.5. No serious pests or diseases affect the plant.

HARVEST AND USE Young branches can be lopped from the plant and brought indoors to provide a pleasant and pervasive scent. To avoid seed discharges, any remaining seedpods should be stripped from these cuttings. The fragrant flowers can also be gathered as a scent agent. This plant is not a spice and should not be consumed.

Witch hazel leaves from the cultivar 'Mohonk Red'

Yellow Anise

SCIENTIFIC NAME: *Illicium parviflorum*
FAMILY: Illiciaceae

Woody Perennial; Evergreen Shrub

Characteristics

Overall Rating	★★
Ease of Care	★★★★
Utility	★
Landscape Value	★★★★
Salt Tolerance	★
Drought Tolerance	★★★
Heat/Humidity Tolerance	★★★
Cold Tolerance	★★★★
Shade Tolerance	★★★★★
Longevity	★★★

This attractive native shrub is available from several nurseries that specialize in native plants. It is considered endangered in the wild. While this plant has a delightful aroma, all parts are toxic. In other words, it must not be thought of as a substitute for the culinary spices anise or star anise. It is nevertheless worth planting for its scent and for its value as a landscape plant.

Known Hazards

Yellow anise is toxic and not for internal consumption. It must not be substituted for the culinary spices anise or star anise. The plant is listed as endangered and must not be collected from the wild.

GEOGRAPHIC DISTRIBUTION Yellow anise is native to central Florida. It prefers moist bottomland and is sometimes found bordering creeks and tributaries of the St. Johns River. It has been reported from Lake, Marion, Orange, Polk, Seminole, and Volusia counties.

PLANT DESCRIPTION Yellow anise is an evergreen shrub that typically attains a height of about 8 feet, but that is capable of growing to 20 feet. It may have one or several trunks. The alternate leaves are ovate and measure 4 to 6 inches in length. They are glossy and somewhat leathery in texture. The yellow flowers, which measure up to 1 inch in diameter, have 6 to 12 petals. The woody seed capsule is star shaped.

SCENT The leaves, especially when crushed or bruised, emit a pleasant, licoricelike fragrance.

VARIETIES A variety dubbed 'Forest Green' has been selected for its dark green foliage.

RELATIVES Yellow anise belongs to the Illiciacea or Schisandraceae family, depending on the system of taxonomy employed. The genus *Illicium* contains about 35 species. Many members are poisonous. Florida anise, *Illicium floridanum*, is protected as a threatened species in Florida. It is indigenous to the Florida Panhandle, ranging east to Wakulla County, and ranging as far west as Louisiana. It prefers shaded ravines and steepheads. Like yellow anise, Florida anise is toxic and must not be ingested. It is covered in a separate section of this book. Star anise, *Illicium veruma*, is the only member of the genus regularly used for culinary purposes. It is native to Southeast Asia. Star anise is also covered within a separate section of this book.

CULTIVATION Yellow anise is a low-maintenance landscape shrub. It will tolerate a wide range of soil types and attains adequate growth on infertile sand. It is also capable of growing in fairly deep shade. Once established, yellow anise is drought resistant. Yellow anise can be propagated by seed, by cuttings, and by air layering. Storing seeds in damp medium in the refrigerator for 3 months increases the germination rate.

HARVEST AND USE Yellow anise can be used as potpourri, as a strewing herb, and for other purposes that take advantage of its scent. Because of its toxic qualities, it cannot be used as a spice and should not be consumed.

Glossary

Achene – A dry, indehiscent fruit formed from one carpel that contains a single seed.

Aerial root – A root produced above ground. Orchids produce aerial roots.

Air layering – A method of propagation through which roots are forced to develop on the branch of a plant. The rooted branch is then severed and planted.

Alkaloids – Complex substances that occur within certain plants that may have medicinal, poisonous, stimulative, narcotic, or hallucinogenic qualities. Examples are caffeine, quinine, and strychnine. Names typically end in "-ine."

Alternate leaves – Leaves that occur singly at the leaf nodes; they do not appear opposite one another along the stem.

Annual – A plant that sprouts, grows, and dies over the course of a single year.

Anther – The enlarged tip of a stamen that produces pollen.

Apex – The tip, often of a leaf or fruit. In a fruit the apex is located at the end distant from the stem insert.

Astringent – A substance that causes tissues to constrict or tighten.

Axil – The juncture of the petiole (leaf stalk) and the stem. Flower buds may develop in leaf axils.

Basal rosette – A group of leaves growing in a circular pattern and emerging directly from the top of the root.

Base – The area of a leaf near the petiole.

Berry – A fleshy fruit of somewhat homogenous texture that does not contain a stone. Most berries have succulent skin and multiple seeds.

Biennial – A plant that grows over the course of two
years, usually flowering and dying at the end of the second growing season.

Bracts – Leaflike structures that underpin or that are part of an inflorescence.

Budding – A propagation technique, similar to grafting, through which a small bud is removed from the selected cultivar and inserted into a notch or cut in the bark of a rootstock.

Bulbil – A small bulb-like structure replacing flowers, prevalent in onions and garlics.

Calyx – The lowermost whorl of sepals (modified leaves) within a flower.

Cambium – The soft, thin layer of tissue lying outside of the wood and inside the inner bark of trees and shrubs.

Cane – A thin, flexible stem growing directly from the ground or a low branch.

Capsule – A fruit that splits along sutures at maturity. A capsule is derived from a compound ovary, made up of 2 or more carpels.

Carcinogenic – A substance that tends to cause or accelerate the development of cancerous cells.

Carpel – The portion of the pistil of a flower that contains the ovules.

Chilling hours – The number of hours at or below 45° F required for bud break, flowering, and fruit set in temperate fruit species.

Chlorosis – A condition, caused by nutritional deficiency or disease, where the leaves fail to produce chlorophyll and turn pale yellow or whitish-green.

Compound leaf – A leaf composed of 2 or more leaflets attached to a single leaf stem or petiole.

Corm – The enlarged, solid, fleshy base of a stem; an underground storage stem.

Corolla – The whorl of petals located above the sepals in a flower.

Cultivar – A cultivated variety; a plant that has been cloned to preserve its genetic characteristics.

Damping-off – A fungal rot that causes the collapse of seedlings shortly after they emerge from the soil.

Deciduous – Describing a plant that sheds its leaves on an annual or seasonal basis.

Dehiscent – Describing a fruit, capsule, or other structure that splits open upon reaching maturity.

Dentate – Describing a leaf with toothlike projections along the margin.

Dioecious – Describing a species that bears male and female flowers on different plants.

Diuretic – A substance that causes or stimulates urination.

Drupe – A fleshy fruit with a stony endocarp containing one or more seeds.

Elliptic – Shaped like an ellipse or elongated oval, tapered at both ends.

Embryo – A rudimentary plant present in the seed before germination.

Emetic – A substance that causes or stimulates vomiting.

Entire – Describing a leaf margin with a smooth edge; not containing notches, teeth or lobes.

Evergreen – Describing a plant that does not lose its leaves on an annual or seasonal basis.

Flower – A reproductive structure, ordinarily composed of sepals, petals, stamens, and pistils, although sometimes lacking one or more of these parts.

Fruit – The mature ovary of a flowering plant that encloses the seeds.

Glabrous – Describing a smooth, hairless surface.

Globose – Round or rounded.

Grafting – A means of propagation through which a branch tip from one plant (the scion) is bonded to the stem and root system of a second plant (the rootstock).

Herb – A short-lived plant with pliable, non-woody stems.

Herbaceous – Non-woody, typically referring to the stems or stalks.

Hesperidium – A specialized berry with a leathery rind and a segmented interior.

Indehiscent – Describing a fruit or pod that does not split open at maturity to discharge its seeds.

Inflorescence – A cluster of flowers.

Infusion – A plant extract, usually made by steeping plant material in hot water.

Invasive exotic – A non-native plant that has escaped cultivation and that is reproducing and spreading.

Lanceolate – Describing a narrow, lance-shaped leaf, broadest at the base and tapered to a long point.

Leaf – A plant organ consisting of a blade and a petiole.

Leaflet – The individual blade of a compound leaf.

Lobed – Describing a leaf with extensions separated by deep indentations, known as sinuses.

Margin – The edge of a leaf.

Monoecious – Bearing separate male and female flowers on the same plant.

Nematodes – Microscopic worms living in the soil, some of which attack plant roots.

Node – The area of a stem where the vascular tissue branches into leaves, buds, or other appendages.

Oblong – Tapered at both ends, but with the sides nearly parallel.

Obovate – Oval, with the broadest part near the apex.

Opposite leaves – Leaves arranged so that 2 occur at each node.

Ovary – The part of the flower that encloses the ovules; the enlarged base of the pistil, which becomes the fruit.

Ovate – Oval, with the broader part near the base.

Ovule – The structure within a flowering plant that gives rise to the seed.

Palmate – Describing leaflets, leaf structures, or leaf veins, arising from and spreading outward from a single point at the base of the leaf.

Pedicel – The flower stalk.

Peduncle – The main stalk of an inflorescence.

Perennial – A plant capable of surviving for more than two growing seasons.

Perfect flower – A perfect flower is hermaphroditic and contains female parts (pistils) and male parts (stamens).

Persistent – Remaining attached.

Petal – A unit of the corolla, a flower appendage located between the sepals and the stamens.

Petiole – The leaf stalk.

Phloem – Stem or trunk tissue involved in the transport of the products of photosynthesis.

Pinnately compound – Containing leaflets arranged oppositely or alternately along the leaf stalk axis.

Pinnately veined – Describing leaves with a middle vein intersected by secondary veins, which radiate toward the margins on each side.

Pistil – The female part of a flower, comprising the central organs, which is made up of an ovary, style, and stigma.

Pod – A dehiscent, often dry, fruit that develops from a single carpel that splits along two parallel sutures.

Pollen – The male microspore of seed plants, produced by the stamens.

Pollination – The process of transferring the pollen from the stamen to the stigma.

Pubescent – Having fine hairs on the surface.

Raceme – A long, often pendulant, unbranched inflorescence.

Rhizome – A horizontal underground stem, such as is found in bananas.

Rootstock – The root system and lower stem of a grafted tree; all portions below the graft union.

Scion – The branch of a cultivar or selected plant that is grafted onto a rootstock.

Sedative – A substance that has a soothing or relaxing effect.

Seed – A fertilized, matured ovule; a multicellular reproductive structure containing the plant embryo.

Sepal – Part of the calyx; the outermost structure of a flower.

Serrate – Describing a leaf margin with sharp, forward-pointing teeth.

Simple leaf – Any leaf that is not compound.

Spathe – A sheathlike leaf partially enclosing an inflorescence.

Stamen – The male pollen-producing organ of a flower, composed of a filament and anther.

Stigma – The sticky tip of the pistil of a flower receptive to pollen.

Strain – A subsubspecies of a plant, or a variant of a cultivar that is nearly identical, not deserving full cultivar status.

Style – Part of the pistil of a flower. The style is a tubular structure that connects the stigma and the ovary.

Subshrub – A plant that is largely herbaceous, but that contains a woody base.

Sucker – A vigorous shoot sprouting from below ground or from older growth.

Taproot – A well-developed, vertical, primary root.

Toothed – Leaves that have small teeth along the margins (same as *Dentate*).

Umbel – A group of flowers that forms on a base of spokelike stems radiating from a single point; umbrellalike in form.

Venation – Referring to the pattern of veins within the blade of a leaf. Venation may be palmate, pinnate, or parallel.

Whorl – A group of leaves, petals, or carpels forming a spokelike pattern around a central axis.

Xylem – Trunk and stem tissue involved in the transport of water and minerals upward to the canopy.

Gardens and Herb Collections

Alfred B. Maclay State Garden
3540 Thomasville Road
Tallahassee, FL 32308

Atlanta Botanical Garden
1345 Piedmont Ave N.E.
Atlanta, GA 30309

Audubon Botanical Garden
5530 Sunset Drive
Miami, FL 33143

Bok Tower Gardens
1151 Tower Boulevard
Lake Wales, FL 33853

Cummer Museum of Art and Gardens
829 Riverside Avenue
Jacksonville, FL 32204

Eden State Gardens
181 Eden Garden Road
Santa Rosa Beach, FL 32459

Edison & Ford Winter Estates and Botanical
Gardens
2350 McGregor Blvd.
Fort Myers, FL 33901

Educational Concerns for Hunger Organization
(ECHO)
Bookstore and Nursery
17391 Durrance Road
North Fort Myers, FL 33917

Epcot/Walt Disney World
"The Land" attraction and ride
Lake Buena Vista, FL 32830

Flamingo Gardens
3750 S. Flamingo Road
Davie, FL 33330

Fruit & Spice Park
24801 S.W. 187th Avenue
Homestead, FL 33031

Harry P. Leu Gardens
1920 N. Forest Avenue
Orlando, FL 32803

Heathcote Botanical Garden
210 Savanna Road
Fort Pierce, FL 34982

Kanapaha Botanical Gardens
4625 S. W. 63rd Blvd.
Gainesville, FL 32608

Key West Botanical Forest and Garden
5210 College Road
Key West, FL 33040

Marie Selby Botanical Gardens
811 South Palm Avenue
Sarasota, FL 34236

McKee Botanical Garden
4871 N. A1A
Vero Beach, FL 32963

Morikami Museum and Japanese Gardens
4000 Morikami Park Road
Delray Beach, FL 33446

Mounts Botanical Garden
531 North Military Trail
West Palm Beach, FL 33415

Pinellas County Extension & Florida Botanical
Gardens
12520 Ulmerton Road
Largo, FL 33774

Ravine State Gardens
1600 Twigg Street
Palatka, FL 32178

Sarasota Jungle Gardens
3701 Bayshore Road
Sarasota, FL 34234

State Botanical Garden of Georgia
2450 S. Miledge Avenue
Athens, GA 30605

Sugar Mill Botanical Gardens
950 Old Sugar Mill Road
Port Orange, FL 32119

Sunken Gardens
1825 4th Street N.
St. Petersburg, FL 33704

Tallahassee Museum of History and Natural
Science
3945 Museum Drive
Tallahassee, FL 32310

Tropical Ranch Botanical Gardens
1905 SW Ranch Trail
Stuart, FL 34997

Nurseries and Seed Companies

Burpee and Company
300 Park Avenue
Warminster, PA 18991
800-888-1447

Cross Country Nurseries
199 Kingwood-Locktown Road
Rosemont, NJ 08556
908-996-4646

Excalibur Nursery
5200 Fearnley Road
Lake Worth, FL 33467
561-969-6988

Garden of Delights Nursery
14560 SW 14th Street
Davie, FL 33325
954-370-9004

Jené's Tropicals
6831 Central Avenue
St Petersburg, FL 33710
727-344-1668

Just Fruits and Exotics
30 St. Francis Street
Crawfordville, FL 32327
850-926-5644

Kilgore Seed Company
1400 W. First Street
Sanford, FL 32771
407-323-6630

Kingfisher Variety Herbs, Palms & Bamboo
Highway 441
Orange Lake, FL
352-591-4344

The Kitazawa Seed Company
P.O. Box 13220
Oakland, CA 94661
510-595-1188

Maggie's Herbs
11400 County Road 13
St. Augustine, FL 32092
904-829-0722

McCrory's Sunny Hill Herb Farm
35152 La Place Court
Eustis, FL 32736
352-357-9876

O'Toole's Herb Farm
305 Artemesia Trail
Madison, FL 32341
850-973-3629

Park Seed Company
1 Parkton Ave
Greenwood, SC 29647
800-213-0076

Pinder's Nursery
5500 SW Martin Highway
Palm City, FL 34990
772-286-0284

Plant Creations
28301 SW 172nd Avenue
Homestead, FL 33030
305–248–8147

Rabbit Hill Gardens Herb Farm
3505 N. Hwy 19-A
Mt. Dora, FL 32757
352-223-4393

Rockledge Gardens
2153 South U.S. Highway 1
Rockledge, FL 32955
321–636–7662

Seeds of Change
P.O. Box 15700
Santa Fe, NM 87506
888-762-7333

Southern Exposure Seed Exchange
P.O. Box 460
Mineral, VA 23117
540-894-9480

Tallahassee Nurseries
2911 Thomasville Road
Tallahassee, FL 32308
850-385-2162

Zone Ten Nursery
18900 S.W. 186 Street
Miami, FL 22187
305–255–9825

References and Further Reading

Bell, C. Ritchie, and Bryan J. Taylor. *Florida Wild Flowers and Roadside Plants*. Chapel Hill, NC: Laurel Hill Press, 1982.

Boning, Charles R. *Florida's Best Fruiting Plants: Native and Exotic Trees, Shrubs, and Vines*. Sarasota, FL: Pineapple Press, 2006.

Brandies, Monica Moran. *Herbs and Spices for Florida Gardens*. Wayne, PA: B.B. Mackey Books, 1996.

Bremness, Lesley. *The Complete Book of Herbs: A Practical Guide to Growing and Using Herbs*. New York, NY: Penguin Group, Penguin Putnam, 1994.

Brennan, Georgeanne, and Mimi Luebbermann. *Little Herb Gardens: Simple Secrets for Glorious Gardens-Indoors and Out*. San Francisco, CA: Chronicle Books, 2004.

Brill, Steve, and Evelyn Dean. *Identifying and Harvesting Edible and Medicinal Plants in Wild (and not so Wild) Places*. New York, NY: Hearst Books, 1994.

Bruce, Hank. *Uncommon Scents: Growing Herbs and Spices in Florida*. Winter Springs, FL: Winner Enterprises, 1996.

Corn, Charles. *The Scents of Eden: A History of the Spice Trade*. Tokyo, Japan: Kodansha International, 1999.

Couplan, François. *The Encyclopedia of Edible Plants of North America*. New Canaan, CT: Keats, 1998.

Crane, Jonathan H., Carlos F. Balerdi, and Gene Joyner. *Publication #HS1056*. Gainesville, FL: Horticultural Sciences Department, Florida Cooperative Extension Service, Institute of Food and Agricultural Sciences, University of Florida, 2005.

Crane, Jonathan H., Carlos F. Balerdi, and Gene Joyner. *Publication #HS1057*. Gainesville, FL: Horticultural Sciences Department, Florida Cooperative Extension Service, Institute of Food and Agricultural Sciences, University of Florida, 2005.

Crawford, Pamela. *Container Gardens for Florida*. Lake Worth, FL: Color Garden Publishing, 2005.

Creasy, Rosalind. *The Edible Flower Garden*. Boston, MA: Periplus Editions, 1999.

Cunningham, Scott. *Cunningham's Encyclopedia of Magical Herbs*. Second edition. St. Paul, MN: Llewellyn Publications, 2003.

Cutler, Karen Davis, and David Cavagnarok. *Burpee: The Complete Vegetable & Herb Gardener: A Guide to Growing Your Garden Organically*. New York, NY: MacMillan, 1997.

DeBaggio, *Thomas. Growing Herbs from Seed, Cutting, and Root: An Adventure in Small Miracles*. Second edition. Loveland, CO: Interweave Press, 2000.

Deuerling, Richard J., and Peggy S. Lantz. *Florida's Incredible Wild Edibles*. Orlando, FL: Florida Native Plant Society, 1993.

Facciola, Stephen. *Cornucopia II: A Source Book of Edible Plants*. Vista, CA: Kampong Publications, 1998.

Foley, Caroline, Jill Nice, and Marcus A. Webb. *New Herb Bible*. New York, NY: Penguin Group, Penguin Putnam, 2002.

Foster, Steven, and James A. Duke. *A Field Guide to Medicinal Plants and Herbs of Eastern and Central North America*. Second edition. New York, NY: Houghton Mifflin, 2000.

Garland, Sarah. *The Complete Book of Herbs and Spices*. New York, NY: The Viking Press, 1979.

Gilbert, Robert A., ed. *Florida Sugarcane Handbook*, SS-AGR-251. Gainesville, FL: Agronomy Department, Florida Cooperative Extension Service, Institute of Food and Agricultural Sciences, University of Florida, 2005.

Guerra, Michael. *The Edible Container Garden: Growing Fresh Food in Small Spaces*. New York, NY: Fireside, 2000.

Haehle, Robert G., and Joan Brookwell. *Native Florida Plants*. Houston TX: Gulf Publishing, 1999.

Halfacre, R.G., and A.R. Showcroft. *Landscape plants of the Southeast*. Raleigh, NC: Sparks Press, 1979.

Hamel, Paul B., and Mary Chiltoskey. *Cherokee Plants: Their Uses: A 400 Year History*. Sylva, NC: Sylva Herald, 1975.

Hemphill, Ian, and Kate Hemphill. *The Spice and Herb Bible*. Toronto, Canada: Robert Rose, Inc., 2006.

Hessayon, Dr. D.G. *The Vegetable and Herb Expert*. New York, NY: Sterling Publishing, 2001.

Hill, Madalene, and Gwen Barclay. *Southern Herb Growing*. Fredericksburg, TX: Shearer Publishing, 1987.

Hutton, Wendy. *Asian Herbs and Spices*. Hong Kong: Periplus Editions, 2003.

Kowalchick, Clair, and William H. Hylton, eds. *Rodale's Illustrated Encyclopedia of Herbs*. Emmaus, PA: Rodale Press, 1998.

Lanza, Patricia. *Lasagna Gardening with Herbs: Enjoy Fresh Flavor, Fragrance, and Beauty with No Digging, No Tilling, No Weeding, No Kidding*! Emmaus, PA: Rodale Press, 2004.

Lawton, Barbara Perry. *Mints: A Family of Herbs and Ornamentals*. Portland, OR: Timber Press, 2002.

Lewis, Eleanore. *Herbs*. Des Moines, IA: Better Homes and Gardens Books, 2002.

MacCubbin, Tom. *The Edible Landscape*. Oviedo, FL: Waterview Press, 1989.

McTrae, Bobbi A. *The Herb Companion Wishbook and Resource Guide*. Loveland, CO: Interweave Press, 1992.

McVicar, Jekka. *New Book of Herbs*. New York, NY: DK Publishing, 2002.

Morton, Julia F. *Fruits of Warm Climates*. Miami, FL: Julia F. Morton, 1987.

Morton, Julia F. *Wild Plants for Survival in South Florida*. Miami, FL: Fairchild Tropical Garden, 1982.

Nelson, Gil. *Florida's Best Native Landscape Plants, 200 Readily Available Species for Homeowners and Professionals*. Gainesville, FL: University Press of Florida, 2003.

Niering, William A., and Nancy C. Olmstead. *National Audubon Society Field Guide to North American Wildflowers, Eastern Region*. New York, NY: Alfred A. Knopf, Inc., 1979.

Norman, Jill. *Herbs and Spices: The Cook's Reference*. New York, NY: DK Publishing, 2002.

Peterson, Lee, and Roger Tory Peterson. *A Field Guide to Edible Wild Plants of Eastern and Central North America*. Boston, MA: Houghton Mifflin, 1978.

Phillips, Roger, and Nicky Foy. *The Random House Book of Herbs*. New York, NY: Random House, 1990.

Platt, Ellen Specter. *Lemon Herbs: How to Grow and Use 18 Great Plants*. Mechanicsburg, PA: Stackpole Books, 2002.

Roth, Sally. *The Successful Herb Gardener*. New York, NY: Hearst Books, 2001.

Rushing, Felder, James A. Fizzel, and Walter Reeves. *50 Great Herbs, Fruits, and Vegetables For Georgia*. Nashville, TN: Cool Springs Press, 2004.

Sahni, Julie. *Savoring Spices and Herbs*. New York, NY: William Morrow and Company, 1996.

Sanecki, Kay N. *Planning and Planting Herb Gardens*. London, UK: Ward Lock, 1996.

Smith, Miranda. *Your Backyard Herb Garden*. Emmaus, PA: Rodale Press, 1997.

Stephens, James M. Publication *#CIR570*. Gainesville, FL: Horticultural Sciences Department, Florida Cooperative Extension Service, Institute of Food and Agricultural Sciences, University of Florida, 1994.

Stephens, James M. Publication #HS580. Gainesville, FL: Horticultural Sciences Department, Florida Cooperative Extension Service, Institute of Food and Agricultural Sciences, University of Florida, 1994.

Stresau, Frederic B. *Florida My Eden*. Port Salerno, FL: Florida Classics Library, 1986.

Tabor, Roger. *Wild About Herbs*. Pleasantville, NY: Reader's Digest, 2002.

Tucker, Arthur O., and Thomas DeBaggio. *The Big Book of Herbs*. Loveland, CO: Interweave Press, 2000.

Van Atta, Marian. *Exotic Foods: A Kitchen and Garden Guide*. Sarasota, FL: Pineapple Press, 2002.

Worden, Eva C., and Sydney Park Brown. *Publication #ENH971*. Gainesville, FL: Environmental Horticulture Department, Florida Cooperative Extension Service, Institute of Food and Agricultural Sciences, University of Florida, 2004.

Index

Note: Numbers in bold refer to pages featuring an image of the term

Florida's Best Fruiting Plants by Charles R. Boning. A comprehensive guide to fruit-bearing plants that thrive in the Florida environment. Discusses exotics and native species, familiar plants, and dozens of rare and obscure plants. (pb)

Tropical Trees of Florida and the Virgin Islands: A Guide to Identification, Characteristics and Uses by T. Kent Kirk. This user-friendly, all-color field guide aids in the identification of more than 90 species of trees native to Florida and the Virgin Islands (and a few widespread exotics). For each species, there are photos of the whole tree, leaves, flowers, and fruit. (pb)

Flowering Shrubs and Small Trees for the South by Marie Harrison. Author and master gardener Marie Harrison offers tips on how to identify, select, and care for more than 100 flowering shrubs and small trees suited to the South. Full-color photos and line drawings throughout. (pb)

Native Bromeliads of Florida by Harry E. Luther and David H. Benzing. Provides the means to identify and appreciate the many unconventional characteristics of Florida's sixteen species (and two hybrids) of native bromeliads, often called "air plants." These include the abundant Spanish moss and the rare, carnivorous *Catopsis berteroniana*. Includes color photographs. (hb)

The Trees of Florida: A Reference and Field Guide by Gil Nelson. A comprehensive guide to Florida's amazing variety of trees, native and exotic, from scrub oak to mangroves, from sabal palm to Florida yew. Field sites for observing the species. For the naturalist, botanist, landscape architect, and weekend gardener. (pb)

The Shrubs & Woody Vines of Florida: A Reference and Field Guide by Gil Nelson. Useful to professional botanists as well as landscape architects and homeowners, this easy-to-use field guide includes more than 550 woody vines and shrubs native to Florida. With color photos and line drawings. (hb, pb)

The Ferns of Florida: A Reference and Field Guide by Gil Nelson. A complete guide to Florida's amazing variety of ferns. Includes notes on each species' growth form and habit, as well as general remarks about its botanical and common names, unique characteristics, garden use, and history in Florida. Color plates feature more than 200 images, some of which include rare species never before illustrated in color. (hb, pb)

Natural Florida Landscaping by Dan Walton and Laurel Schiller. This book will help you make a plan that will work for your yard and choose the native plants that will thrive there in order to create a beautiful and environmentally sensitive landscape. (pb)

The Art of South Florida Gardening, Second Edition, by Harold Songdahl and Coralee Leon. Gardening advice specifically written for the unique conditions of south Florida. This practical, comprehensive guide, written with humor and know-how, will teach you how to outsmart the soil, protect against pests and weather, and select the right trees and shrubs for Florida's climate. (pb)

100 Orchids for Florida by Jack Kramer. 100 beautiful orchids you can grow in Florida, chosen for their beauty, ease of cultivation, and suitability to Florida's climate. (pb)

Groundcovers for the South by Marie Harrison. Presents a variety of plants that can serve as groundcovers in the American South. Each entry gives detailed information on ideal growing conditions, plant care, and different selections within each species. Color photographs and line drawings make identification easy. (pb)

Southern Gardening: An Environmentally Sensitive Approach by Marie Harrison. A comprehensive guide to beautiful, environmentally conscious yards and gardens. Suggests useful groundcovers and easy-care, adaptable trees, shrubs, perennials, and annuals. (pb)

Gardening in the Coastal South by Marie Harrison. A master gardener discusses topics such as salt tolerance, pesticide use, beneficial insects, invasive exotics, and gardening for butterflies and birds. Color photos and pen-and-ink illustrations round out the text. (pb)

Flowering Trees of Florida by Mark Stebbins. Written for both the seasoned arborist and the weekend gardener alike, this comprehensive guide offers 74 outstanding tropical flowering trees that will grow in Florida's subtropical climate. Full-color photos throughout. (pb)

Ornamental Tropical Shrubs by Amanda Jarrett. Eighty-three shrubs that display beautiful flowers and/or leaves in the subtropical and tropical zones. This book includes a full profile for each shrub, including drought and salt tolerance, flowers and fruits, potential problems, and much more. Explains how to use shrubs in garden design. Full-color photos throughout. (hb, pb)